# Mel Bochner

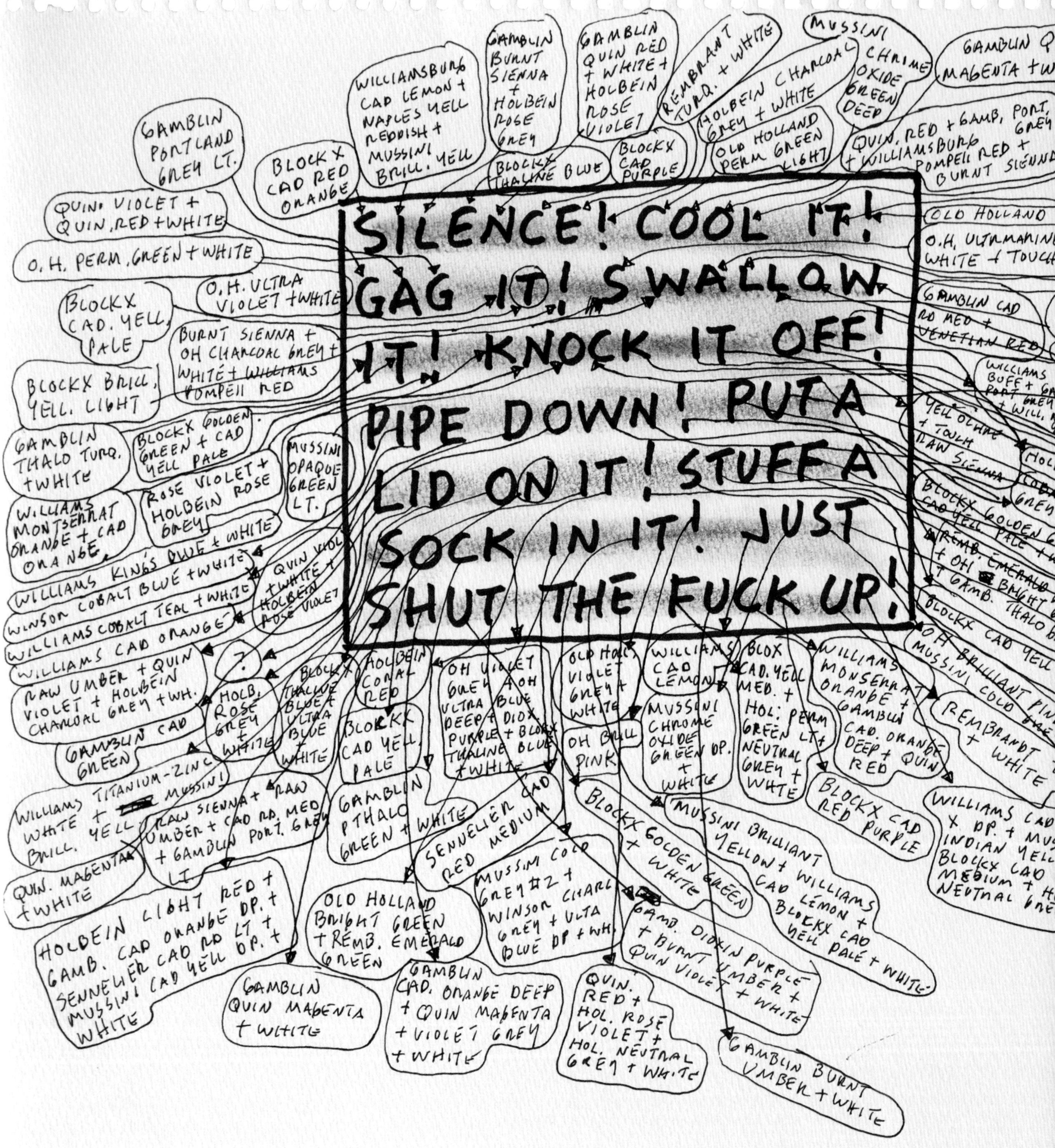

SILENCE! COOL IT! GAG IT! SWALLOW IT! KNOCK IT OFF! PIPE DOWN! PUT A LID ON IT! STUFF A SOCK IN IT! JUST SHUT THE FUCK UP!

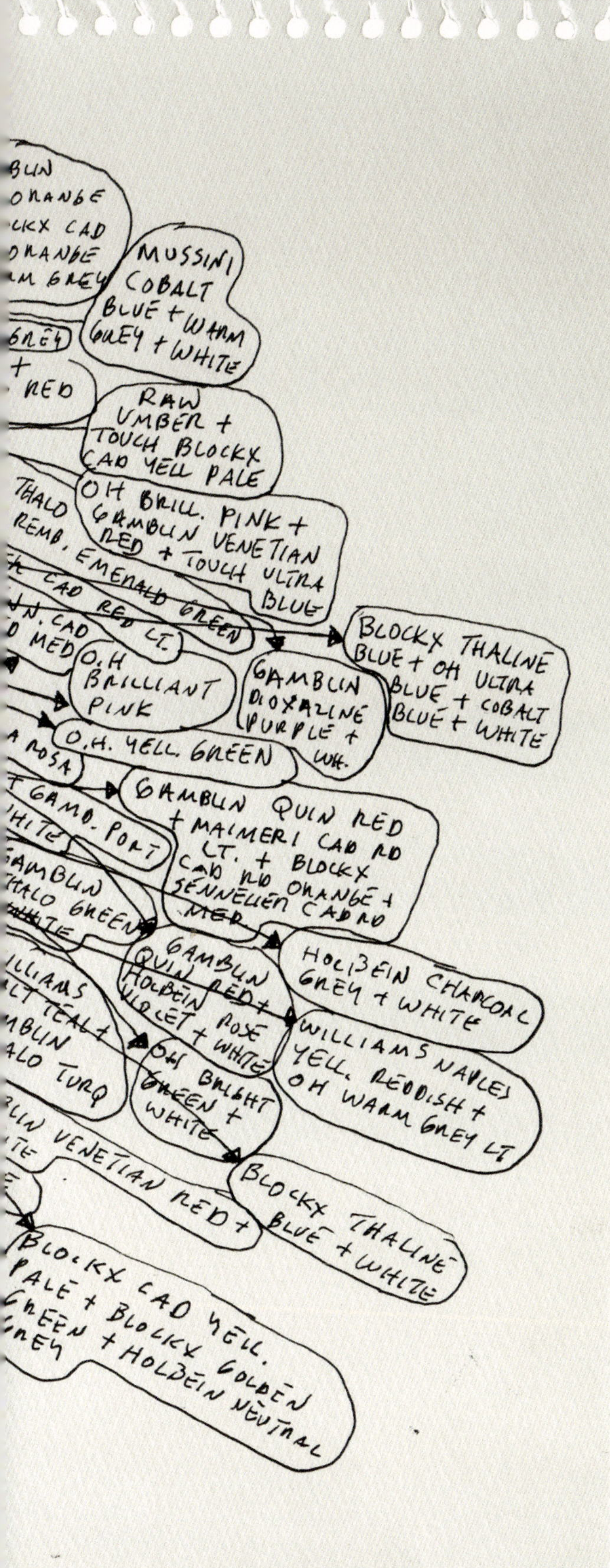


# Mel Bochner

**Strong Language**

**NORMAN L. KLEEBLATT**

WITH A TEXT BY **MEL BOCHNER**

**THE JEWISH MUSEUM, NEW YORK**
UNDER THE AUSPICES OF THE JEWISH THEOLOGICAL SEMINARY OF AMERICA

**YALE UNIVERSITY PRESS, NEW HAVEN AND LONDON**

This book has been published in conjunction with the exhibition
**"Mel Bochner: Strong Language"**
organized by The Jewish Museum, New York, May 2–September 7, 2014.



The Jewish Museum
Director of Publications: Eve Sinaiko

Yale University Press
Publisher, Art and Architecture: Patricia Fidler
Senior Editor, Art and Architecture: Michelle Komie
Managing Editor, Art and Architecture: Kate Zanzucchi
Associate Design and Production Manager: Sarah Henry

Designed and typeset by Katy Homans in Din and Garamond types
Printed in China by Regent Publishing Services Limited

The Jewish Museum
1109 Fifth Avenue
New York, New York 10128
thejewishmuseum.org

Yale University Press
PO Box 209040
New Haven, Connecticut 06520-9040
yalebooks.com/art

Library of Congress Control Number: 2013952437
ISBN 978-0-300-19734-1

A catalogue record for this book is available from the British Library.

The paper in this book meets the requirements of ANSI/NISO Z39.48-1992 (Permanence of Paper).

10 9 8 7 6 5 4 3 2 1

Cover: (front) *Dollar Hash Exclamation Plus*, 2011 (see page 107);
(back) *Enough Said*, 2012, 24 × 30 in. (58.4 × 76.2 cm). Private collection
Frontispiece: Working drawing for *Silence!*, 2011 (see page 70)

# Contents

# Donors and Lenders to the Exhibition

**DONORS**

**Mel Bochner: Strong Language** is made possible by the Melva Bucksbaum Fund for Contemporary Art.

Leadership support is provided by the Barbara S. Horowitz Contemporary Art Fund. Generous additional support is provided by Michael Kapland and Bonnie Postel in loving memory of their parents Dr. Jack Allen and Shirley H. Kapland, Suzanne F. Cohen, Alice and Nahum Lainer, Jill and Peter Kraus, and Judith Racht and Irving Stenn, Jr.

The exhibition is supported, in part, by an award from the National Endowment for the Arts.

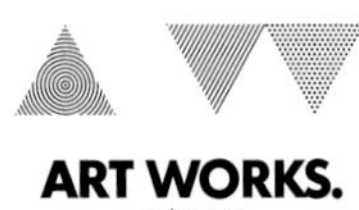

**ART WORKS.**
arts.gov

**LENDERS**

Piera Bochner

Melva Bucksbaum and Raymond Learsy, New York

Suzanne F. Cohen, Baltimore

Collection of the artist

Beth Rudin DeWoody

Hadley Martin Fisher Collection

Peter Freeman

Peter Freeman, Inc., New York and Paris

Danielle and David Ganek

Glenstone Foundation, Potomac, Maryland

Andrea and Jim Gordon, Chicago

Betty and Edward Harris, Chicago

Akira Ikeda Gallery, New York

The Jewish Museum, New York

Wendy Evans Joseph and Jeffrey Ravetch

Jill and Peter Kraus, New York

Evelyn and David Lasry

Los Angeles County Museum of Art

Sandro and Fiamma Manzo

Lizbeth Marano

The Museum of Modern Art, New York

Leslie and Alan Pearson

Pergamont Collection

Private collections

Smithsonian American Art Museum, Washington, DC

Irving Stenn, Jr., Chicago

Two Palms

# Foreword

In 1964 a young artist from Pittsburgh, fresh out of art school and recently arrived in New York, got a job as a security guard at The Jewish Museum. He worked in this capacity for a year or so until he was caught napping behind a Louise Nevelson sculpture, and fired.

Fortunately, Mel Bochner's relationship with The Jewish Museum did not end with that episode. Two years later he visited the museum to see the pioneering exhibition "Primary Structures" and write an article about it for *Arts Magazine*. He saw something thrilling in the Minimalist works on display—a paradigm shift in contemporary art—and wrote one of the most influential and perceptive reviews of the show. His incisive text remains a landmark of sixties criticism. He was twenty-five.

By then, of course, he was breaking new artistic ground himself, thinking about what might come after Minimalism and exploring the complex relationships between the visual and the intellectual; between language, measurement, and thought. In a career that spans half a century, his passion for these issues has never abated. Language in particular remains a consistent through-line in his work, the starting point for many inquiries and the focus of many experiments.

Jewish culture is often considered more verbal than visual. The long tradition of Jewish intellectuals, storytellers, and comedians fits within this notion. Bochner both embraces and challenges that idea, and his obsession with the interface of language and art may be seen within this context. It was in this spirit that the museum acquired his painting *The Joys of Yiddish* in 2012, marking another happy encounter between the artist and the institution.

We are delighted, now, to welcome Mel Bochner back to The Jewish Museum, this time as neither guard nor critic but as protagonist of an in-depth survey of his word-based art, beautifully and perceptively curated by Norman L. Kleeblatt with the assistance of Stephen Brown. In focusing on his paintings on language—and *of* language and *with* language—we celebrate both the artist and a fundamental aspect of Jewish culture.

**CLAUDIA GOULD**
Helen Goldsmith Menschel Director
The Jewish Museum

# Preface and Acknowledgments

In June 2011, I began a discussion with Mel Bochner about acquiring one of his recent thesaurus paintings. We did not have a specific canvas in mind, but the curatorial staff was enthusiastic about the possibilities, as was Claudia Gould, the recently appointed director of the museum; her only stipulation was that we acquire a major work. Soon thereafter, the museum purchased Bochner's newly minted *Joys of Yiddish*. Our acquisition coincided with an exhibition at the National Gallery of Art in Washington, DC, curated by James Meyer—who, coincidentally, had worked at The Jewish Museum at an early point in his career, just as Bochner had. The exhibition was thoughtful, intelligent, and visually seductive. It became evident that it was high time to show Bochner on his home turf, in New York.

What approach should The Jewish Museum take? Some aspects of Bochner's fifty-year career have been explored frequently, especially his early work. With the close collaboration of the artist, we arrived at a presentation suited to this institution. My heartfelt thanks go to Mel Bochner for his artistic and intellectual generosity and for his confidence in me. He has been a wonderful partner, thoughtful and witty. The dialogue he encouraged and his unerring eye have helped shape a unique view of his art. It has been a true pleasure to work with him on all aspects of this show and catalogue. I also thank Lizbeth Marano, whose understanding of her husband's vision and career surfaced frequently throughout our work together.

Always close at hand, his studio assistants, Nicholas Knight and James Powers, helped to organize images and information. I appreciate their understanding of Bochner's work; they offered insights that were added to the mix. Peter Freeman, the artist's gallerist in New York, has been a generous lender and advisor; I thank him, his wife, Lluisa Sarries i Zgonic, and his excellent staff for their collegiality, in particular Kerry Andresen, Suzanne Imber, and Greg Lofthouse. Evelyn and David Lasry of Two Palms have helped in many ways, not only through their technical and artistic support for Bochner's virtuoso printmaking but also by lending to and supporting our venture in many ways.

I warmly acknowledge Claudia Gould, Helen Goldsmith Menschel Director, for her unswerving belief in the project, in Bochner's work, and in me. Jens Hoffmann, Deputy Director, Exhibitions and Public Programs, and Ruth Beesch, Deputy Director, Program Administration, have been unfailing in their support and assistance, aesthetic and practical. I have also depended on several talented curatorial fellows and interns: Chana Boruchov, Lulu Krause, Robert Liles, and Daniel Roza. Jennifer Ayres and Julie Maguire, exhibitions coordinator and senior registrar, along with the former director of exhibitions and collections, Jane Rubin, handled with aplomb the complexities of mounting the exhibition. This volume has benefited from the professionalism, expertise, and lucid editing of Eve Sinaiko, and from the fine work of our colleagues at Yale University Press: Patricia Fidler, Michelle Komie, Sarah Henry, and Heidi Downey. The book has been beautifully designed by Katy Homans. Al Lazarte, senior director of operations and exhibition services, ensured, as he does for all exhibitions at the museum, that this show was impeccably fabricated and detailed. To other staff of the museum, in development, marketing, and operations, I offer thanks for the excellent support they have provided.

As in a number of my previous projects, the architect Calvin Tsao has been a great partner for the artist and me. Having admired many of Calvin's projects at the museum, Bochner felt that he would be the perfect choice to realize our vision. Zack McKown enthusiastically welcomed the project, and the team of Christina Gaiger and Paul Lee produced a superb installation; I warmly thank them and Colette Mullan at Tsao McKown for facilitating this productive liaison.

I have benefited greatly from other recent Bochner exhibitions and from their informative publications, not only the show in Washington but also James Rondeau and Johanna Burton's wonderful 2007 project for the Art Institute of Chicago — one of the first museum exhibitions to showcase the thesaurus paintings — and the traveling show and accompanying publication organized by Achim Burchardt-Hume, Ulrich Wilmes, and João Fernandes in 2012. For valuable insights and discussion that have enriched my thinking on Bochner, I thank David Joselit.

The generosity of lenders and supporters, both institutional and individual, has been crucial to this exhibition. The owners of artworks have agreed to do without them for a time so that the public may enjoy them. My colleagues and I offer our heartfelt thanks for their gracious support.

**NORMAN L. KLEEBLATT**
Susan and Elihu Rose Chief Curator

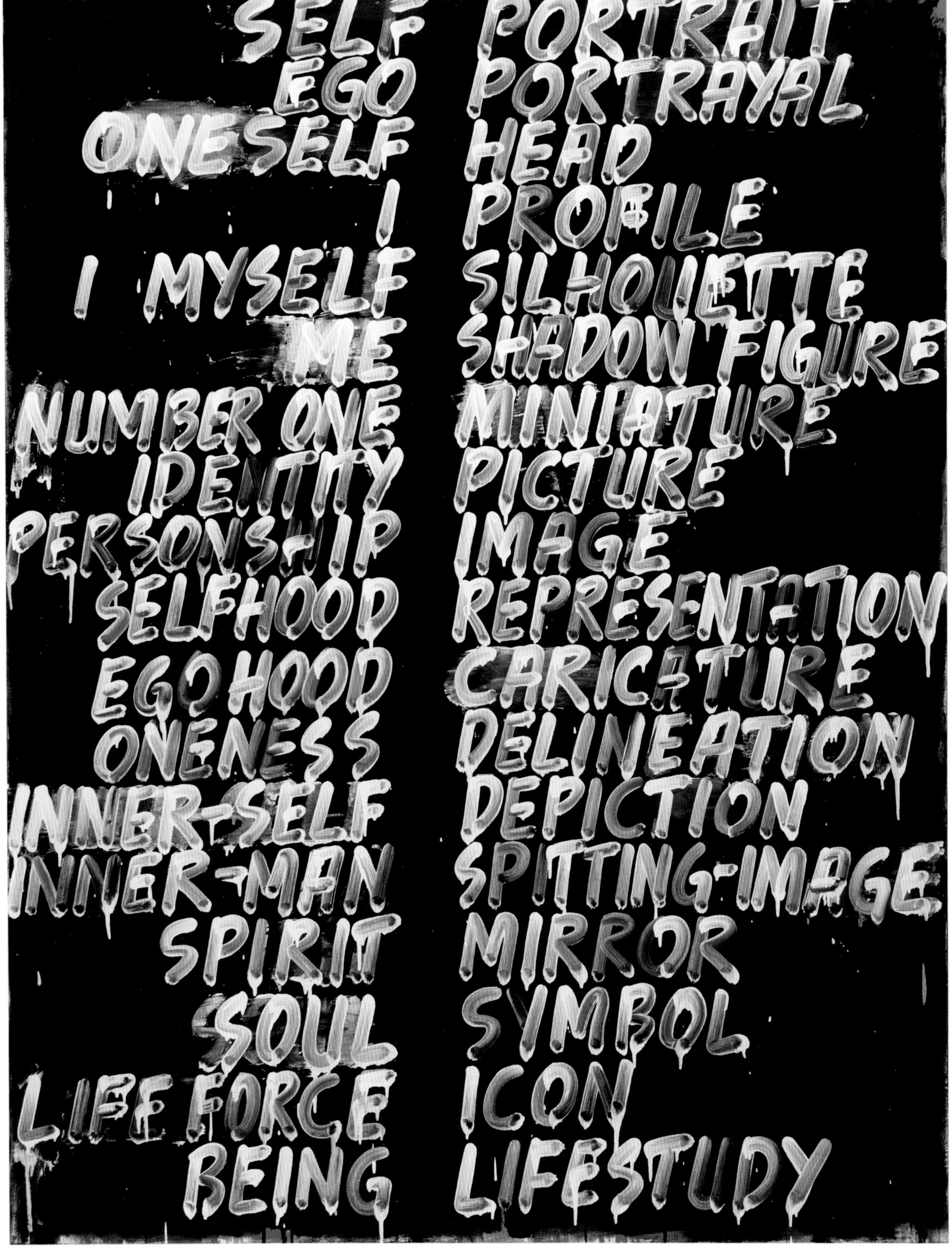

SELF                PORTRAIT
EGO                 PORTRAYAL
ONESELF             HEAD
I                   PROFILE
I MYSELF            SILHOUETTE
ME                  SHADOW FIGURE
NUMBER ONE          MINIATURE
IDENTITY            PICTURE
PERSONSHIP          IMAGE
SELFHOOD            REPRESENTATION
EGOHOOD             CARICATURE
ONENESS             DELINEATION
INNER-SELF          DEPICTION
INNER-MAN           SPITTING-IMAGE
SPIRIT              MIRROR
SOUL                SIMBOL
LIFE FORCE          ICON
BEING               LIFESTUDY

# Mel Bochner
## Strong Language

**NORMAN L. KLEEBLATT**

Artist and writer, Mel Bochner is celebrated for his key role in the evolution of Conceptual art in the 1960s and 1970s. During those years he produced work that dealt with ideas and concepts on the one hand, including philosophical and mathematical theories, and on the other the pragmatic application of systems of measurement and counting. In doing so he continually dealt with issues of original and reproduction, the real and the fabricated. Words and language played significant roles as medium, subject, and method for his art from his earliest days. Despite this, he has consistently questioned the definition of Conceptualism—art in which the idea is more important than the material work itself—and its relevance to his work.[1]

Bochner's work, however, has always been rooted in physicality. Looking back on that time, he recalls "always thinking of myself as a painter . . . a painter who just didn't happen to paint."[2] This dichotomy should not be considered unusual in an artist more interested in the materiality of ideas than in the immateriality of the underlying concepts. Bochner makes the conceptual physical, the idea visible. If contradictions inevitably arise, he embraces them.[3] His work must be understood as hybrid, combining the traditional and the experimental, the intellectual and the sensual, rigor and humor. His career consists of looking both forward and back, even more so after his return to painting. Over the years he has established a dialogue between the assimilation and critique of various modern and contemporary art movements while simultaneously experimenting with and building on his own earlier work.

In about 1979 he returned to painting on canvas (a medium largely rejected by the Conceptualists) and, more recently, to a highly tactile, painterly version of printmaking. In paintings, drawings, and prints he has continued his lifelong exploration of the connection between the visual and the verbal, notably in an ongoing series of canvases based on *Roget's Thesaurus.* The word "thesaurus" means treasure or treasury; for Bochner the volume is a "warehouse for words," a text ready-made for use in his witty, billboardlike pictures. In each work he groups a collection of synonyms or related phrases drawn from an entry in Roget, arrayed in a carefully calculated sequence. In *Silence!,* for example (page 72), a string of words runs from left to right and top to bottom, ranging from the formal to the vernacular, from familiar slang to obscenity. The sequence starts with the sibilant "silence" and ends with a vulgar, guttural "shut the fuck up!" High-key colors on delectable backgrounds in equally vivid hues add a seductive complexity. The effect is to draw the eye wildly over the composition as the mind attempts simultaneously to absorb both vibrating colors and staccato text. Here, as throughout the series, the word acts as both idea and image.

### CONCEPT, WORD, IMAGE

The thesaurus works move Bochner's practice away from a predominantly Conceptual expression to an approach that emphasizes lush painterly technique. Nevertheless, the Conceptual aspects so central to the artist's thinking over the decades remain deeply embedded.

An excellent example of such refractions, dichotomies, and contradictions is the recent *Self/Portrait.* The picture is a painterly reinvention of a tiny, highly personal work

*Self/Portrait,* 2013

Oil on canvas, 75 × 58 in. (190.5 × 147.3 cm)
Collection of the artist

from the beginning of Bochner's career, one that has become iconic in the early history of Conceptual art. The original *Self/Portrait* of 1966 was an ink drawing on graph paper, although "notation" or "diagram" might be a better description. In it, two lists of words are strung vertically, with "self" at the top of the left column, and "portrait" at top right. Read vertically, they are lists of synonyms for these two terms. Read horizontally, they generate unusual combinations of concepts, sometimes forging amalgams or neologisms, or simply presenting disjunctive mishmashes. The image is neither exclusively literary nor painterly; it is neither a self-portrait in the traditional sense nor a descriptive word-portrait such as a memoirist might write. Instead, it is an evocation of the self and its mimetic representation.

Both the 1966 and 2013 self-portraits are linguistic examinations of a standard artistic genre. Both interpolate their textual references onto the self-portrait's internal meanings as visual depiction and pictorial description. They provide no personal disclosures, no mimetic allusions, but offer a generalized chain of personal and psychological attributes (on the left) and a list of standard concrete and abstract nouns (on the right). In a traditional self-portrait the artist may use a mirror to gain access to his own image, so that the looking-glass mediates between the seen and the depicted. In these two works the gap between the columns serves that same reflective function—both linking and separating the categories of "self" and "portrait."

The only hint that these images depict a specific individual—Bochner himself—is in their title. Further, Bochner has created a number of face-offs between the personal and the general that make the identity of the "self" enigmatic.[4] Because he himself is invisible in these self-portraits, the works become theoretical studies of the meanings and limits of self-perception and self-depiction. Here "self" and "portrait" are fused to create a hybrid of word, sign, and image that displaces the traditional self-portrait.

Bochner's original drawing is intimate and modest, a work to be appreciated in private. By contrast, his recent painting is meant for public consumption: monumental in size and impact, with lusciously gestural brushwork. Yet in both versions the word list, poised between the writer's thought and painter's processes, comes across as a deliberation or exploration—something jotted, tentative, meditative. The painting is executed with a high degree of finish but designed to resemble a chalkboard—a place where words are temporary: scribbled, erased, added to, or replaced. In emphasizing the painted surface Bochner calls attention to the systematic nature of painting itself, to the grammar of brushstroke, facture, surface, tonality. "Painting," he has remarked, is "a language, a way to express, contradict, or deny. . . . Painting itself is a dictionary."[5] The choice of term is not accidental: a dictionary, like a thesaurus, is a tool for organizing an organic language into a formal structure. Bochner's abiding interest in systems—linguistic, philosophical, mathematical, representational—persists throughout his work.

Something purposefully retro is at play in the 2013 *Self/Portrait:* the blackboard is a schoolroom artifact and a relic of the predigital era. It evokes nostalgia, a concept verboten in the modernist ethos that prevailed when Bochner came to artistic maturity. The

SELF PORTRAIT
EGO PORTRAYAL
ONESELF HEAD
I PROFILE
I MYSELF SILHOUETTE
ME SHADOW FIGURE
NUMBER ONE MINIATURE
YOURS TRULY SKETCH
IDENTITY PICTURE
PERSONALITY IMAGE
PERSONSHIP LIKENESS
SELFHOOD REPRESENTATION
EGOHOOD CARICATURE
ONENESS DELINEATION
SELF-IDENTITY ILLUSTRATION
INNER-SELF DEPICITION
INNER-MAN SPITTING-IMAGE
PYSCHE REFLECTION
SPIRIT MIRROR
SOUL SYMBOL
ANIMA MASK
LIFE FORCE ICON
BEING LIFESTUDY

*Self/Portrait*, 1966

Ink on graph paper, 5⅜ × 4½ in. (13.6 × 11.4 cm)
Private collection, New York

 It offers a glance backward to the artist's early work yet is positioned firmly within Bochner's current painting vocabularies. In the course of his career Bochner has often revisited earlier ideas and reformulated earlier works, using different scales, media, techniques, and strategies. Significantly, such changes generate new concepts and meanings.

## EARLY THESAURUS WORKS

As the 1966 drawing and the 2013 painting indicate, Bochner's interest in language—particularly synonyms—is longstanding. In the course of his articulation, theorizing, and problematizing of the essence of language he has explored the interconnections between written language and visual depiction. Doing this, he finds points of contact between them and reveals the ways they remain separate. He thus "demonstrates the insufficiency of any language system, any theory, *any form* to capture [the] persistent disjunctions among the different ways . . . of being in the world."[6] The 1966 self-portrait is one in a group of small text-based portraits of other artists and writers, made between 1966 and 1968. These exquisite works, made on the scale of traditional portrait miniatures, constitute an early use of the thesaurus and, according to the artist, prompted his interest in language. Each is a set of words, drawn in ink and configured into a specific shape, and each portrays an artist of Bochner's circle or one of his cultural heroes: Ad Reinhardt, Eva Hesse, Sol LeWitt, Robert Smithson, Dan Flavin, Donald Judd, Marcel Duchamp, Jasper Johns, Jorge Luis Borges. Unique to Bochner as they are, they can be seen as part of a rethinking in the 1960s of the nature of drawing—a trend to "disengag[e] drawing from expression" and from the personal character and dramatic gestures of Abstract Expressionism.[7]

Just as he remade *Self/Portrait* forty-seven years later, he has also revisited two other of his early portraits. In 2001 he re-created portraits of Eva Hesse and Robert Smithson, close friends who had died in 1970 and 1973, respectively. Both newer works are on paper but are much larger than the 1966 originals. They are more loosely drawn, using the soft, tactile medium of charcoal rather than ink. As in all of Bochner's frequent reworkings of his older artworks, these drawings accrue additional meanings: they are elegiac memorials to deceased friends rather than playful and personal homages.[8]

The text-based portraits began as an outgrowth of Bochner's work in the 1960s with geometric and other mathematical configurations and related diagrammatic problem solving. They began as lists of synonyms taken ready-made from the thesaurus and were initially intended as notes or thought exercises, not necessarily as works of art.

At that time Bochner had already begun working with words in place of numbers. The first of his word drawings, *Cause and Effect* (page 6), is a hand-cut ring of graph paper with five phrases in a continuous loop. These move through the experiences of friction, heat, and pain to the emotions of caring, tenderness, and love, and back again. In both sentiment and form the work calls to mind the medieval image of the Ouroboros, the serpent biting its

***Portrait of Ad Reinhardt, 1966***

Ink on graph paper, 10¾ × 3¾ in. (27.3 × 9.5 cm)
Private collection

| | |
|---|---|
| QUIESCENCE | SILENCE |
| STILLNESS | SOUNLESSNESS |
| QUIETNESS | TONELESSNESS |
| QUIETUDE | MUTENESS |
| CALMNESS | DUMBNESS |
| RESTFULNESS | SPEECHLESSNES |
| PEACEFULNESS | APHONIA |
| PLACIDNESS | GAG |
| TRANQUILITY | MUZZLE |
| SERENITY | HUSH |
| PEACE | SOFTEN |
| COMPOSURE | DAMPEN |
| REST | DEAFEN |
| REPOSE | SUBDUE |
| MOTIONLESS | MUM |
| IMMOBILITY | SUPPRESS |
| INACTION | REPRESS |
| FIXATION | NOISELESS |
| FIXITY | LULL |
| STANDSTILL | MUFFLE |
| STAND | DEADEN |
| STOP | SOFTEN |
| DEADLOCK | INAUDIBLE |
| INERT | SHUT-UP |
| INERTIA | UNSAID |
| PASSIVENESS | SMOTHER |
| TORPID | STIFLED |
| LANGUID | UNHEARD |
| STAGNATION | QUIET |
| STASIS | DUMMY-UP |
| CALM | UNUTTERED |
| TRANQUIL | UNEXPRESSED |
| FIXED | ATONIC |
| STATIC | MUTE |
| LEADEN | TACITURN |
| DULL | RETICENT |
| LIFELESS | INCOMMUNICATIVE |
| IMMOTIVE | RETICENCE |
| SILENT | QUIESCENT |

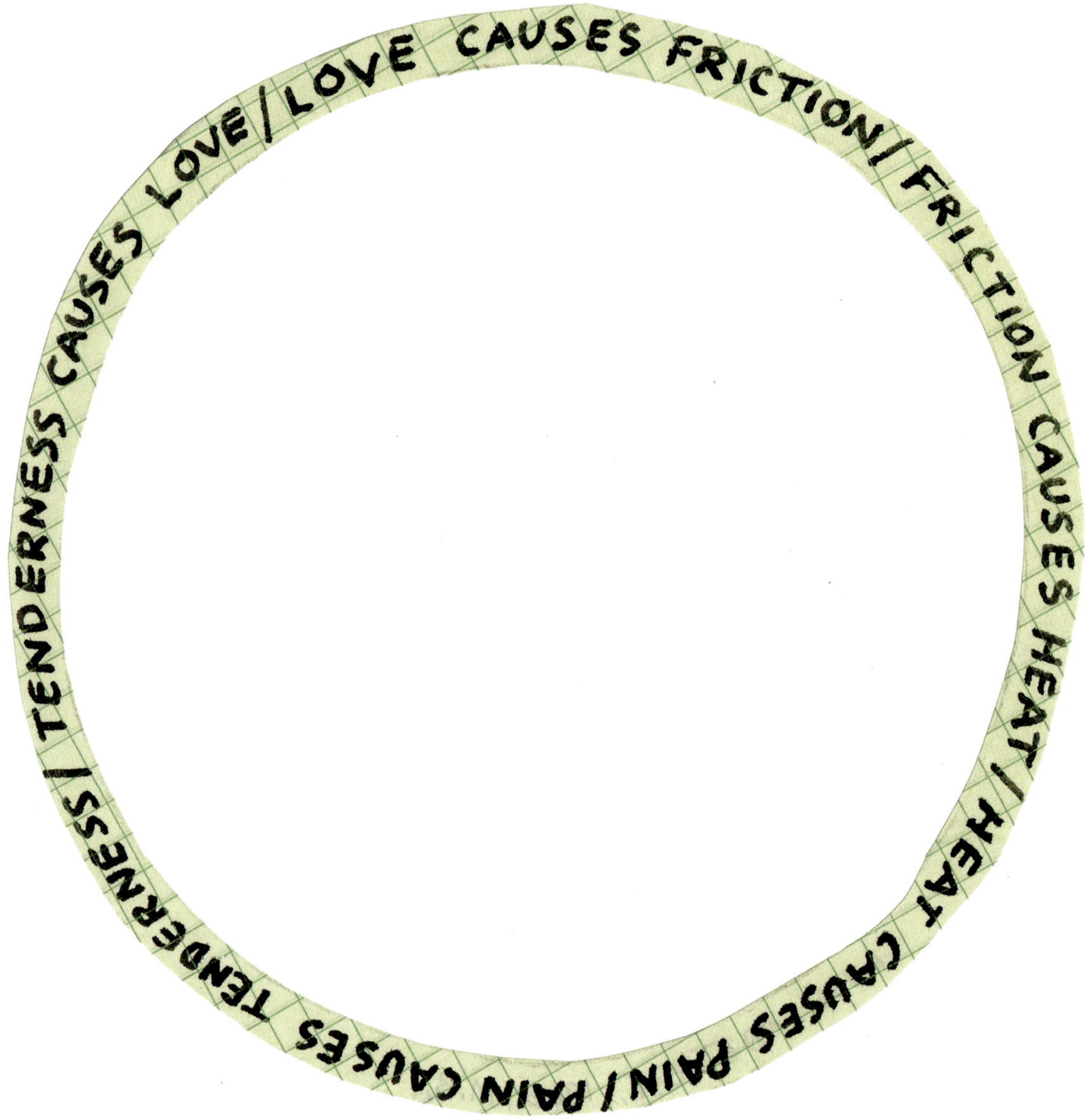

*Cause and Effect,* **1966**

Ink on graph paper (cut out), 5⅞ in. (14.9 cm) in
diameter
Private collection

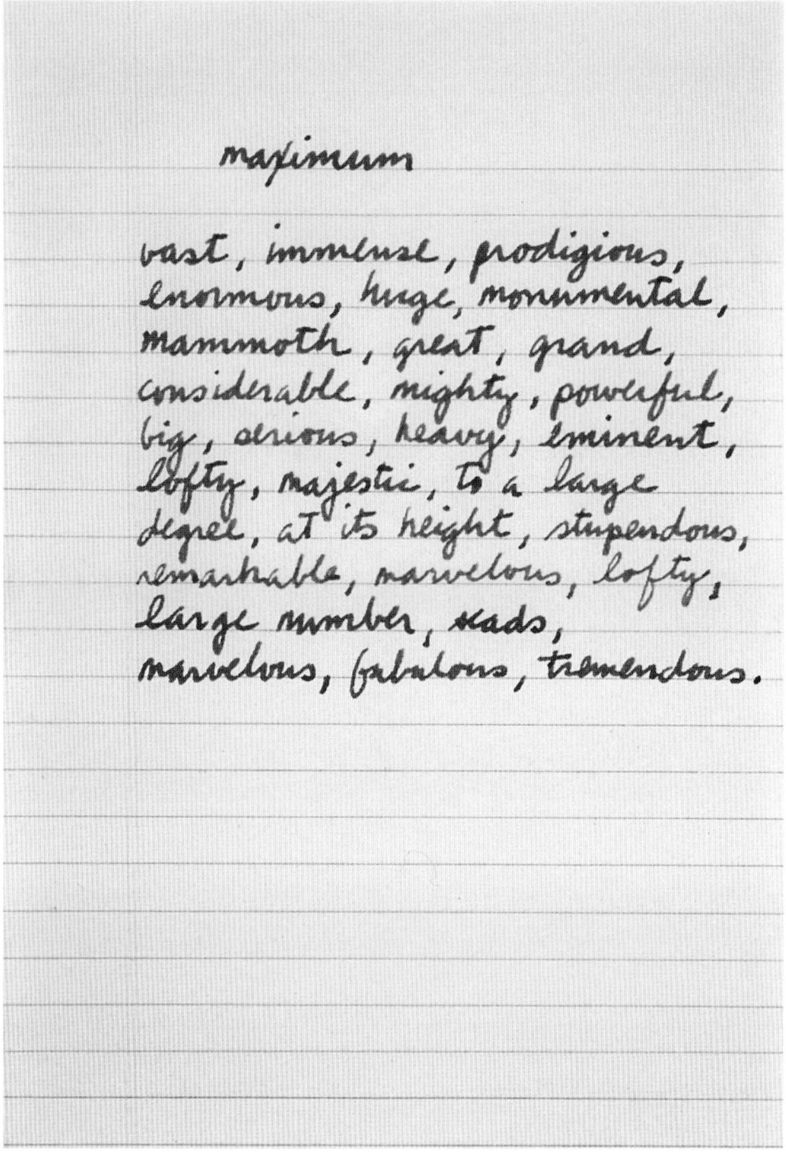

maximum

vast, immense, prodigious,
enormous, huge, monumental,
mammoth, great, grand,
considerable, mighty, powerful,
big, serious, heavy, eminent,
lofty, majestic, to a large
degree, at its height, stupendous,
remarkable, marvelous, lofty,
large number, scads,
marvelous, fabulous, tremendous.

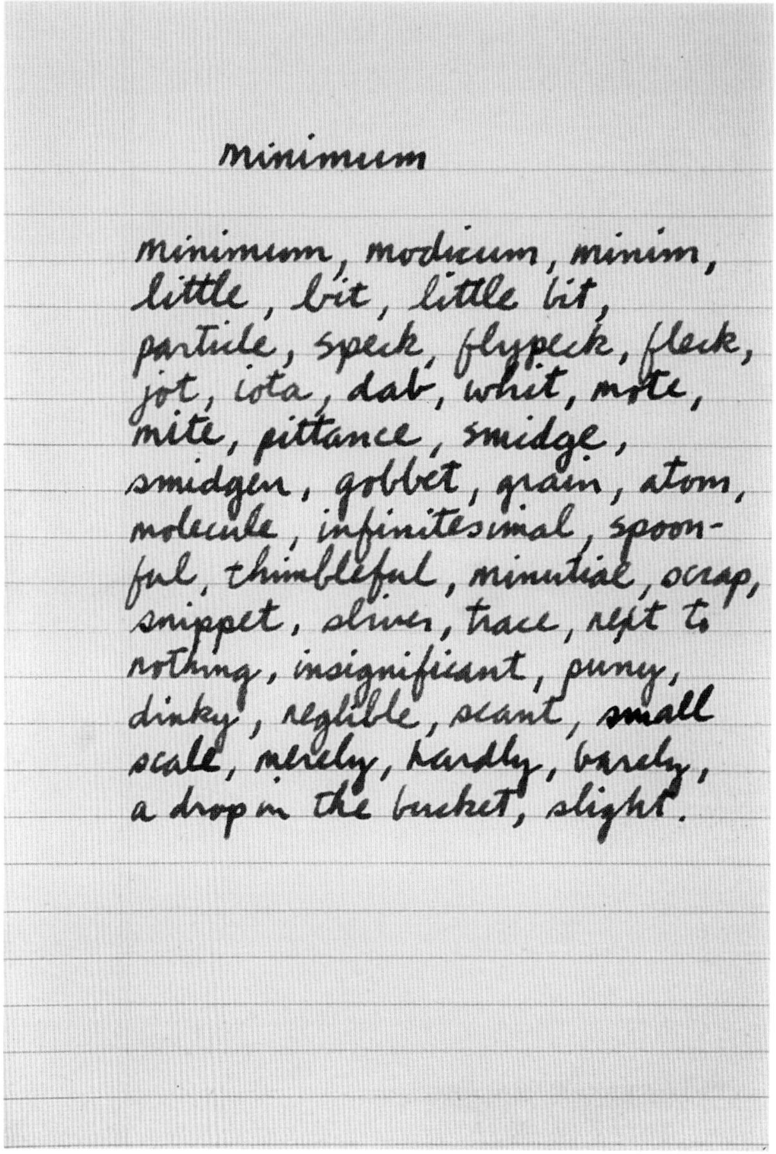

minimum

minimum, modicum, minim,
little, bit, little bit,
particle, speck, flyspeck, fleck,
jot, iota, dab, whit, mote,
mite, pittance, smidge,
smidgen, gobbet, grain, atom,
molecule, infinitesimal, spoon-
ful, thimbleful, minutia, scrap,
snippet, sliver, trace, next to
nothing, insignificant, puny,
dinky, negligible, scant, small
scale, merely, hardly, barely,
a drop in the bucket, slight.

*Maximum/Minimum, 1966*

Ink on two sheets of lined paper, each 7⅛ × 5 in. (18.1 × 12.7 cm)
Private collection

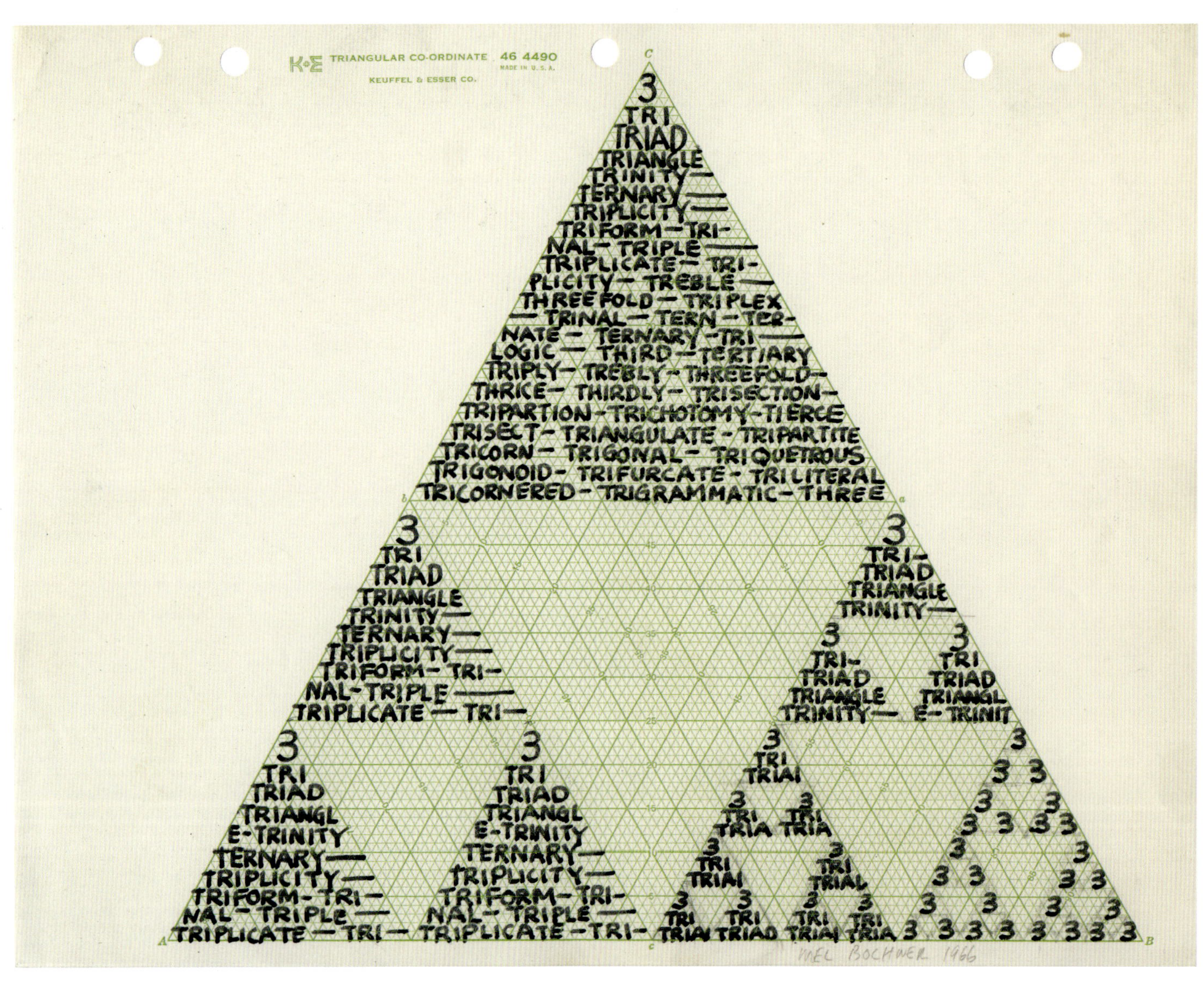



***3*, 1966**

Ink on graph paper, 8½ × 11 in. (21.6 × 27.9 cm)
Irving Stenn, Jr., Chicago

***Portrait of Sol LeWitt*, 1966**

Ink on graph paper, 5¼ × 5½ in. (13.3 × 13.9 cm)
Private collection

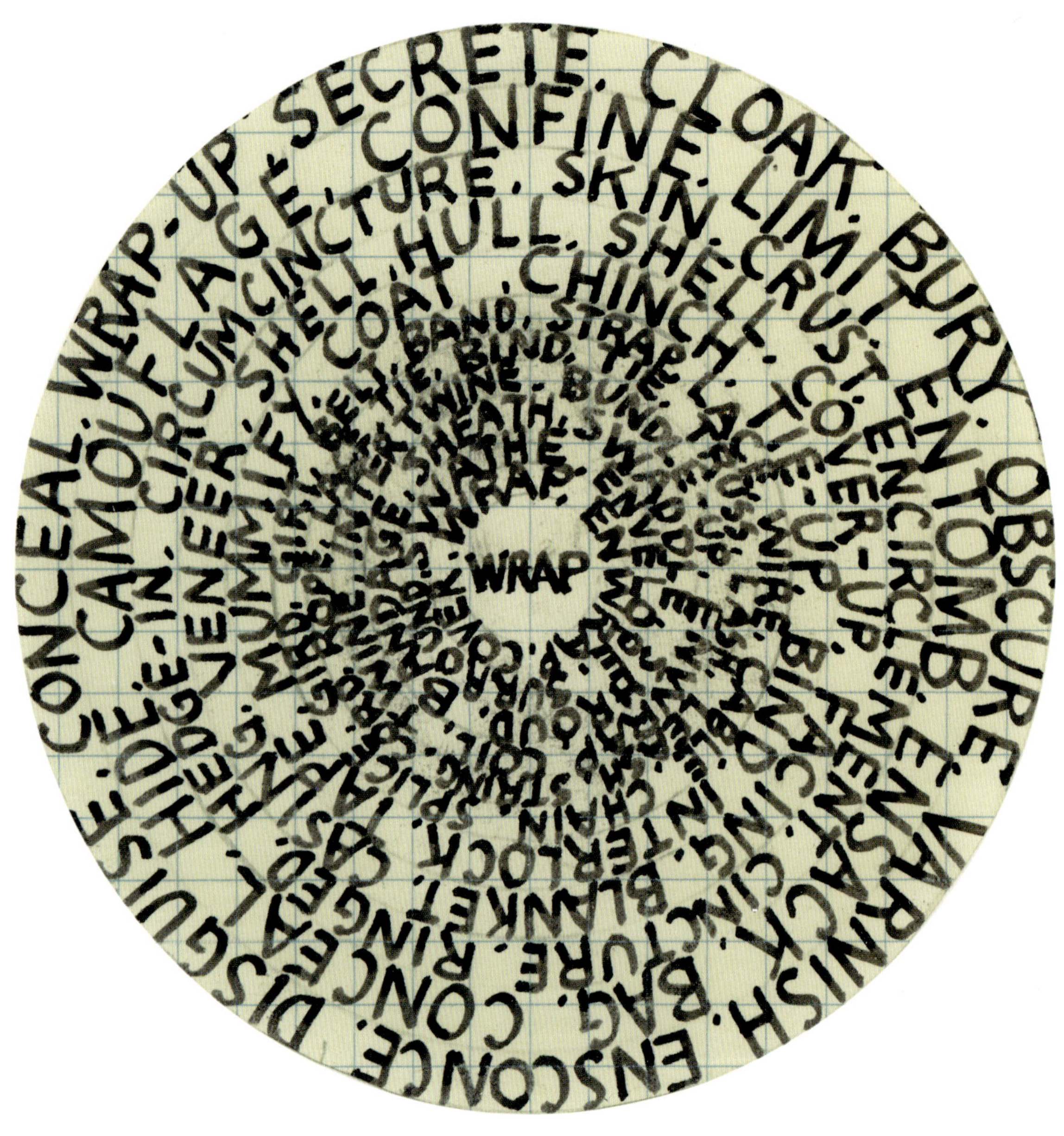

*Portrait of Eva Hesse,* **1966**

Ink on graph paper, 4⅜ in. (11.1 cm) in diameter
Private collection

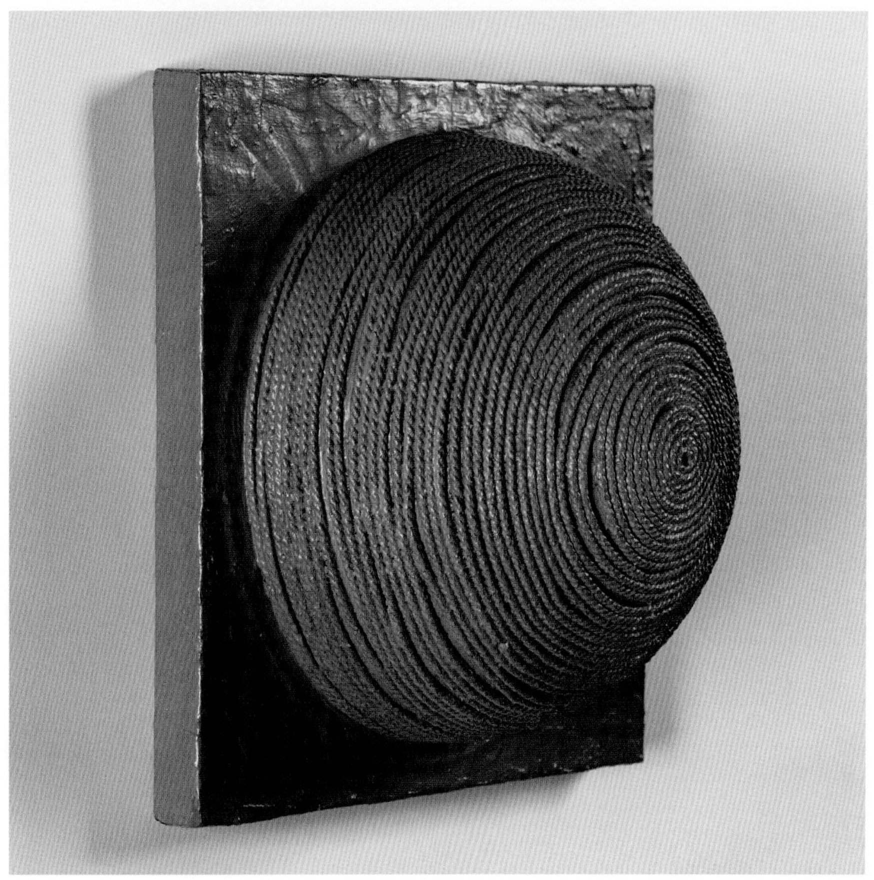

own tail—a symbol with ancient roots and multiple meanings, often referring to eternity, cycles of creation, or esoteric wisdom. The work is not quite six inches in diameter, the handwritten words minute, suggesting that medieval micrography may also have been a source.[9] Such referents are not random: Bochner has always been attuned to the long history of art and culture and has perennially explored the complex relationship of thought to image, philosophy to art.

If *Cause and Effect* is a concept drawing or diagram, *3,* which follows it (page 8), explicitly merges geometry with words, the mathematical with the linguistic. Bochner considers this his first thesaurus drawing. It is thus a bridge between his works based on numbers and his engagement with language. The thesaurus-style word portraits of Reinhardt, Hesse, LeWitt, Smithson, and others followed soon after.[10]

Each word portrait incorporates a list of synonyms applicable to the sensibilities of the sitter. The words are laid out in a shape typical of that artist's signature works. *Portrait of Ad Reinhardt* (page 5) presents two columns of words headed with "quiescence" and "silence." Though rectangular in format, they are, like *Cause and Effect,* circular in concept: each list of terms ends with the word that appears at the top of the other column. The two columns are strictly rectangular, divided by a center gap, a layout that repeats the bifurcated, often quadripartite organization of Reinhardt's paintings. Bochner's choice of language also alludes to the nearly imperceptible differences in value and form in Reinhardt's subtle monochromes.

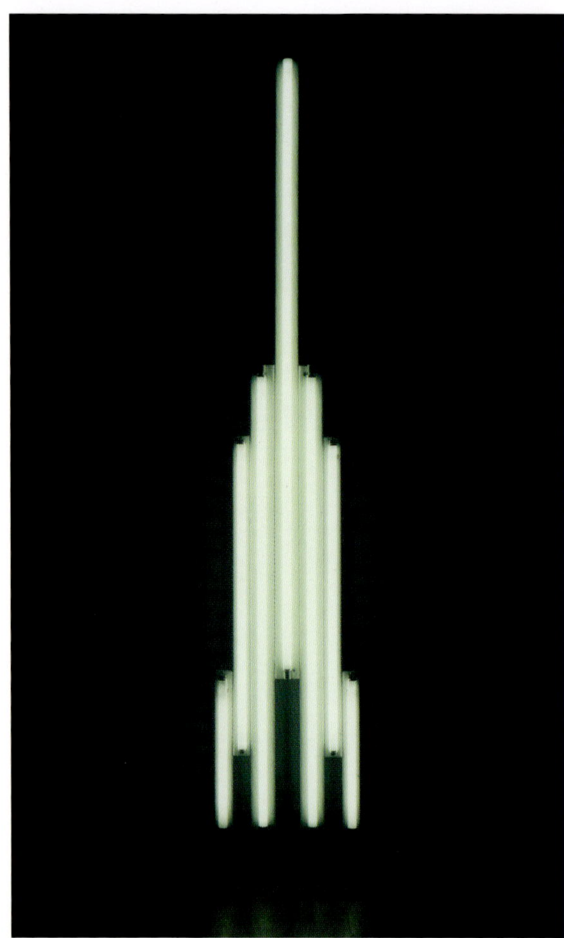

Dan Flavin, *Monument for V. Tatlin,* 1966–69
Mixed media, 120¼ × 23 × 3½ in. (305.4 ×
58.4 × 8.9 cm)
Tate, London

"Wrap" is the operative word at the center of the concentric circles that form
Eva Hesse's portrait (page 10). Its format not only mimics the definition of the term but
re-creates in miniature the spherical organization that Hesse was using in her sculpture at
that moment in her career.

In the portrait of Robert Smithson (page 18), two blocks of words linked at every
fifth line compose a shape reminiscent of the industrial boxes, filled with rubble, that
Smithson was then making. As the titular word "Repetition" suggests, the words are meant
to be read in a continuous loop, beginning at the top of the page and threading between
one column and the other. The last word, "encore," is followed by a comma, inviting the eye
to start again at the top. But where the portraits of Reinhardt and Hesse use mostly objective, respectful vocabularies, Smithson's words and phrases are full of vernacular and slang—
"humdrum," "the same old song," "rehash," "ditto." This lighthearted spirit may reflect
Bochner and Smithson's close friendship, their collaborations and escapades. Roguish
phrases, vulgarities, and obscenities, which first appear here, become central in Bochner's
subsequent thesaurus paintings.

Dan Flavin's portrait is formally and linguistically more complex. The shape is a set
of narrow horizontal rectangles in staggered lengths, like a sideways ziggurat—a direct reference to Flavin's fluorescent light sculptures. Here, Bochner uses full sentences and phrases

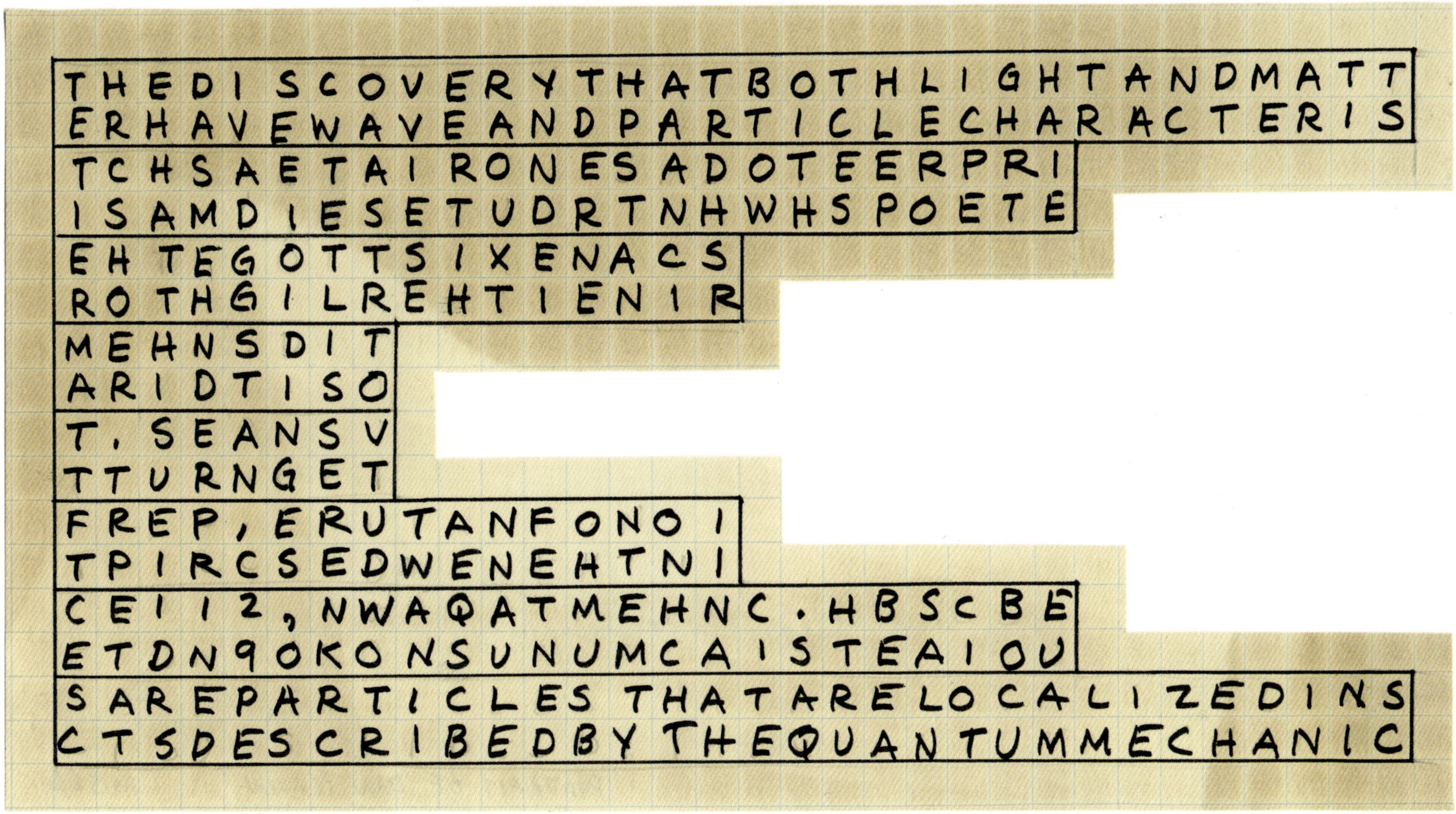

THEDISCOVERYTHATBOTHLIGHTANDMATT
ERHAVEWAVEANDPARTICLECHARACTERIS
TCHSAETAIRONESADOTEERPRI
ISAMDIESETUDRTNHWHSPOETE
EHTEGOTTSIXENACS
ROTHGILREHTIENIR
MEHNSDIT
ARIDTISO
T.SEANSV
TTURNGET
FREP,ERUTANFONOI
TPIRCSEDWENEHTNI
CEII2,NWAQATMEHNC.HBSCBE
ETDN9OKONSUNUMCAISTEAIOU
SAREPARTICLESTHATARELOCALIZEDINS
CTSDESCRIBEDBYTHEQUANTUMMECHANIC

***Portrait of Dan Flavin*, 1968**

Ink on graph paper (cut out), 4½ × 8½ in. (11.4 × 21.6 cm)
Private collection

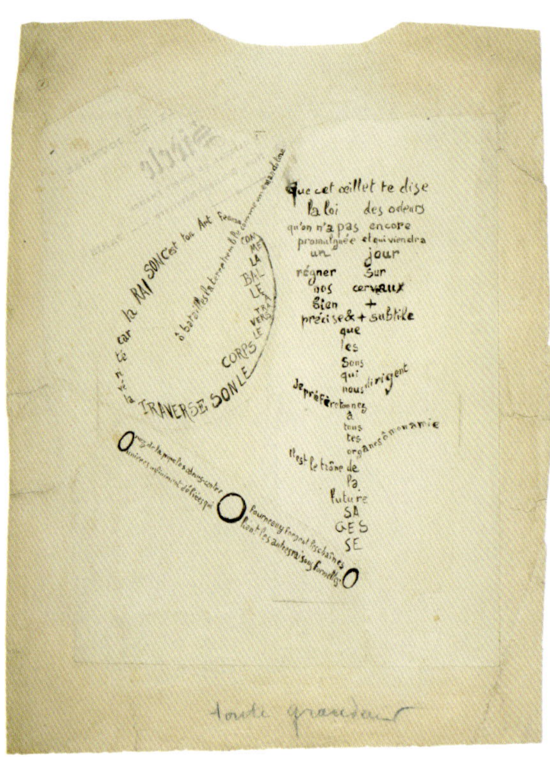

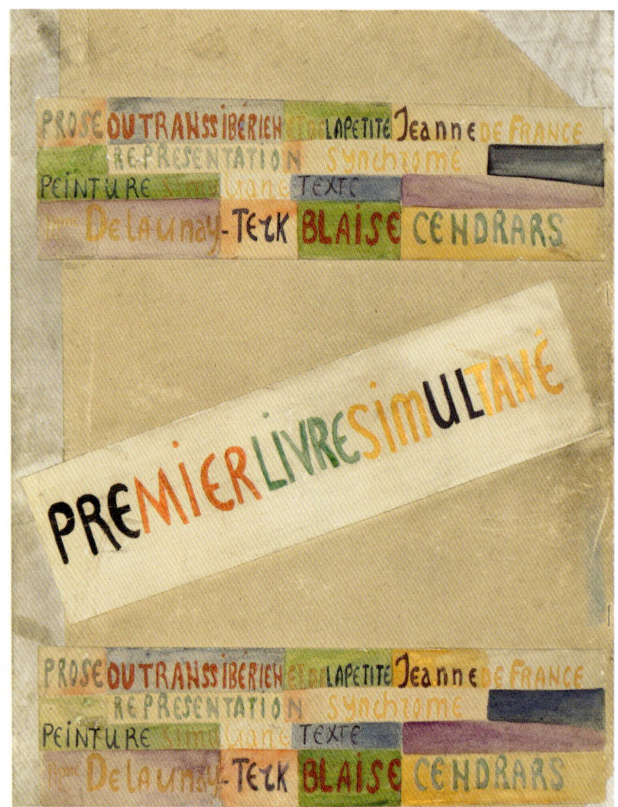


Guillaume Apollinaire, *The Mandolin, Carnation, and Bamboo,* ca. 1915/17
Ink calligram, 10¾ × 8¼ in. (27.5 × 20.9 cm)
Musée National d'Art Moderne, Centre Georges Pompidou, Paris

Sonia Delaunay-Terk, prospectus for
*The Prose of the Trans-Siberian and of Little Jehanne of France,* 1913
Watercolor and collage on cardboard,
21 × 14½ in. (53.3 × 36.8 cm)
Los Angeles County Museum of Art, Modern and Contemporary Art Council Fund (M.2013.74.1)

rather than discrete words. Some passages are clear and simple to read, but in some sections the letters are arranged brainteaser fashion, in a complicated serpentine layout, so that the statement becomes a complex puzzle. The text concerns the nature of light and matter as described by quantum mechanics.[11] Bochner seems to be suggesting that Flavin's sculptures, which must be switched on to exist, fuse the materiality of matter and the immateriality of light.

Most of the portraits are drawn on graph paper, whose gridded geometry lends them both a mathematical precision and a gamelike playfulness, as if they were crosswords or acrostics. The implication is that the viewer/reader is invited to participate in their completion. This concept of viewer engagement has remained a tenet of Bochner's art.

Early on, he also became interested in the way abstract mental processes and actual physical space converge in a work of art.[12] Likewise, the interface of the verbal and the visual has long fascinated him. While he was still a student, a 1959 article in *Art News Annual* introduced him to Stéphane Mallarmé, Guillaume Apollinaire, and pattern poetry — poems laid out to form a shape or image with symbolic meaning. In these shaped poems literal description becomes visual representation.[13] Their complexity, combined with a disarming visual simplicity, appealed to Bochner, and by 1966 he may have seen in them a paradoxical relationship with the shaped canvases then central to avant-garde painting.

One way to approach Bochner's fascination with words and language is to see it in an art-historical context, both modernist and traditional. The precedent of Pablo Picasso's iconic Analytic Cubist pictures and collages or the assemblage paintings of Jasper Johns has

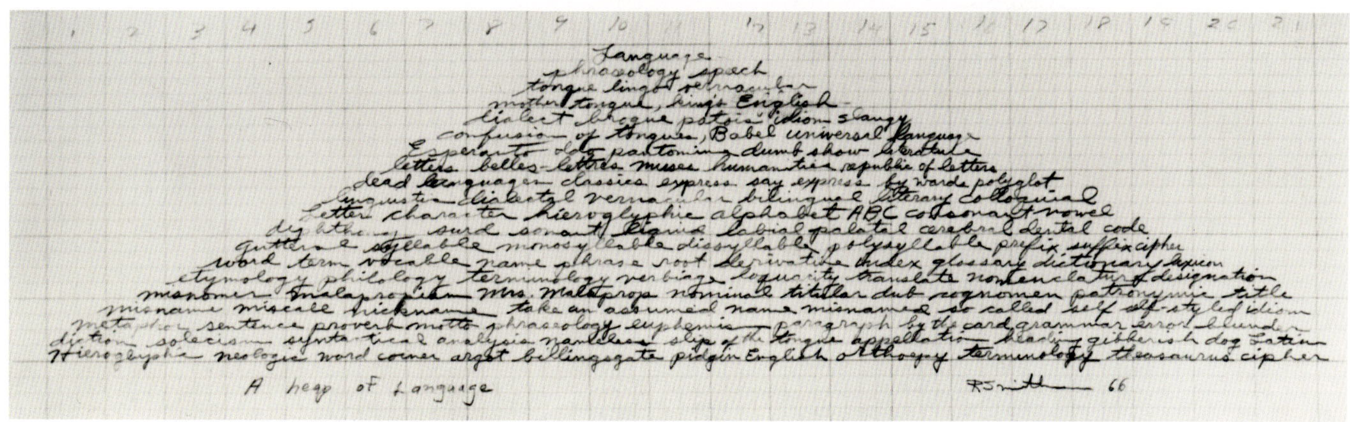

Robert Smithson, *A Heap of Language,* 1966
Pencil on paper, 6½ × 22 in. (16.5 × 55.9 cm)
The Over Holland Collection

Richard Serra, *Verb List,* 1967
Graphite on paper, two sheets, each 10 × 8 in.
(25.4 × 20.3 cm)
The Museum of Modern Art, gift of the artist in
honor of Wynn Kramarsky

Carl Andre, *words men word court proofs years
hair men cell,* 1962
Typed carbon paper transfer on paper,
11 × 8½ in. (27.9 × 21.6 cm)
The Museum of Modern Art, The Judith
Rothschild Foundation Contemporary Drawings
Collection Gift (purchase, and gift, in part, of
The Eileen and Michael Cohen Collection)

often been noted. Given his voracious appetite for art of the past, even certain classics, from Simone Martini to Rembrandt, may be relevant.[14] Bochner himself acknowledges the impact of Johns at a transformative moment in his career.

Two threads in early twentieth-century modernism provide particularly interesting analogies. The visual poetry of the French avant-garde, particularly Apollinaire, has been mentioned (page 14). An unexpected second point of entry is the work of the Orphist painter Sonia Delaunay-Terk, who in 1913 illustrated a book-length poem of Blaise Cendrars, *The Prose of the Trans-Siberian and of Little Jehanne of France,* working collaboratively with him. It is a long, vertical work on paper, rather like a scroll; Cendrars's words run down the right side and Delaunay-Terk's jewel-toned abstract watercolors down the left, intertwined with the verses.[15] In a painted advertising flier for the work she places Cendrars's words individually and in groups in blocks of color, using letters in contrasting tones (page 14). Her claim that "*the simultaneous contrast of colors* and the *text* form depths and movements of novel inspiration" could easily be applied to Bochner's thesaurus paintings.[16] Delaunay-Terk's experiments, like Bochner's, lie at the interface between the verbal and the visual—and both artists use the sensual and structural aspects of color as a fundamental element. Like a number of book artists of the period, Delaunay-Terk explores hybrid forms that merge the two systems of expression, so that images are not mere illustrations for words but are integral to the act of reading, and vice versa. The importance of such explorations for Bochner's practice is clear.

A drawing made in 1966 by Bochner's friend Robert Smithson suggests a shared interest in the nexus of the verbal and the visual. *A Heap of Language* (page 15) piles up words about language into the shape of a literal heap, reminiscent of Smithson's sculptures of displaced, accumulated stones and other materials. However, Smithson's and Bochner's playful romance with words and texts differs greatly in tone and concept from the more ascetic strategies for language of their fellow Conceptual artists.[17] Like the Smithson drawing, Bochner's thesaurus portraits of 1966–68 are at once intimate and ironic, serious and witty. With this series he establishes a dualistic, hybrid approach to art making that simultaneously embraces the high intellectual and the bawdy—a double thread evident throughout his oeuvre.

A number of artists in the sixties were producing small language-based works on paper that were as much about thinking as about making art. This was a rejection of the grand scale and heroic gesture of Abstract Expressionist painting, with its insistence on a separation from the other arts—for example, literature and music. Carl Andre's concrete poems, made on a typewriter, collapse the distinction between concept and creation, writing and drawing. Words, for Andre, are units of composition, like the tiles or bricks of his floor sculptures (page 15).[18]

Made later, in 1967, Richard Serra's *Verb List* (page 15) explores the conjunction of word and image in a strikingly different way. The drawing is a handwritten list of 108 words (84 verbs and 24 potential contexts) that describe the actions Serra will perform on specific materials to make sculptures. In contrast to Bochner's portraits, which capture both the mature personalities of the artists and the signature forms of their works, this list is a script for the making of the work of art.[19]

**Minimal Art—The Movie, 1966**

Ink and pencil on notebook paper, 6 × 3½ in. (15.2 × 8.9 cm)
Collection of the artist

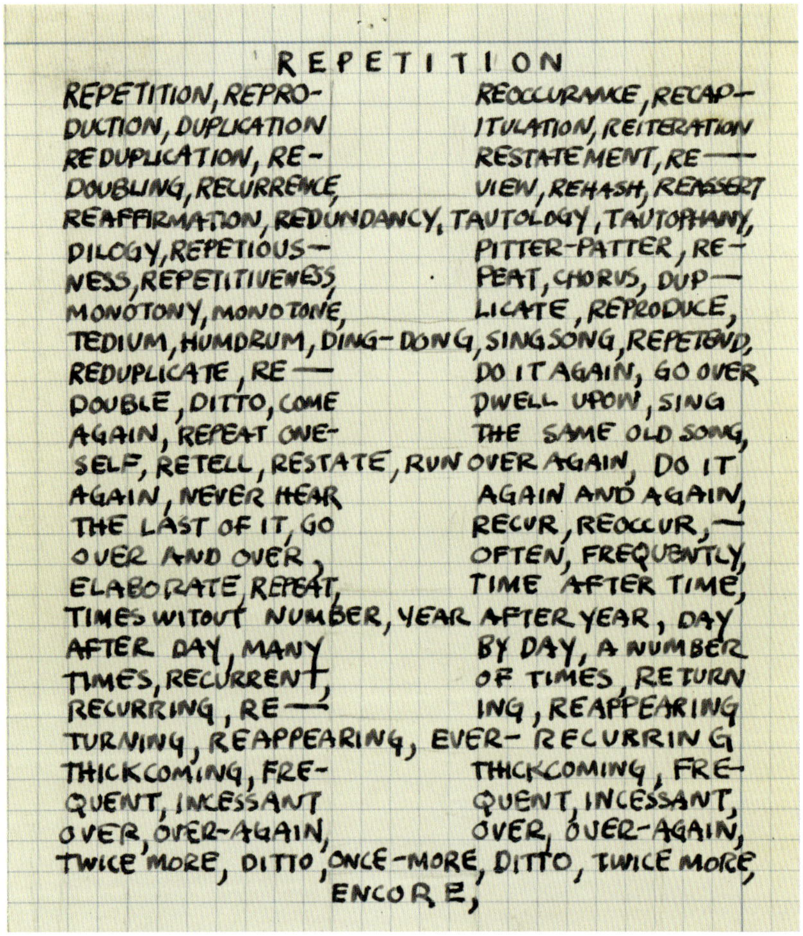

REPETITION

REPETITION, REPRO-
DUCTION, DUPLICATION
REDUPLICATION, RE-
DOUBLING, RECURRENCE,
REAFFIRMATION, REDUNDANCY,
DILOGY, REPETIOUS-
NESS, REPETITIVENESS,
MONOTONY, MONOTONE,
TEDIUM, HUMDRUM, DING-DONG,
REDUPLICATE, RE-
DOUBLE, DITTO, COME
AGAIN, REPEAT ONE-
SELF, RETELL, RESTATE,
AGAIN, NEVER HEAR
THE LAST OF IT, GO
OVER AND OVER,
ELABORATE, REPEAT,
TIMES WITOUT NUMBER,
AFTER DAY, MANY
TIMES, RECURRENT,
RECURRING, RE-
TURNING, REAPPEARING,
THICKCOMING, FRE-
QUENT, INCESSANT
OVER, OVER-AGAIN,
TWICE MORE, DITTO,

REOCCURANCE, RECAP-
ITULATION, REITERATION
RESTATEMENT, RE--
VIEW, REHASH, REASSERT
TAUTOLOGY, TAUTOPHANY,
PITTER-PATTER, RE-
PEAT, CHORUS, DUP-
LICATE, REPRODUCE,
SINGSONG, REPETEND,
DO IT AGAIN, GO OVER
DWELL UPON, SING
THE SAME OLD SONG,
RUN OVER AGAIN, DO IT
AGAIN AND AGAIN,
RECUR, REOCCUR, —
OFTEN, FREQUENTLY,
TIME AFTER TIME,
YEAR AFTER YEAR, DAY
BY DAY, A NUMBER
OF TIMES, RETURN
ING, REAPPEARING
EVER-RECURRING
THICKCOMING, FRE-
QUENT, INCESSANT,
OVER, OVER-AGAIN,
ONCE-MORE, DITTO, TWICE MORE,
ENCORE,

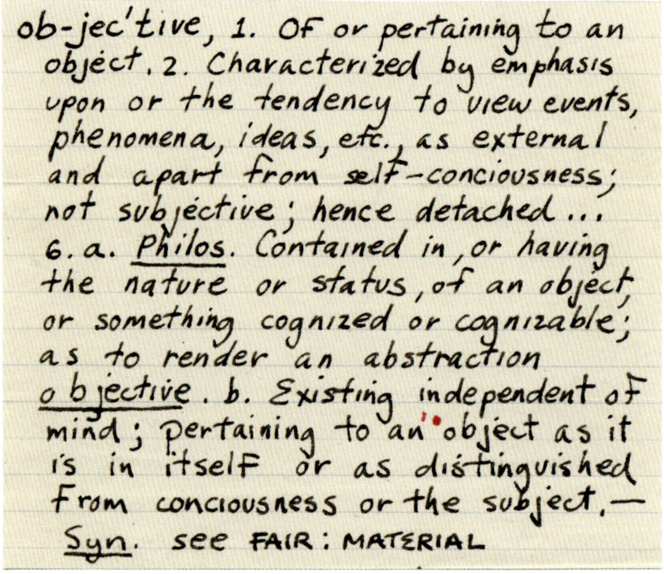

ob-jec'tive, 1. Of or pertaining to an
object. 2. Characterized by emphasis
upon or the tendency to view events,
phenomena, ideas, etc., as external
and apart from self-conciousness;
not subjective; hence detached ...
6. a. Philos. Contained in, or having
the nature or status, of an object,
or something cognized or cognizable;
as to render an abstraction
objective. b. Existing independent of
mind; pertaining to an object as it
is in itself or as distinguished
from conciousness or the subject. —
Syn. see FAIR: MATERIAL

*Portrait of Robert Smithson*, **1966**

Ink on graph paper, 7⅝ × 6¾ in. (19.3 × 17.1 cm)
Private collection

*Portrait of Donald Judd*, **1968**

Ink on lined paper, 5½ × 6½ in. (13.9 × 16.5 cm)
Private collection

ORTHOGONAL ROUTES FOR/OF DUCHAMP
RE- "(BLOSSOMING) ABC"

```
  1            2            3            4
TOMAKE       CSNIGN       EASTRI       ITEBAH
ANINSC       OITPIR       GERHAV       PLAHCA
RIPTIO       .E.I,N       DNOLON       E-THGI
NOFITC       CIHWNI       SSHOUL       ROTTFE
TITLE,       ORGEHT       ICUNIT       LMORFR
).MOVI       LAFOPU       PHABET       EDROTC

  5            6            7            8
CUNITW       LIWDNA       ITPIRC       LIUQER
PEBLLI       LBEDIS       SNIEHT       OFDEEN
RESENT       DECALP       ARDSC,       EHTOTG
NI(EY)(CL)   FROMAT       OMATOW       NIDDRO
(NN)(OO)     OCANDB       RF,ECN       CCA,DL
THEGRO       ACKAGA       IN.-SI       UOHSNO
CBAPPU

  9           10           11           12
IBRIUM       ABA)[R       (ALPHA       OLEVED
OFTHEP       NAROLL       ERBOX]       OT).CD
LATD,D       GNIHTY       OFLETT       NABSDR
ISPLAC       HTNO.)       [ASORT       AWOTOG
EACSTA       TALPSI       WILLBE       LLIWHC
BILISE       ATA.DE       .THERE       IHWTEB

 13           14           15           16
PANDST       :NOITP       IFICAN       IRCSNI
ER(YDU       PHOTOG       M,SIGN       IHTYLL
PRESEN       CIHPAR       R(FOR        ARUTPL
NOITAT       METHOD       (overlap:    UCSTNE
OFTHIS       MRETED       RESIL/THUN/  SERPER
IRCSNI       INTHEA       OEMI)        .)..EC
                          ICUNIT
                          LPHBET
```

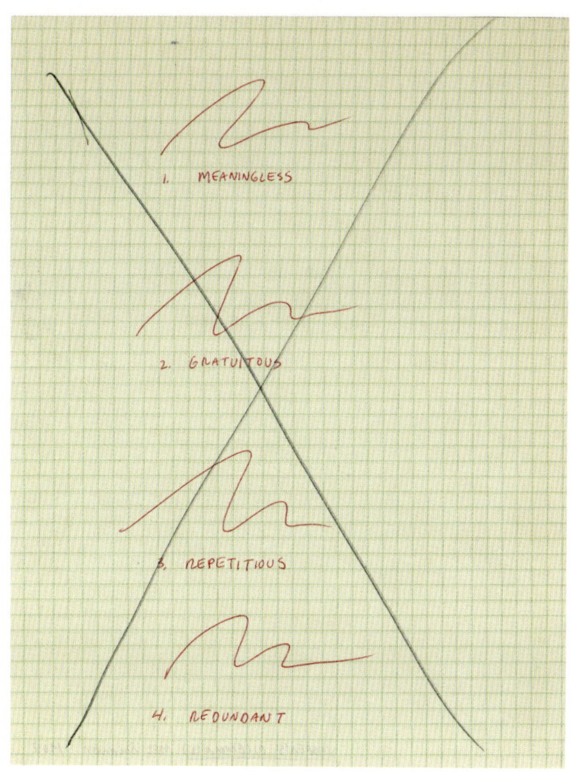



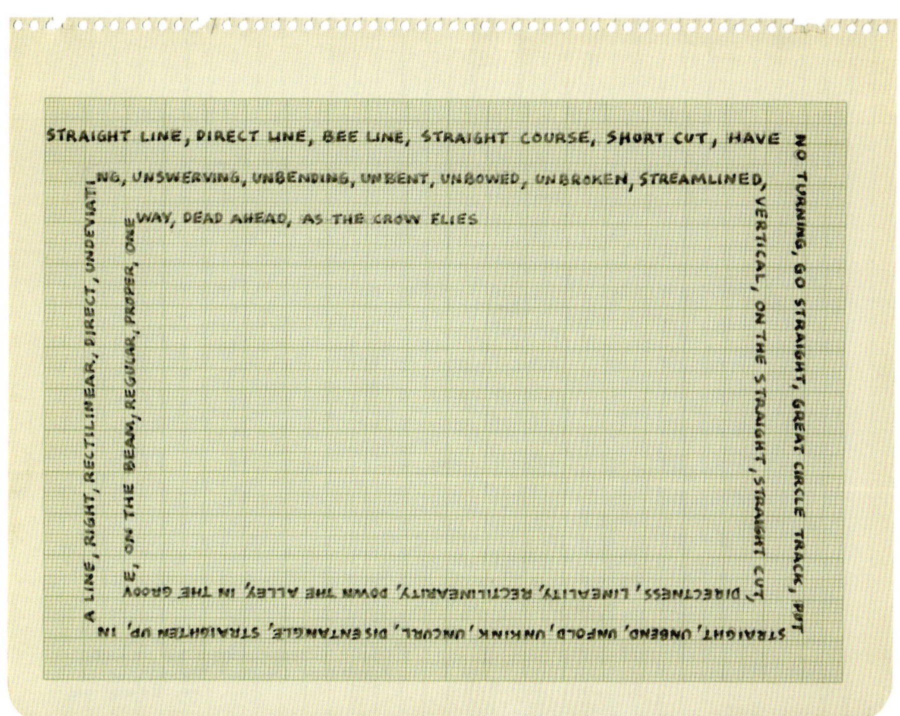



*Portrait of Marcel Duchamp,* 1968

Ink on graph paper, 11 × 8½ in. (27. × 21.6 cm)
Private collection

*Jasper's Dilemma (2),* 1968

Ballpoint pen and graphite on graph paper,
9¾ × 7½ in. (24.8 × 19.1 cm)
Private collection

*Portrait of Borges,* 1968

Ink on graph paper, 8½ × 11 in. (21.6 × 27.9 cm)
Private collection

Bochner reviewed the Jewish Museum's exhibition "Primary Structures" in *Arts Magazine,* June 1966

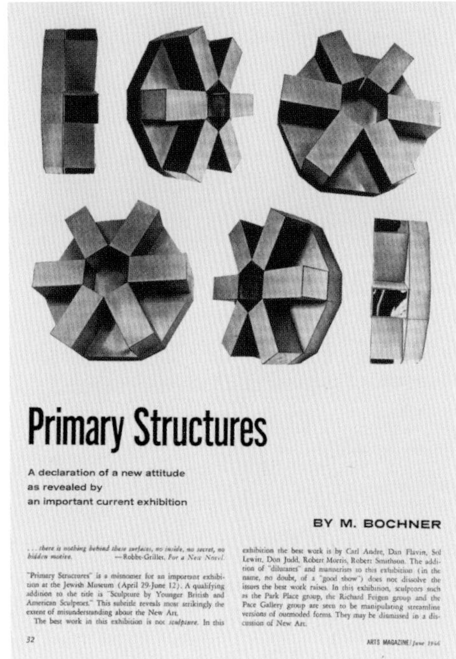

# Primary Structures

A declaration of a new attitude
as revealed by
an important current exhibition

## BY M. BOCHNER

*. . . there is nothing behind these surfaces, no inside, no secret, no hidden motive.* —Robbe-Grillet, *For a New Novel.*

"Primary Structures" is a misnomer for an important exhibition at the Jewish Museum (April 29-June 12). A qualifying addition to the title is "Sculpture by Younger British and American Sculptors." This subtitle reveals most strikingly the extent of misunderstanding about the New Art.

The best work in this exhibition is not *sculpture.* In this exhibition the best work is by Carl Andre, Dan Flavin, Sol Lewitt, Don Judd, Robert Morris, Robert Smithson. The addition of "dilutants" and mannerists to this exhibition (in the name, no doubt, of a "good show") does not dissolve the issues the best work raises. In this exhibition, sculptors such as the Park Place group, the Richard Feigen group and the Pace Gallery group are seen to be manipulating streamline versions of outmoded forms. They may be dismissed in a discussion of New Art.

32

ARTS MAGAZINE/June 1966

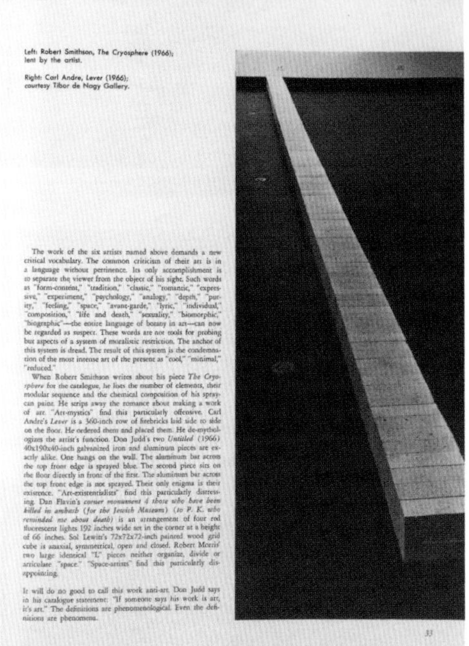

Left: Robert Smithson, *The Cryosphere* (1966); lent by the artist.

Right: Carl Andre, *Lever* (1966); courtesy Tibor de Nagy Gallery.

The work of the six artists named above demands a new critical vocabulary. The common criticism of their art is in a language without pertinence. Its only accomplishment is to separate the viewer from the object of his sight. Such words as "form-content," "tradition," "classic," "romantic," "expressive," "experiment," "psychology," "analogy," "depth," "purity," "feeling," "space," "avant-garde," "lyric," "individual," "composition," "life and death," "sexuality," "biomorphic," "biographic"—the entire language of botany in art—can now be regarded as suspect. These words are not tools for probing but aspects of a system of moralistic restriction. The anchor of this system is dread. The result of this system is the condemnation of the most intense art of the present as "cool," "minimal," "reduced."

When Robert Smithson writes about his piece *The Cryosphere* for the catalogue, he lists the number of elements, their modular sequence and the chemical composition of his spray-can paint. He strips away the romance about making a work of art. "Art-mystics" find this particularly offensive. Carl Andre's *Lever* is a 360-inch row of firebricks laid side to side on the floor. He ordered them and placed them. He de-mythologizes the artist's function. Don Judd's two *Untitled* (1966) 40x190x40-inch galvanized iron and aluminum pieces are exactly alike. One hangs on the wall. The aluminum bar across the top front edge is sprayed blue. The second piece sits on the floor directly in front of the first. The aluminum bar across the top front edge is not sprayed. Their only enigma is their existence. "Art-existentialists" find this particularly distressing. Dan Flavin's *corner monument 4 those who have been killed in ambush (for the Jewish Museum) (to P. K. who reminded me about death)* is an arrangement of four red fluorescent lights 192 inches wide set in the corner at a height of 66 inches. Sol Lewitt's 72x72x72-inch painted wood grid cube is anaxial, symmetrical, open and closed. Robert Morris' two large identical "L" pieces neither organize, divide or articulate "space." "Space-artists" find this particularly disappointing.

It will do no good to call this work anti-art. Don Judd says in his catalogue statement: "If someone says his work is art, it's art." The definitions are phenomenological. Even the definitions are phenomena.

Bochner has continued to employ systems of mathematics, geometry, and measurement in his work, and these remain important avenues. But his practices related to words, texts, and language follow a somewhat different route, culminating in a series of thesaurus paintings begun shortly after the turn of this century. In addition to those sources he also draws upon his own early art criticism, as well as artworks he made in the form of magazine layouts that incorporate texts and images. In all these efforts he refuses to maintain a firewall between the visual and the verbal.

Throughout his career, Bochner has written on art, beginning with short reviews of contemporary artists' exhibitions in New York galleries for *Arts Magazine* in 1965. Over the years he has contributed a substantial bibliography of reviews and essays to numerous publications. In the sixties and seventies it became common for artists to act as journalists and critics. Indeed, it was a hallmark of the Conceptual movement to bypass both art historians and art critics as analysts and interpreters; instead, the Conceptual artists themselves stepped into those roles.[20] Along with Donald Judd, Dan Graham, Joseph Kosuth, and Smithson, a host of other opinionated and erudite Conceptualists acted as both critics and theorists.

One of Bochner's first important articles for *Arts Magazine* was a review of "Primary Structures," the landmark 1966 exhibition of Minimalist sculpture at The Jewish Museum. His obsession with lists of words is already on display, and he is especially attuned to the terminology used to describe art. Writing on the way Minimalism resists traditional art-critical terminology, he remarks: "Such words as 'form-content,' 'tradition,' 'classic,' 'romantic,' 'expressive,' 'experiment,' 'psychology,' 'analogy,' 'depth,' 'purity,' 'feeling,' 'space,' 'avant-garde,' 'lyric,' 'individual,' 'composition,' 'life and death,' 'sexuality,' 'biomorphic,' 'biographic'—the entire language of botany in art—can now be regarded as suspect."[21] Although

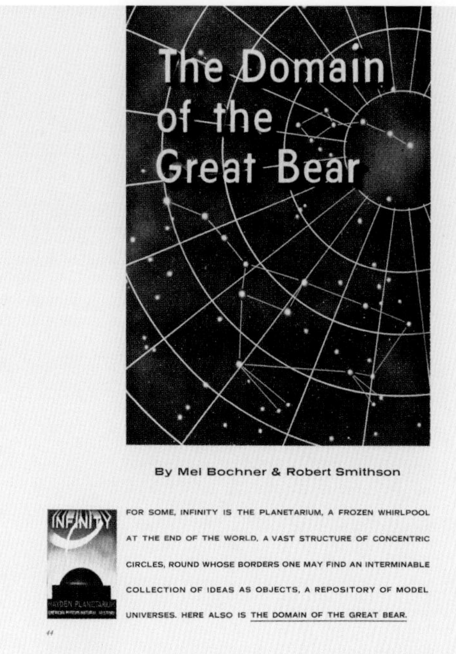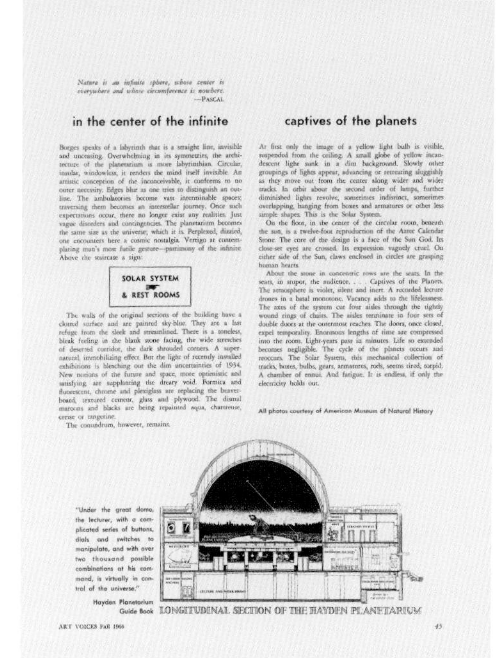

this is a collection of descriptors, not synonyms, Bochner's interest in listing definitions and vocabularies, and his sensitivity to the importance of verbal nuance, is clear. Such lists of synonyms and definitions pepper his writing about art. In fact a 1966 review of a show entitled "Eccentric Abstraction" starts with the definition: "Eccentric means off-center, idiosyncratic, perverse."[22] A review of Sol LeWitt's sculpture, also from 1966, begins: "Sol LeWitt: Grid. Cube. White. Wood. Intersection. Joint. Obstruction. White wood grid cubes and other structures which are not cubes. On the floor. In corners. Against walls. Floor to wall. Wall to wall. Ceiling to floor."  The block of text with its very short units of prose—single words and brief phrases—deliberately imitates LeWitt's work. The connection to Bochner's own portrait of LeWitt is self-evident.[23]

## CRITICISM AND ART, CRITICISM AS ART

Already playing with language and trying new means of reviewing exhibitions, Bochner sought to push further. "I became more interested in testing the boundary between writing-as-criticism and writing-as-visual-art."[24] In this spirit he collaborated with Smithson on a self-proclaimed "literary hoax," an artwork disguised as an article published in *Art Voices* magazine. The eight-page piece, entitled *The Domain of the Great Bear (Project for a Magazine),* is ostensibly about New York's American Museum of Natural History, and it incorporates the museum's own educational and promotional texts and photographs. But the true aim of this hybrid literary and critical animal was to create a work of art that, according to Bochner, "would fly under the radar." It sought to scrutinize the nature of creativity and distribution as well as the boundaries between original and reproduction. In doing so it perplexed most readers. As a collaborative enterprise, it additionally dismantled the western ideal of the solitary artist genius, of authorship in general, and of personal

# MISUNDERSTANDINGS
## (A THEORY OF PHOTOGRAPHY)
## MEL BOCHNER

PHOTOGRAPHS PROVIDE FOR A KIND OF PERCEPTION THAT IS MEDIATED INSTEAD OF DIRECT... WHAT MIGHT BE CALLED 'PERCEPTION AT SECOND HAND.'

JAMES J. GIBSON

THE PHOTOGRAPH KEEPS OPEN THE INSTANTS WHICH THE ONRUSH OF TIME CLOSES UP; IT DESTROYS THE OVERTAKING, THE OVERLAPPING OF TIME.

MAURICE MERLEAU-PONTY

IN MY OPINION, YOU CANNOT SAY YOU HAVE THOROUGHLY SEEN ANYTHING UNTIL YOU HAVE A PHOTOGRAPH OF IT.

EMILE ZOLA

LET US REMEMBER TOO, THAT WE DON'T HAVE TO TRANSLATE SUCH PICTURES INTO REALISTIC ONES IN ORDER TO 'UNDERSTAND' THEM, ANY MORE THAN WE NEED TRANSLATE PHOTOGRAPHS INTO COLORED PICTURES, ALTHOUGH BLACK-AND-WHITE MEN OR PLANTS IN REALITY WOULD STRIKE US AS UNSPEAKABLY STRANGE AND FRIGHTFUL. SUPPOSE WE WERE TO SAY AT THIS POINT: 'SOMETHING IS A PICTURE ONLY IN A PICTURE-LANGUAGE.'

LUDWIG WITTGENSTEIN

I WANT TO REPRODUCE THE OBJECTS AS THEY ARE OR AS THEY WOULD BE EVEN IF I DID NOT EXIST.

TAINE

PHOTOGRAPHY IS THE PRODUCT OF COMPLETE ALIENATION.

MARCEL PROUST

I WOULD LIKE TO SEE PHOTOGRAPHY MAKE PEOPLE DESPISE PAINTING UNTIL SOMETHING ELSE WILL MAKE PHOTOGRAPHY UNBEARABLE.

MARCEL DUCHAMP

THE TRUE FUNCTION OF REVOLUTIONARY ART IS THE CRYSTALLIZATION OF PHENOMENA INTO ORGANIZED FORMS.

MAO TSE-TUNG

PHOTOGRAPHY CANNOT RECORD ABSTRACT IDEAS.

ENCYCLOPEDIA BRITANNICA

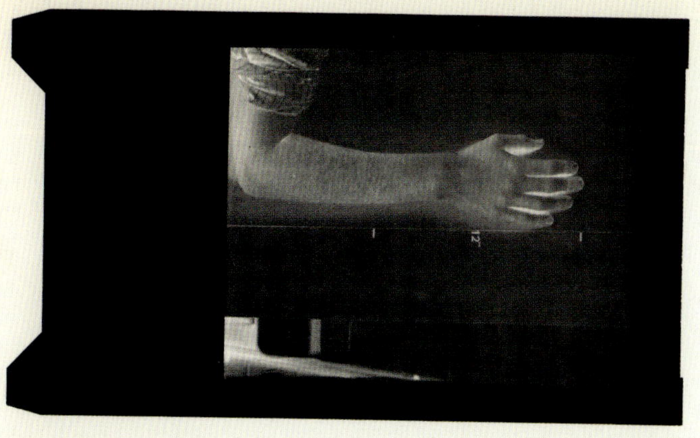

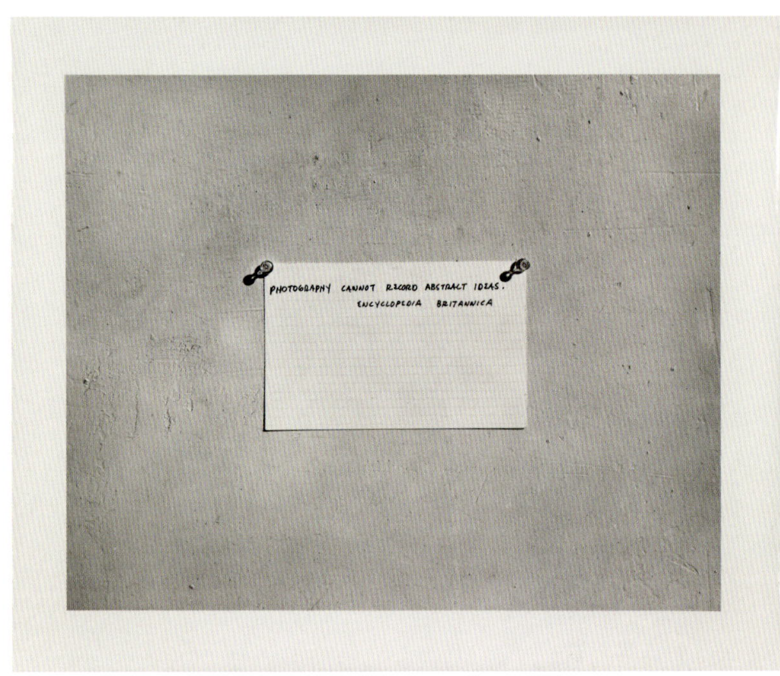


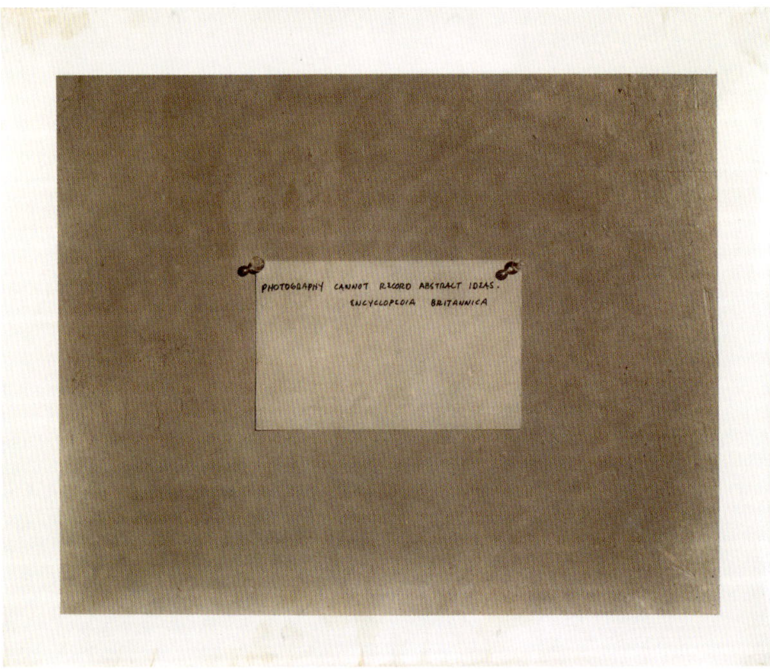


***Photography Before the Age of Mechanical Reproduction,* 2011**

Suite of six photographs: albumen, platinotype, collodion-chloride, gelatin,
salt, and cyanotype, each 20 × 24 in. (50.8 × 61 cm)
Two Palms

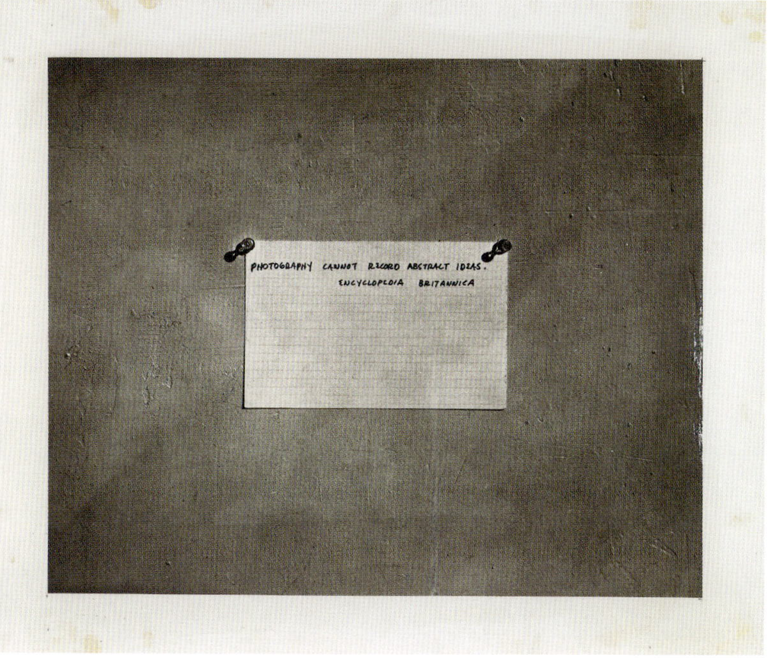

PHOTOGRAPHY CANNOT RECORD ABSTRACT IDEAS.
ENCYCLOPEDIA BRITANNICA

PHOTOGRAPHY CANNOT RECORD ABSTRACT IDEAS.
ENCYCLOPEDIA BRITANNICA


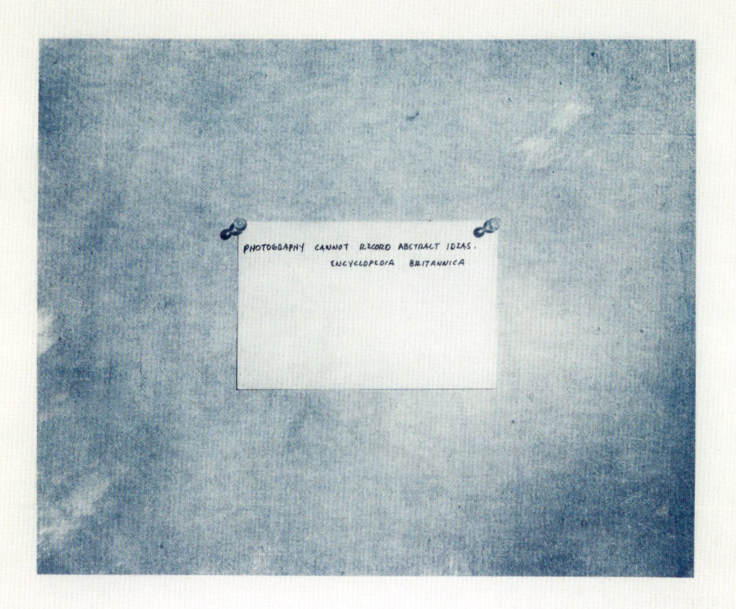

PHOTOGRAPHY CANNOT RECORD ABSTRACT IDEAS.
ENCYCLOPEDIA BRITANNICA

PHOTOGRAPHY CANNOT RECORD ABSTRACT IDEAS.
ENCYCLOPEDIA BRITANNICA

expression in particular. In effect, the article used reproductive means and mass markets as a newfound medium for making art and in the process undermined the function of the art magazine itself. The artists deployed pastiche, parody, and montage; among other things, they imitated and critiqued other contemporary critics' and artists' styles. And the design had an intentionally camp, dated look.[25]

In Bochner's and Smithson's hands the mundane vehicle of the magazine article became a self-reflexive work of art—a parody of the standard mechanisms by which art is made, displayed, collected, and disseminated. Acknowledging the radical changes that mass culture imposed on creativity, they diverted the usual means of artistic production directly into channels of marketing and reproduction. Though this purposefully deceptive artistic venture was recognized by few at the time, today it is revered as a transformative strategy and an icon of the period.[26]

Bochner's ventures into photography continued his project of undercutting the borders between reality and imagination, authenticity and fabrication, intellectual inquiry and archival documentation. *Misunderstandings (A Theory of Photography)* builds upon ideas and tactics used in *The Domain of the Great Bear.* Nine texts handwritten by Bochner on note cards each record a statement about photography (page 23). These are ascribed to Émile Zola, Ludwig Wittgenstein, Maurice Merleau-Ponty, Marcel Proust, Hippolyte Taine, the *Encyclopedia Britannica,* Marcel Duchamp, Mao Tse-Tung, and James J. Gibson. A tenth image is a negative of the artist's own hand. This was made from a photograph of a Polaroid (a photographic process that has no negative). The ten components were then subject to further reproduction: editioned as a suite of offset lithographs the size of the cards, which were placed in a manila envelope inscribed with the title (also offset).

To make a negative of a Polaroid belies the truth to materials so important to the history of modernism; not only that, but three of the nine written statements are inventions of the artist.[27] *Misunderstandings* is an understatement: the work is composed of partial truths and outright fictions that demonstrate the unreliability of both text and technology. Its status is further complicated by the fact the note cards and the negative of the Polaroid are printed reproductions: they are mechanical copies of what appear to be ordinary handwritten notes or perhaps study aids. By the end of the process Bochner had created an artwork that felt ephemeral and that once again interrogated the meaning of originality.

In 2011 the artist revisited this piece in *Photography Before the Age of Mechanical Reproduction* (page 24) as part of his ongoing rethinking and reformulation of earlier work. Collaborating with Barret Oliver, a master printer, he rephotographed one of the original printed note cards for *Misunderstandings* ("photography cannot record abstract ideas") six times, using six different antiquated processes: albumen, platinotype, collodion-chloride, gelatin, salt, and cyanotype. Bochner describes the results: "In the original 1970 photograph, the note card became an abstraction of itself, floating in the center of the black background, indexical, but devoid of any context. In the new series, the note card . . . is seen as an object pinned to a wall, with its shadow cast by an actual light source—the sun. Simultaneously index and icon, it becomes a self-contradictory documentation of itself, unmoored from any specifiable historical time frame."[28]

In this remaking he again shows that objectivity is virtually impossible in art in general, and photography in particular. Likewise, Bochner explores how different technologies impose new meanings on the same simple object. Here, he says, he was less interested in making photography than in "taking it apart." In dismantling the premises on which photography rests he is reexamining the way materials change meanings and generate new interpretations.

Key to understanding Bochner's language-based works is his wall piece *Language Is Not Transparent,* first created in 1970 and remade by the artist many times in the past forty years (pages 29–31). He painted a black rectangle directly on a white gallery wall; three sides are straight-edged, but the bottom of the rectangle is unevenly brushed and paint has been allowed to drip down the wall. As if it were a lesson on a blackboard, Bochner chalked an inscription on the paint:

I. LANGUAGE

IS NOT

TRANSPARENT

In the painted portion of this work he is taking the high seriousness of Abstract Expressionism to task.[29] The rectangular part, along with the black trickles, is a pastiche of the style's gestural qualities, its personal and existential associations, and its iconic drips—characteristics that became fetishized modes of expression. It's as if Hans Hofmann's colored blocks were married to Willem de Kooning's splashes of paint. The text, meanwhile, questions Conceptualism's lofty ideas about the objectivity of language. As so often in Bochner's work, *Language Is Not Transparent* embodies contradictions.

The hand-wrought words and painted surface imply the presence of the artist, while the artwork's placement directly on the wall negates its status as an independent, commodifiable creation. Bochner uses the traditional mechanism of the sinopia, or transfer sketch—a technique as old as mural painting. Yet this wall painting also traffics in the artist's lifelong interest in the way new situations can transform meaning. In *Language Is Not Transparent* each iteration draws attention to the variant details of its manufacture and different aspects of ephemerality: a baseboard that collects drips, a nearby corner, an architecturally striking ceiling. Bochner's repeated remaking of this work is distinguished in fundamental ways from the precise replicas demanded by his Conceptualist colleagues: happenstance is inherent in his program of making and remaking. *Language Is Not Transparent* can never look the same twice.

The bald yet enigmatic statement reminds us that language is shaped by cultural associations and contexts and is neither neutral nor inert. As Bochner put it, "Language forms a crust over thought, and predetermines not only *how* we see, but *what* we see."[30]

***Language Is Not Transparent*, 1970**

Installed in the exhibition "Language IV," Dwan Gallery, New York
Chalk on paint on wall, 72 × 48 in. (182.9 × 121.9 cm)
Los Angeles County Museum of Art, Modern and Contemporary Art Council

1. LANGUAGE IS NOT TRANSPARENT

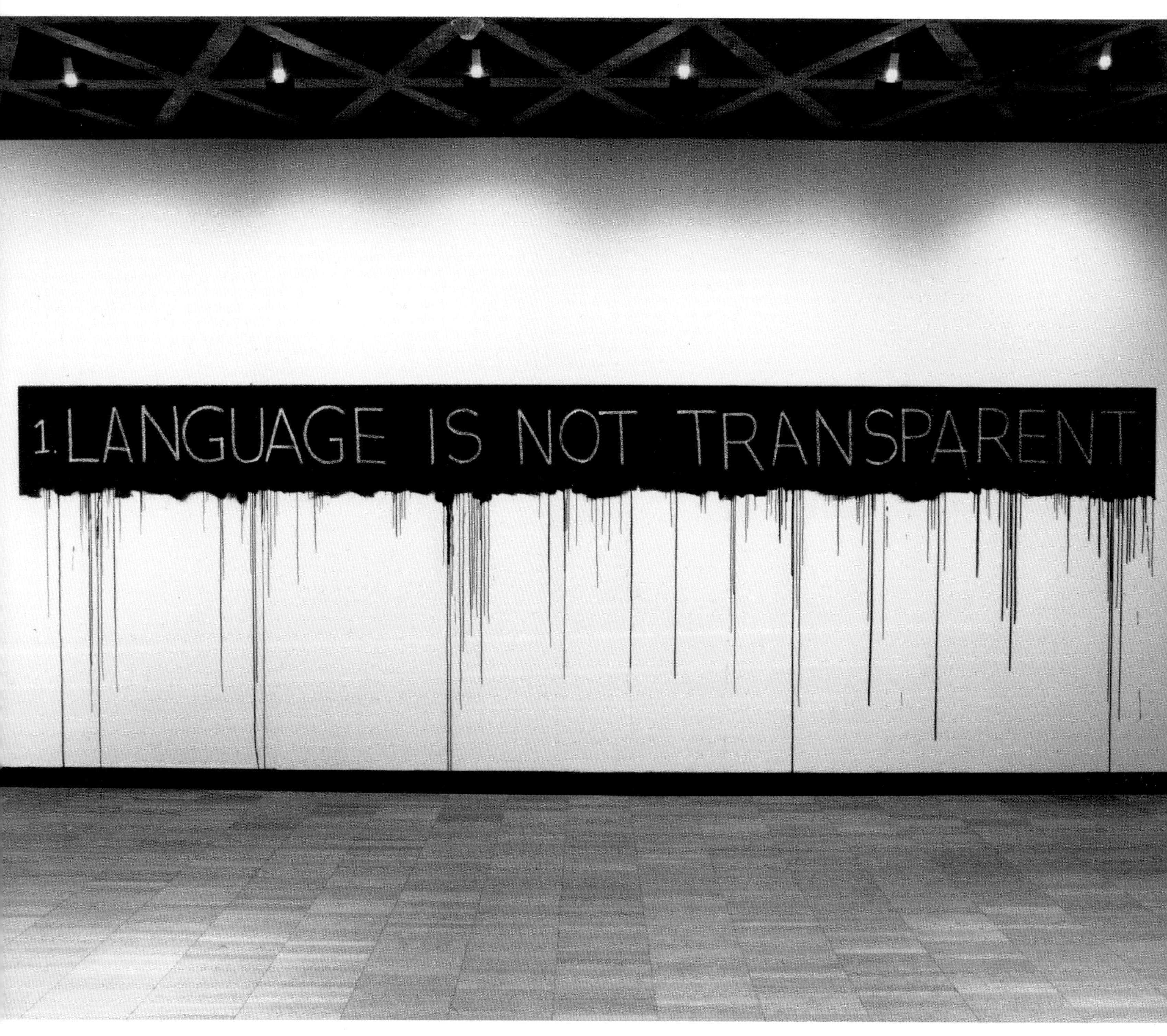


***Language Is Not Transparent*, 1995**

Installed in the exhibition "Mel Bochner: Thought Made Visible
1966–1973," Yale University Art Gallery, New Haven

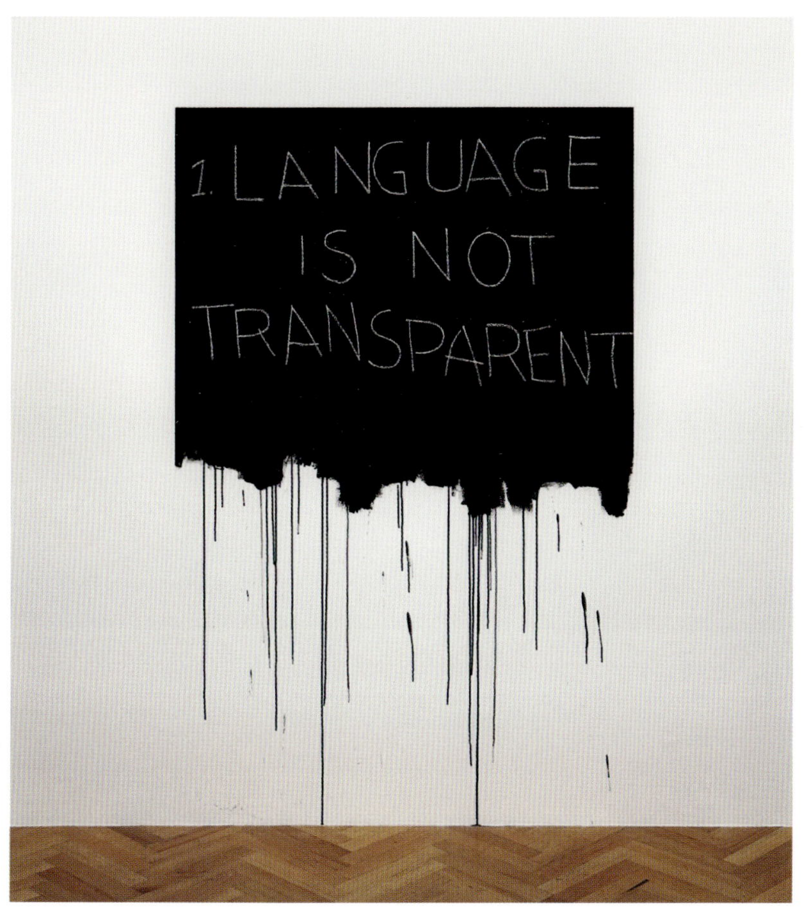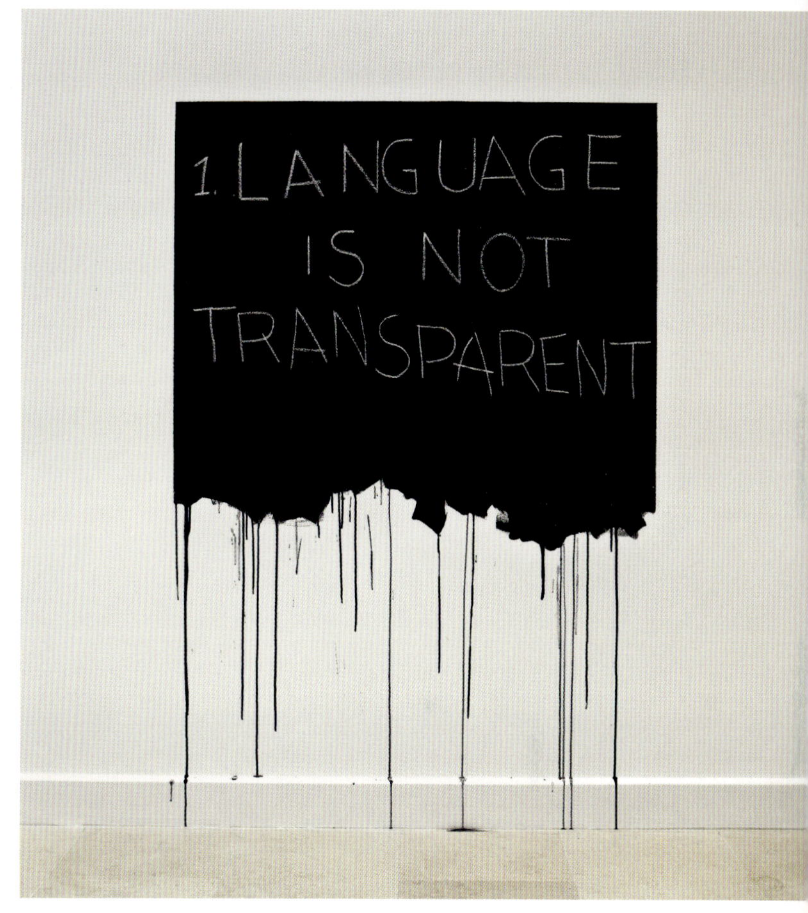



***Language Is Not Transparent*, 2006**

Installed in the exhibition "Mel Bochner: Language, 1966–2006,"
Art Institute of Chicago

***Language Is Not Transparent*, 2010**

Installed in the exhibition "Double Bind/Stop Trying to Understand Me,"
Villa Arson, Nice

LANGUAGE IS NOT TRANSPARENT
LANGUAGE IS NOT TRANSPARENT
LANGUAGE IS NOT TRANSPARENT
LANGUAGE IS NOT TRANSPARENT
LANGUAGE IS NOT TRANSPARENT
MEL BOCHNER, 1969

## PHILOSOPHY OF LANGUAGE

*Language Is Not Transparent* evolved from a small-scale work of the same title made in 1969: four note cards bearing the eponymous phrase, produced with a cheap commercial rubber stamp of the sort commonplace in offices at the time. This gadget, and the action associated with it, gave Bochner's ambiguous theorem, "language is not transparent," the dubious authority of the administrator who stamps invoices "paid" or "overdue." It also plays on the idiom "to rubber-stamp," with its implication of the mechanical, worthless official endorsement. Bochner's satiric use of both tool and gesture evokes H. L. Mencken's cynical phrase "the rubber stamp of criticism."

The first card is stamped once; each successive card is more heavily printed; the final one is so dense that it is almost illegible. Thus the meaning of the phrase is canceled out as the text becomes more and more opaque. This was one of Bochner's first uses of repeated and overprinted texts. He pushed this strategy further in a series of paintings based on writings of the philosopher Ludwig Wittgenstein.

Wittgenstein was important to many artists and intellectuals during the 1960s and early 1970s. Bochner at this time was reading Wittgenstein's *Philosophical Investigations* and *On Certainty* and using those texts to develop his own thinking and art practice. Wittgenstein urged an incessant questioning of ideas and assumptions; Bochner was drawn to his refusal to "stamp anything 'case closed.'"[31] The artist's exploration of the limits of written and spoken language, as well as the vocabularies of art, owes much to this notion.

A key concept for Wittgenstein is the idea that language cannot fully represent the things it stands for and is therefore by nature ineffective — in fact, amorphous. While words that describe tangible objects are less prone to this problem, words that attempt to describe abstract ideas inevitably fail.[32] That distinction pervades Bochner's lifelong investigation into how language operates. In 1995 he addressed the problem concretely in a work based on a quotation from Wittgenstein, "Nothing we do can be defended absolutely and finally. But only by reference to something else that is not questioned. . . ."[33] The English text in black is superimposed on the German in red, which in turn is painted onto two upside-down sheets of the *New York Times* (from two different dates), creating a palimpsest effect (page 35). This overlapping and illegibility mirror Wittgenstein's proposition that knowledge and behavior are always contingent. The work may be seen as a prelude to more complex interactions with the philosopher.

Wittgenstein continues to inspire Bochner, who has returned to his writings time and again. A late book, *Remarks on Colour,* provides the central text and intellectual underpinning of a series of paintings titled *If the Color Changes,* made between 1997 and 2000 (pages 36–43). These form an important way station on Bochner's journey to his unmitigated obsession with the intersection of color and language.

Like much of Wittgenstein's work, the book on color is dense and elliptical. The author seeks to establish connections between the perception of color and its description in language.[34] This philosophical exploration offered Bochner a way to embrace color more vigorously than he had done before. His paintings of the mid-1990s are, all of a sudden,

*Language Is Not Transparent,* **1969**

Rubber stamp on four note cards, each 5 × 8 in. (12.7 × 20.3 cm)
Collection of the artist

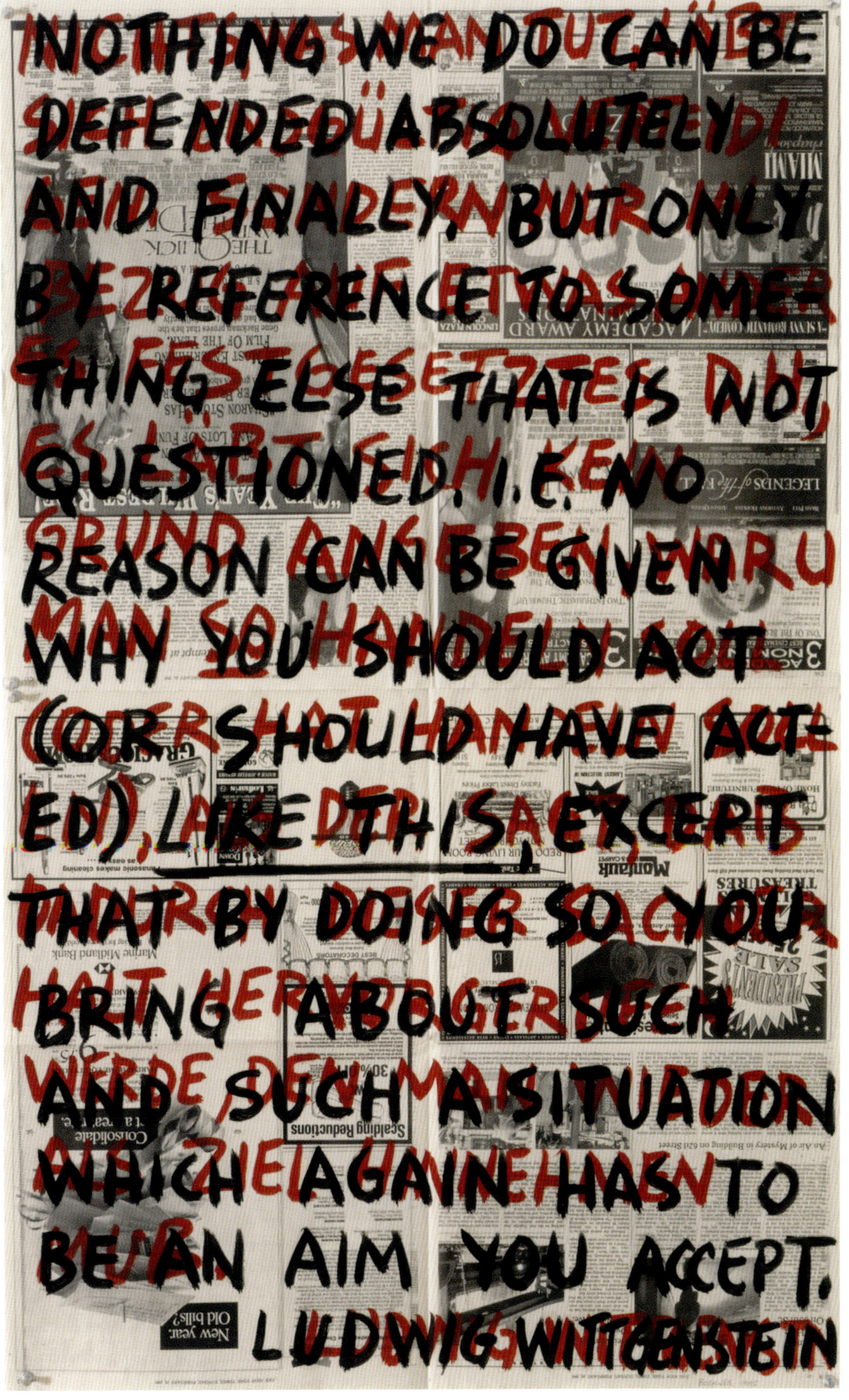

NOTHING WE DO CAN BE DEFENDED ABSOLUTELY AND FINALLY, BUT ONLY BY REFERENCE TO SOMETHING ELSE THAT IS NOT QUESTIONED. I.E. NO REASON CAN BE GIVEN WHY YOU SHOULD ACT (OR SHOULD HAVE ACTED), LIKE THIS EXCEPT THAT BY DOING SO YOU BRING ABOUT SUCH AND SUCH A SITUATION WHICH AGAIN HAS TO BE AN AIM YOU ACCEPT. LUDWIG WITTGENSTEIN

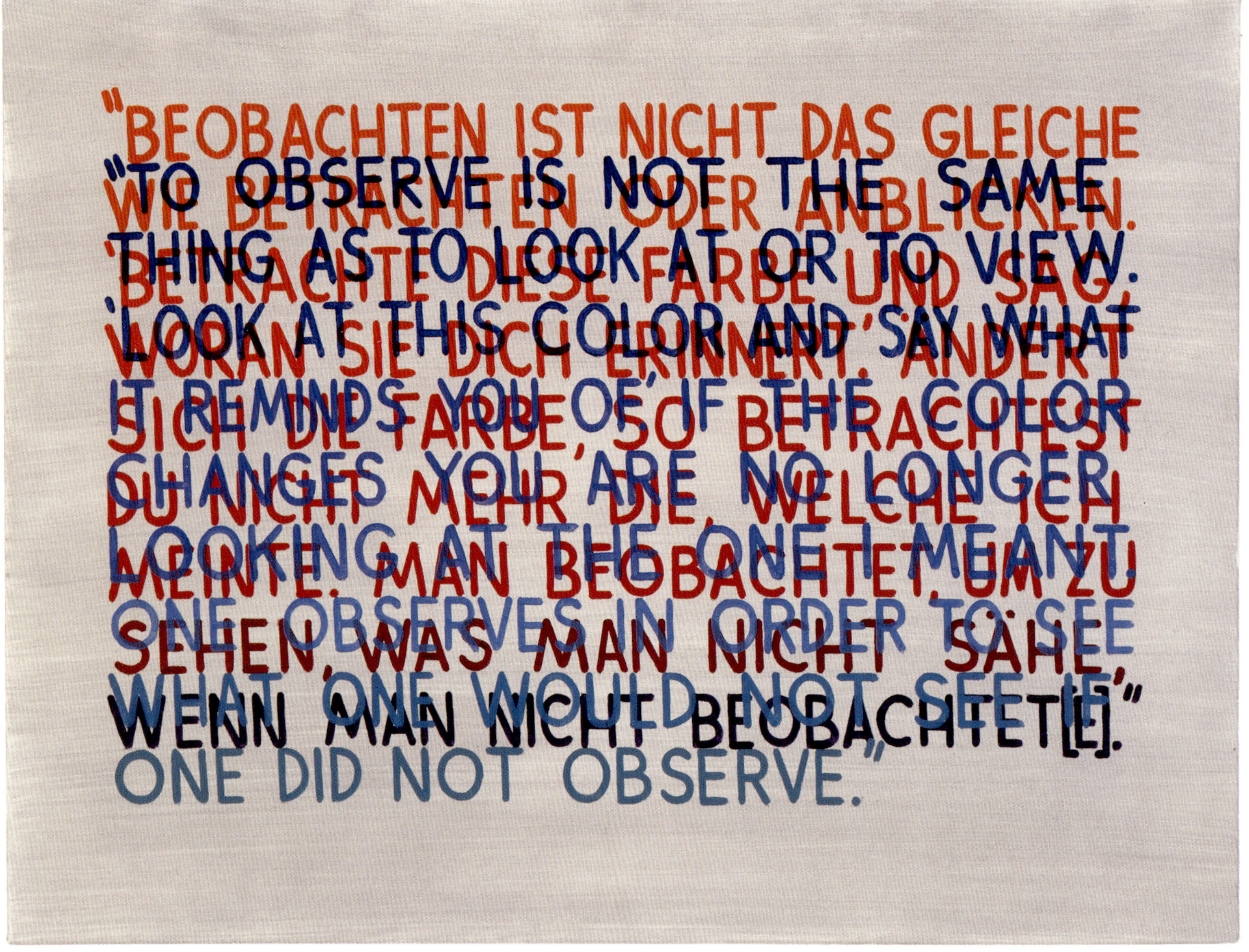



*If the Color Changes (#1)*, 1997

Oil and alkyd on canvas, 36 × 48 in. (91.4 × 121.9 cm)
Private collection

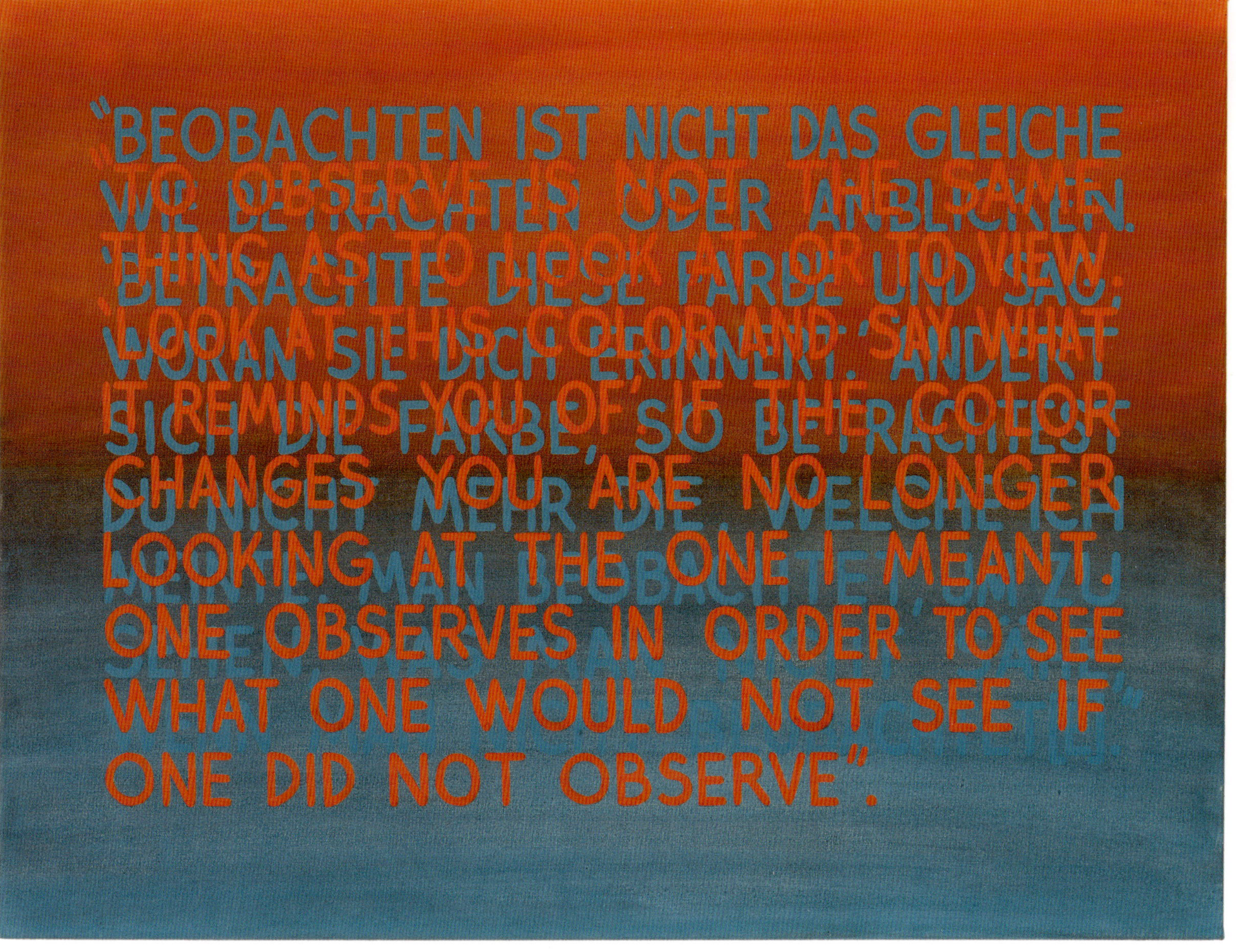


*If the Color Changes (#2), 1997*

Oil on canvas, 36 × 48 in. (91.4 × 121.9 cm)
Private collection

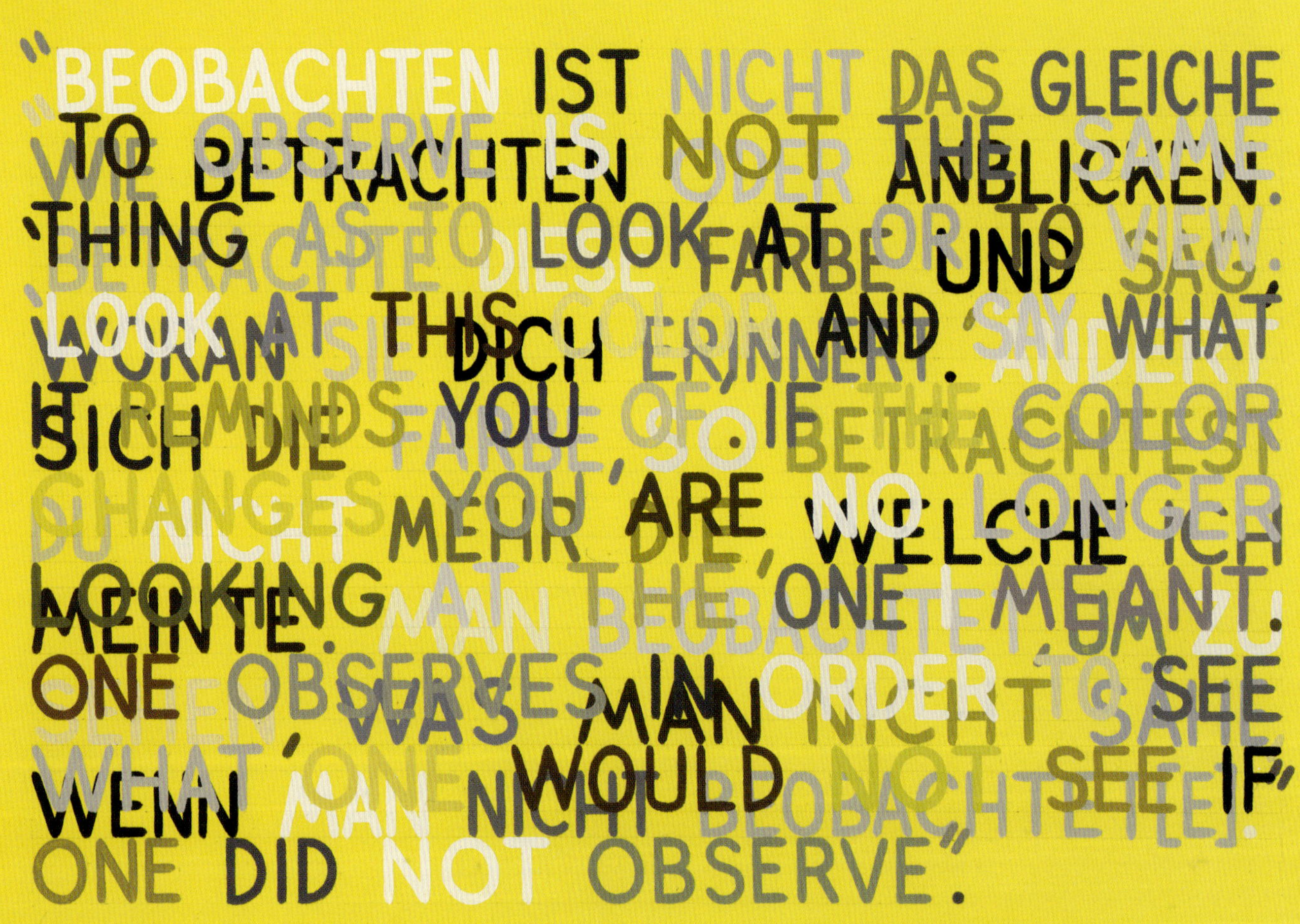


***If the Color Changes (#5)*, 1998**

Oil on canvas, 36 × 48 in. (91.4 × 121.9 cm)
Private collection, Monaco

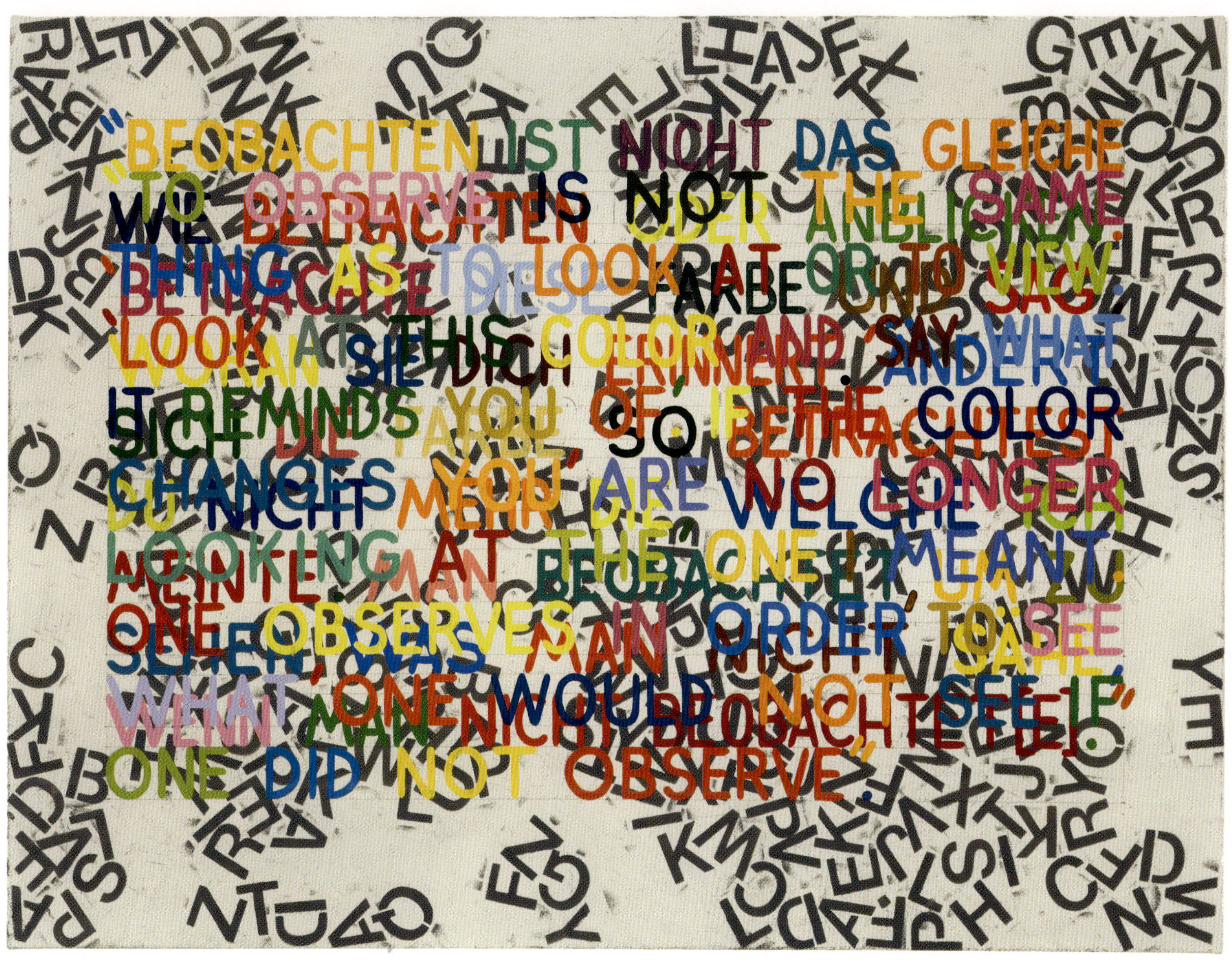

***If the Color Changes (#9), 1999***

Oil on canvas, 36 × 48 in. (91.4 × 121.9 cm)
Private collection

brilliantly hued and freely coloristic. The series *If the Color Changes* takes as its starting point a Wittgenstein quotation: "To observe is not the same thing as to look at or to view. 'Look at this color and say what it reminds you of.' If the color changes you are no longer looking at the one I meant. One observes in order to see what one would not see if one did not observe."[35]

The paintings take up the challenge of interpreting this. Bochner blazons the passage on a series of ten canvases, each iteration using a different combination of colored letters and backgrounds. The English translation overlaps the original German text: as in the scrambled letters of Bochner's portrait of Flavin (see page 13), the interlocking texts are difficult to decipher.

Bochner turns painting into an experiment in the visual manifestation of language. By doing so he inevitably describes both the limitations of language and the possibilities of painting. With all intended irony he takes this highly theoretical, convoluted text as an artistic sanction for his shift to high key, wildly bright, and often cacophonous color.

In most of the pictures color obstructs legibility: words layered over each other in hues of similar value or in complementary colors create a dynamic that makes them virtually unreadable. The paintings, with their tangled, superimposed texts, themselves become expressions of the opacity of Wittgenstein's thought. They are challenging to read, perceive, experience—or, in Wittgenstein's term, to observe.

Contributing to this visual confusion is the use of lively colored backgrounds, which add formal and optical challenges to the already complex imagery. These range from a simple black, white, or bicolor field to rainbow stripes or variegated disks. One painting's ground has soft gradations of color from red to blue. In another, green and blue letters are overlaid on a grid of multicolor circles in varied sizes. That picture pulsates with collisions of rhythmic forms and effervescent colors. The backdrops add yet another level of distancing—Bochner calls it his "delaying mechanism." Presenting visual feast and mental conundrum, Bochner complicates, even confuses, the interface between reading and seeing.

The backgrounds play off a whole range of references to late modernist painting: Color Field, Op, geometric abstraction, and monochrome painting are but a few of the movements Bochner riffs on as he repurposes them. He is alluding to an ongoing debate that began in the 1960s and 1970s about whether painting was still a viable means of expression, and how it might be reinvigorated.

Bochner's use in the 1990s of painterly approaches from the 1970s was tongue in cheek, but his underlying interest in the problem of color was serious. His aim, he says, was "to get at the difficulty of saying anything about color." The series "deals with the conflict between color-as-experience and color-as-grammar."[36] He uses the intersections of color, form, and language to entangle these radically different modes of perception. Simply put, the works both conceal and reveal. Once again, *If the Color Changes* is a game: the works force the viewer to unravel their visual and textual mysteries.

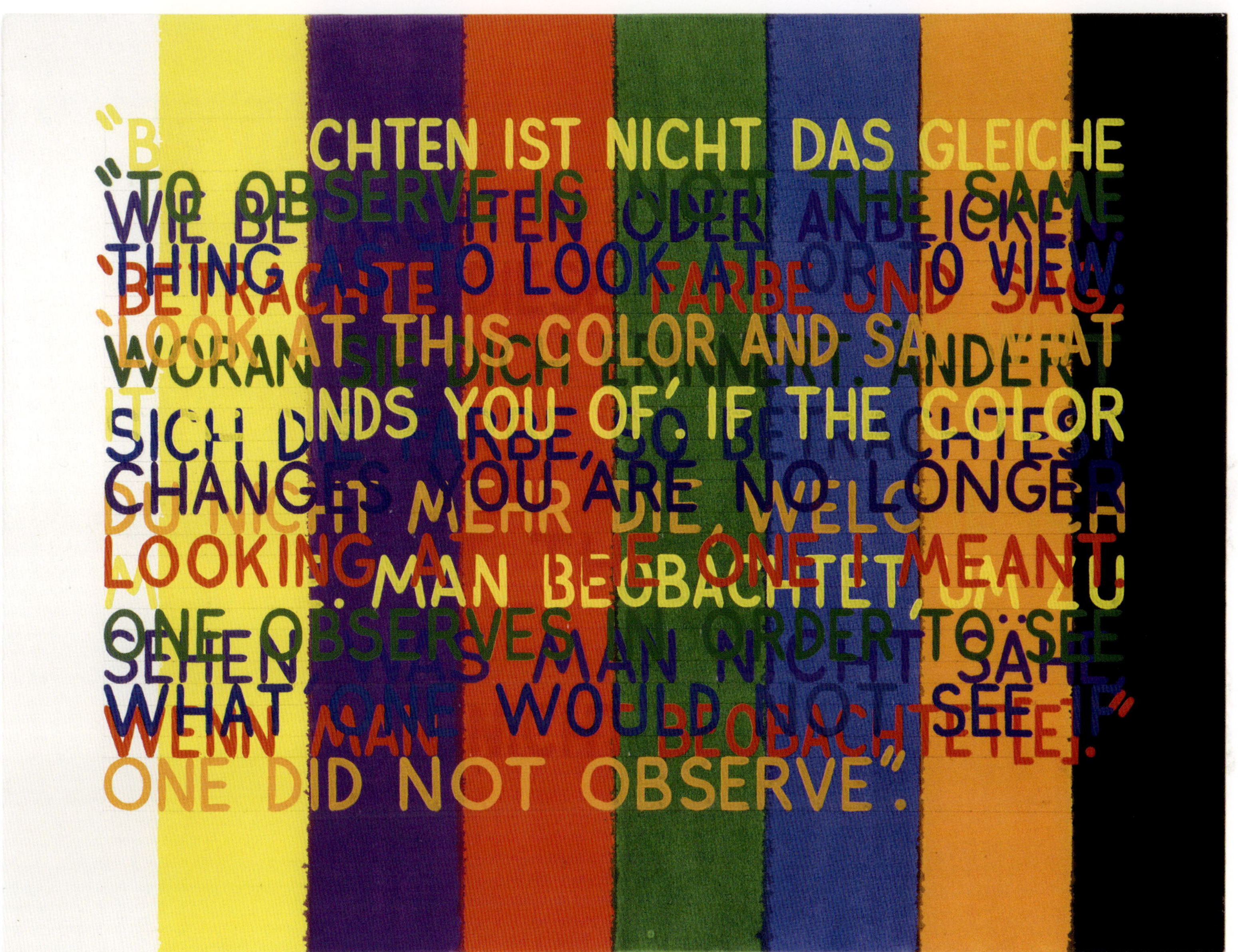



*If the Color Changes (#7),* **1998**

Oil on canvas, 36 × 48 in. (91.4 × 121.9 cm)
Collection of the artist

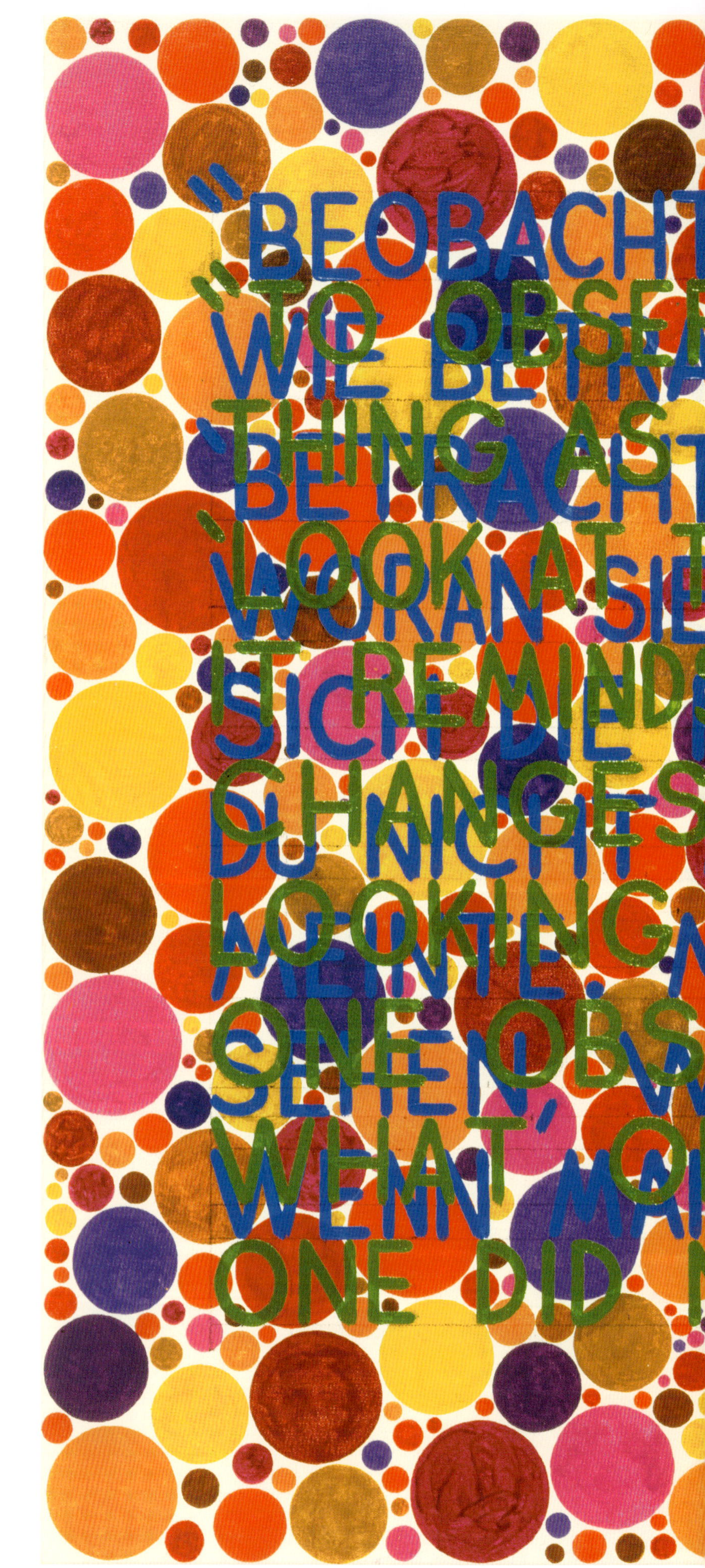

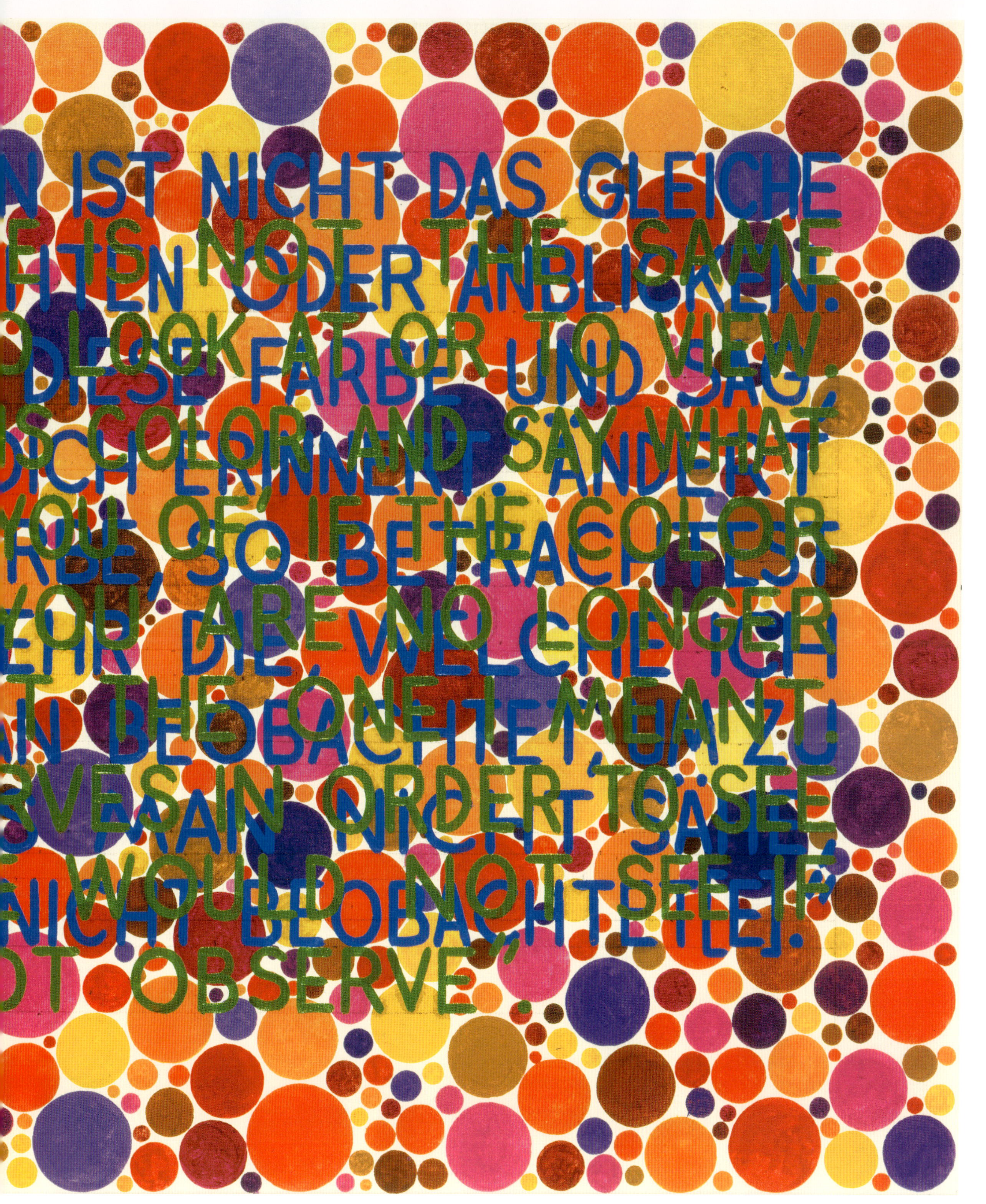

## THE WORD WAREHOUSE

*If the Color Changes* posited the near impossibility of grasping the verbal and the visual simultaneously, and yet contended that they were inseparable. This perceptual split—the problem of synchronizing textual comprehension and visual perception—became the cornerstone of Bochner's thesaurus paintings. The series, an extended examination of the issue, began seriously around 2002 and continues, although it builds upon the artist's earlier use of synonym lists, definitions, and other word clusters. He has made myriad paintings, as well as prints and drawings, using the thesaurus.

The project was launched after the publication in 2001 of the sixth edition of Roget's classic thesaurus. The new volume was more inclusive and less constrained in its vocabulary, incorporating more slang, vernacular, jargon, and—most strikingly to the artist—vulgarities and obscenities of all sorts. Its permissiveness spurred him to broaden his linguistic references to align with his newly open attitude toward color.

Bochner's thesaurus project may be considered a "painterly Readymade," with all the hybrid and contradictory aspects that coinage implies. That is, a painterly approach is applied to a found subject, image, or process—in his case the readily available collections of synonyms in *Roget's Thesaurus.*[37] The thesaurus paintings raise the same linguistic, visual, and phenomenological concerns explored in *If the Color Changes,* but at a new level of complexity. Bochner creates visual and verbal snares for his viewers, who are asked to negotiate a path between brushwork and color on the one hand, and word and meaning on the other. The works, harking back to the early word portraits, are built on the idea of collections of synonyms, but these now no longer depict an individual artist or his or her work. Rather, they stand on their own as the visible manifestation of an idea or sequence of ideas. The words on the canvas range from the familiar to the offbeat, the understandable to the esoteric, the comforting to the embarrassing. These word pictures can be read as both abstract and representational.[38]

One of the paintings leading up to the thesaurus series was the deceptively simple *Un-able* (page 46). Given the dizzying complexity of the *If the Color Changes* series, its format and concept are remarkably straightforward: a tall, narrow canvas divided into candy-colored horizontal bands, each with a single word in a contrasting or complementary hue, all painted in a goofy, childlike facture. All the words are terms of negation, denial, or frustration. The title, with its sly hyphen, suggests the potential unfeasibility of the entire project—the effort to give visual and intellectual form to that which can be neither expressed nor executed. Any action, any perception, Bochner suggests, can be un-done. The unpainted block of white primer at the bottom of the stack is the direct visual materialization of that impossibility.

*No* was made in the same year but is more complex. A catalogue of synonyms—from NO, NEGATIVE at upper left to OVER MY DEAD BODY, MY ASS at lower right—are painted with homestyle lettering in a tactile, disarming manner. The panel is bifurcated: red on the left and orange on the right. Six rows of alternating blue and yellow texts down either side create a vibrating optical effect, as if the viewer were seeing colored rectangles. The eye

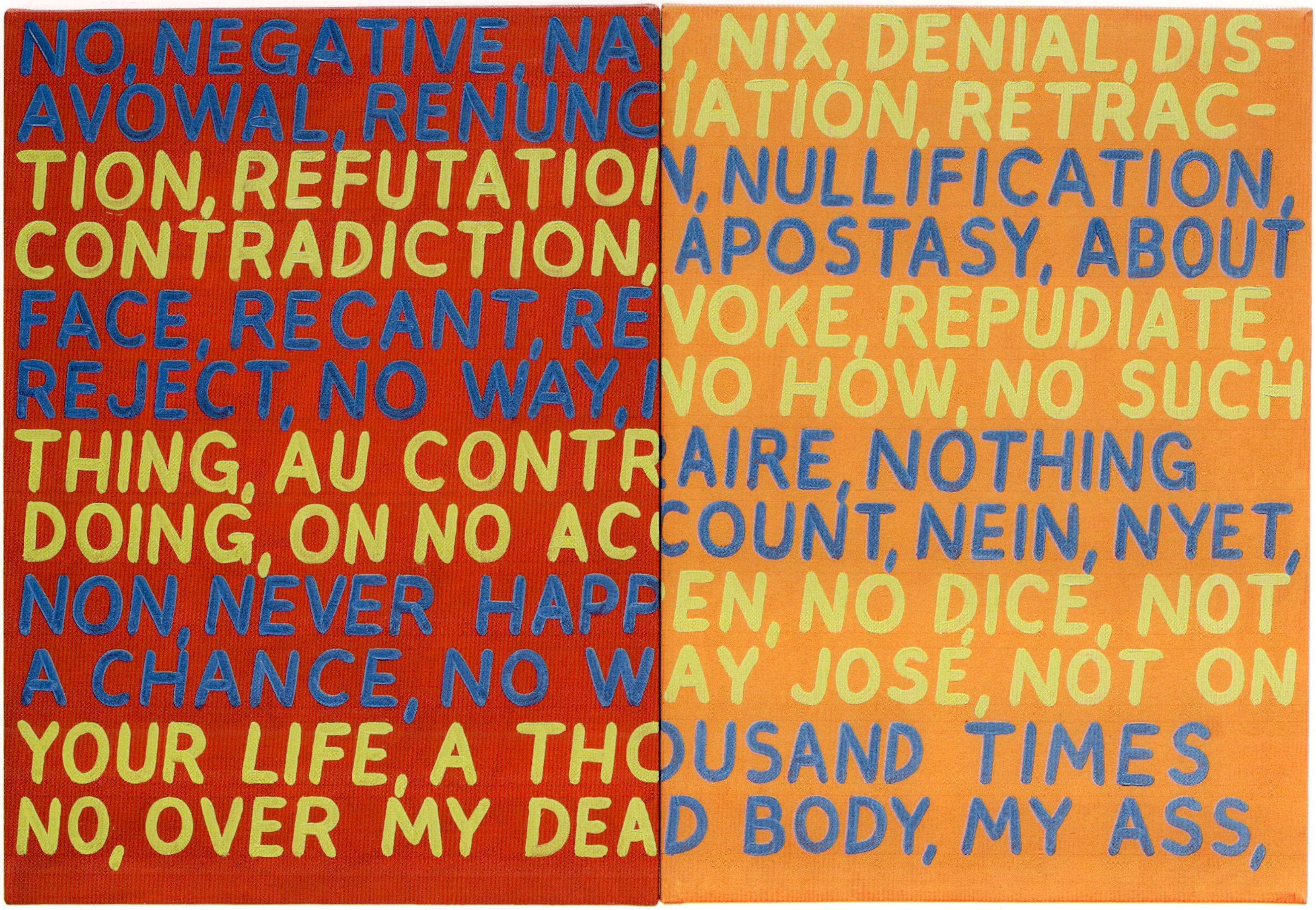

***No,*** 2002

Oil and acrylic on two canvases, 24 × 36 in. (60.9 × 91.4 cm)
Sandro and Fiamma Manzo

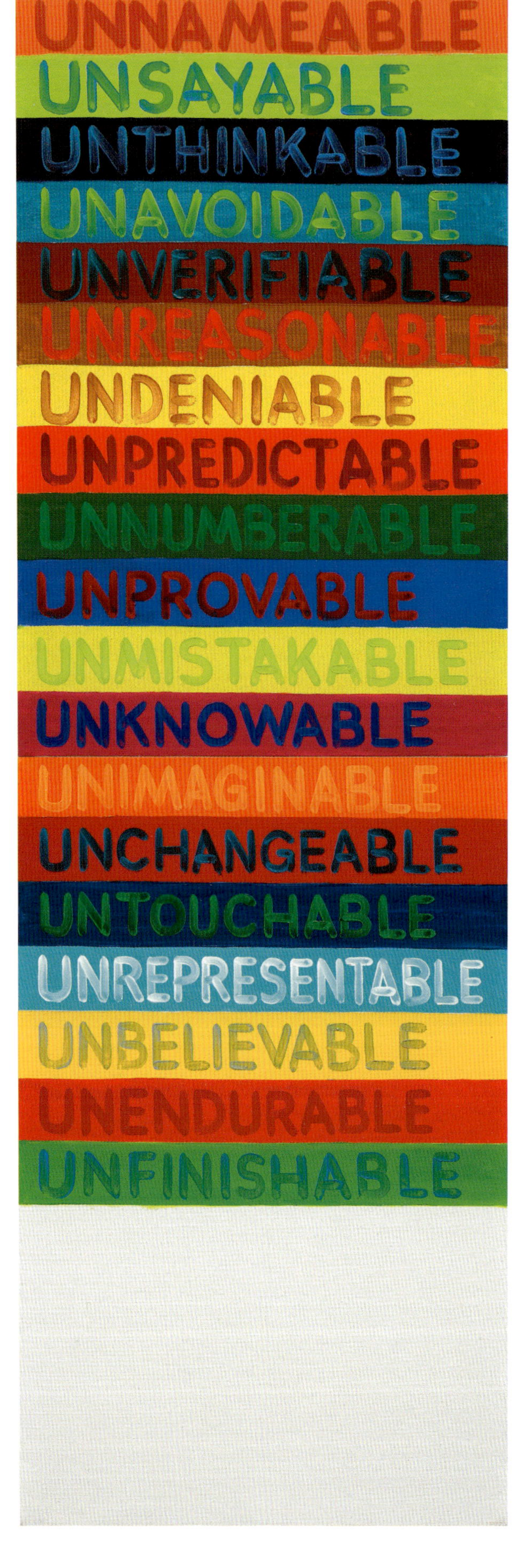

UNNAMEABLE
UNSAYABLE
UNTHINKABLE
UNAVOIDABLE
UNVERIFIABLE
UNREASONABLE
UNDENIABLE
UNPREDICTABLE
UNNNUMBERABLE
UNPROVABLE
UNMISTAKABLE
UNKNOWABLE
UNIMAGINABLE
UNCHANGEABLE
UNTOUCHABLE
UNREPRESENTABLE
UNBELIEVABLE
UNENDURABLE
UNFINISHABLE

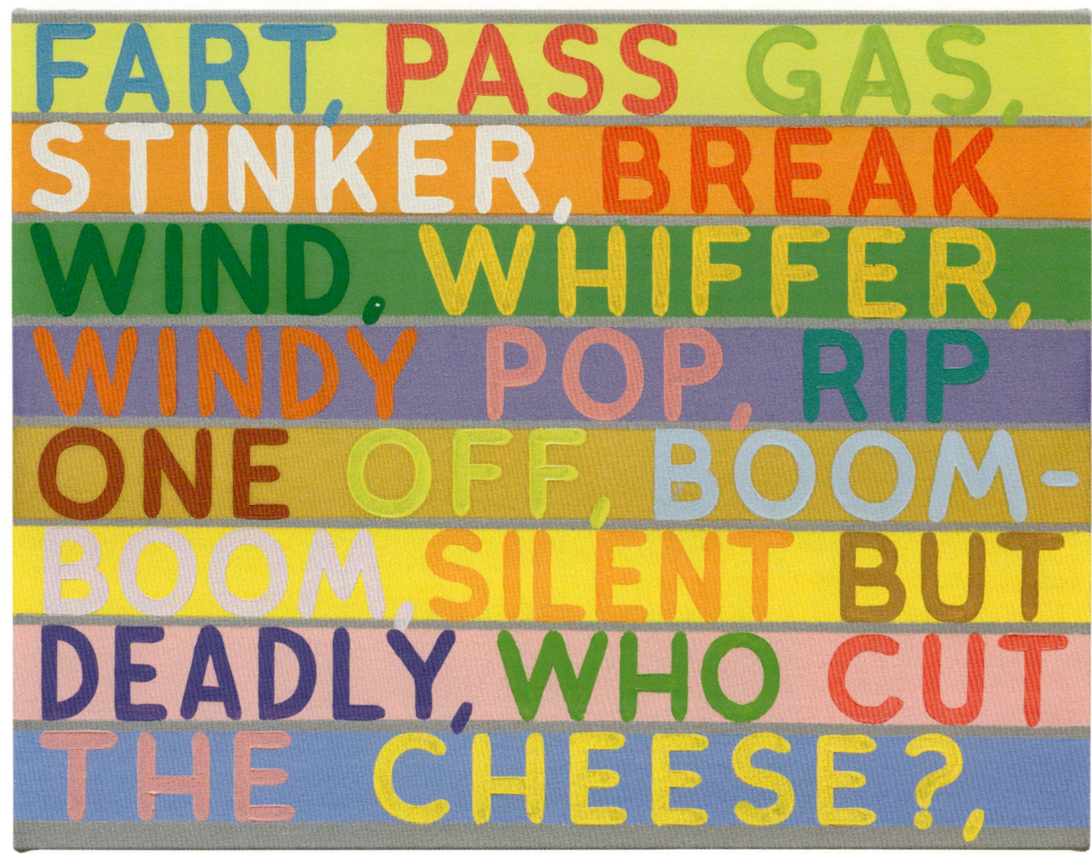



**Un-able, 2002**

Oil on two canvases, 60 × 20 in. (152.4 × 50.8 cm)
Leslie and Alan Pearson

**(Small) Fart, 2003**

Oil and acrylic on canvas, 18 × 24 in. (45.7 × 60.9 cm)
Piera Bochner

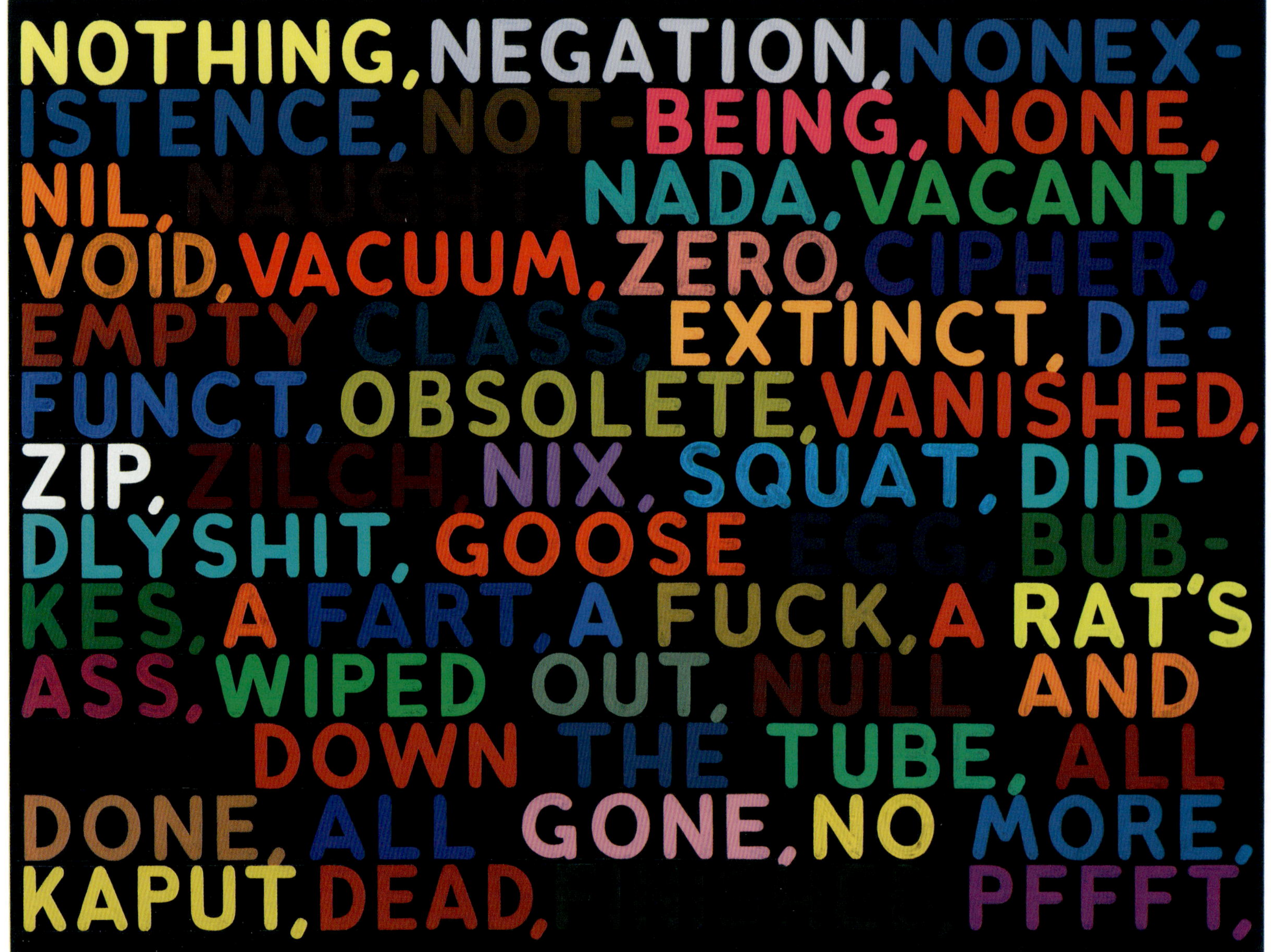


*Nothing*, 2003

Oil on canvas, 45 × 60 in. (114.3 × 152.4 cm)
Jill and Peter Kraus, New York

moves up and down to experience the color but left to right to read the text. Color and words compete aggressively for the viewer's attention. Bochner notes that his color strategy is meant "to divert the text from any responsibility to meaning."[39]

By 2003 the thesaurus pictures have become steadily more sophisticated in their visual articulation and textual locution. *Nothing* flaunts a smooth paint application on a sleek black background. Its language echoes Bochner's earlier interests, particularly the writers who had inspired him at the start of his career: here, as in paintings like *No, Die,* and *Useless,* he is channeling Samuel Beckett's abjection and nihilism. Beginning with the word NOTHING, he takes the reader through a litany of negatives, from the existential (NONEXISTENCE, NEGATION, VOID) to the commonplace (A RAT'S ASS, NULL AND VOID, KAPUT, DEAD, FINISHED), ending with the inchoate utterance PFFFT. While the thesaurus is the source, this stunning arc of words is Bochner's own fabrication. He traces the descent of language from presence to absence (or existence to disappearance) in a carefully mediated serial progression.

The games with color and perception continue. Some words pop out in yellow on the black background like a beacon (NOTHING, NO, KAPUT); others are so close in tone to the background that they nearly vanish (NAUGHT, EGG, VOID, FINISHED). Of course, the minute the viewer succeeds in deciphering such hidden texts, the painterly and chromatic qualities of the picture immediately interfere with the urge to read; and vice versa. One is never able to truly experience image and text in unison. As he often does, Bochner is playing with the classic relationship of figure to ground.[40] As always in his art, there is a sense of intellectual provocation and cultural appraisal, woven together with wit and deadpan humor. Bochner himself cautions that these works may be read as up- or downbeat according to the sensibility of the viewer.[41] The collision between painting and language positions the viewer at the complex, disorienting interface between the perceptual and conceptual.

Bochner's process for the thesaurus paintings emerges from his earlier interest in serial concepts and attitudes.[42] In densely annotated notebooks and preparatory drawings, he hones, analyzes, develops, organizes, and reorganizes his verbal inventory. He often chooses words with personal and autobiographical associations, and they come to him from many sources: "Reading, thinking about the state of the world; a casual comment by a friend; a conversation overheard on the subway; or sometimes they just seem to pop into my head from nowhere."[43]

In *Money* and *Useless* (pages 52, 53) color-play and wordplay are more modulated. As elsewhere in the corpus, each word is painted a single color, but the tones are softer, more subtle, and closer in value. This permits delicate, shifting chromatic relationships to develop. *Die* (page 57), in sharp contrast, uses carnival colors on a bubblegum-pink ground for a series of acerbic metaphors for mortality. KICK THE BUCKET, it recommends cheerfully; PUSH UP DAISIES. Where the first two canvases produce an atmospheric, almost luminous effect, the latter has a Pop quality. It is striking that in such formally similar works the changes in palette arouse such contrasting impressions. Is this effect produced by the colors alone? How much does language contribute to our response?

**Meaningless, 2003**

Oil and acrylic on canvas, 45 × 60 in. (114.3 × 152.4 cm)
Private collection

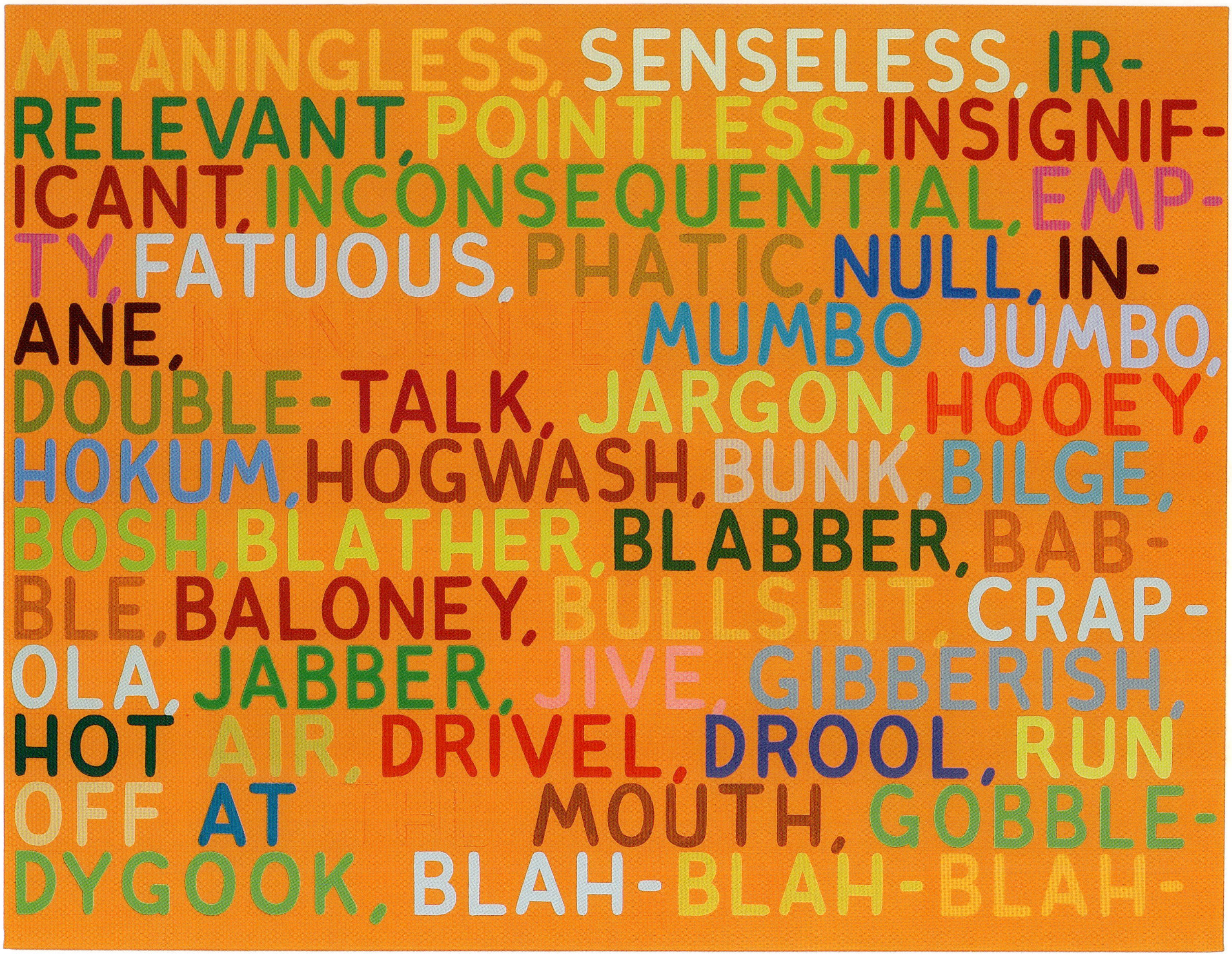

MEANINGLESS, SENSELESS, IR-
RELEVANT, POINTLESS, INSIGNIF-
ICANT, INCONSEQUENTIAL, EMP-
TY, FATUOUS, PHATIC, NULL, IN-
ANE, NONSENSE MUMBO JUMBO,
DOUBLE-TALK, JARGON, HOOEY,
HOKUM, HOGWASH, BUNK, BILGE,
BOSH, BLATHER, BLABBER, BAB-
BLE, BALONEY, BULLSHIT, CRAP-
OLA, JABBER, JIVE, GIBBERISH,
HOT AIR, DRIVEL, DROOL, RUN
OFF AT THE MOUTH, GOBBLE-
DYGOOK, BLAH-BLAH-BLAH-

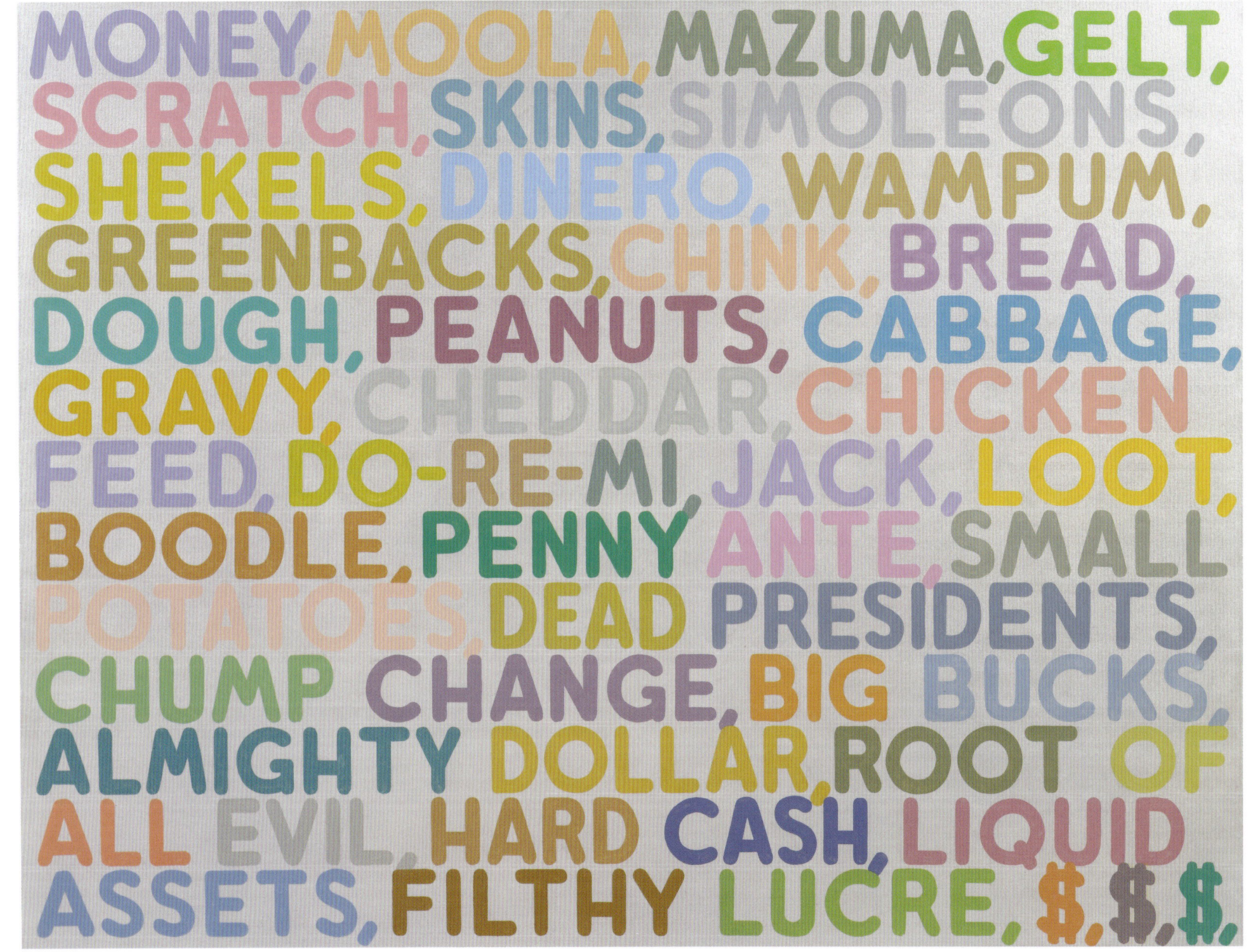


***Money*, 2005**

Oil and acrylic on canvas, 60 × 80 in. (152.4 × 203.2 cm)
Smithsonian American Art Museum, Washington, DC

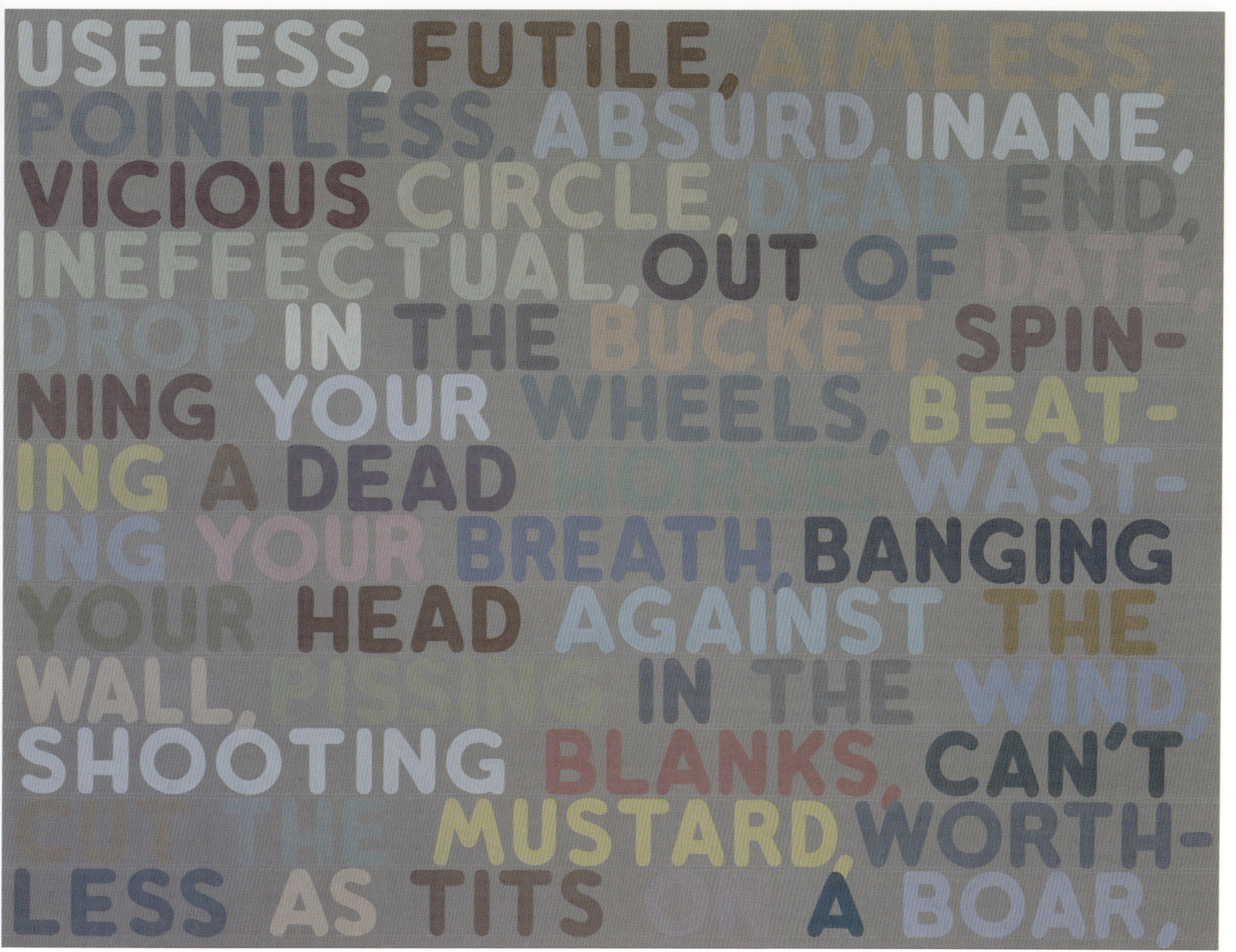


*Useless,* 2005

Oil and acrylic on canvas, 60 × 80 in. (152.4 × 203.2 cm)
Betty and Edward Harris, Chicago

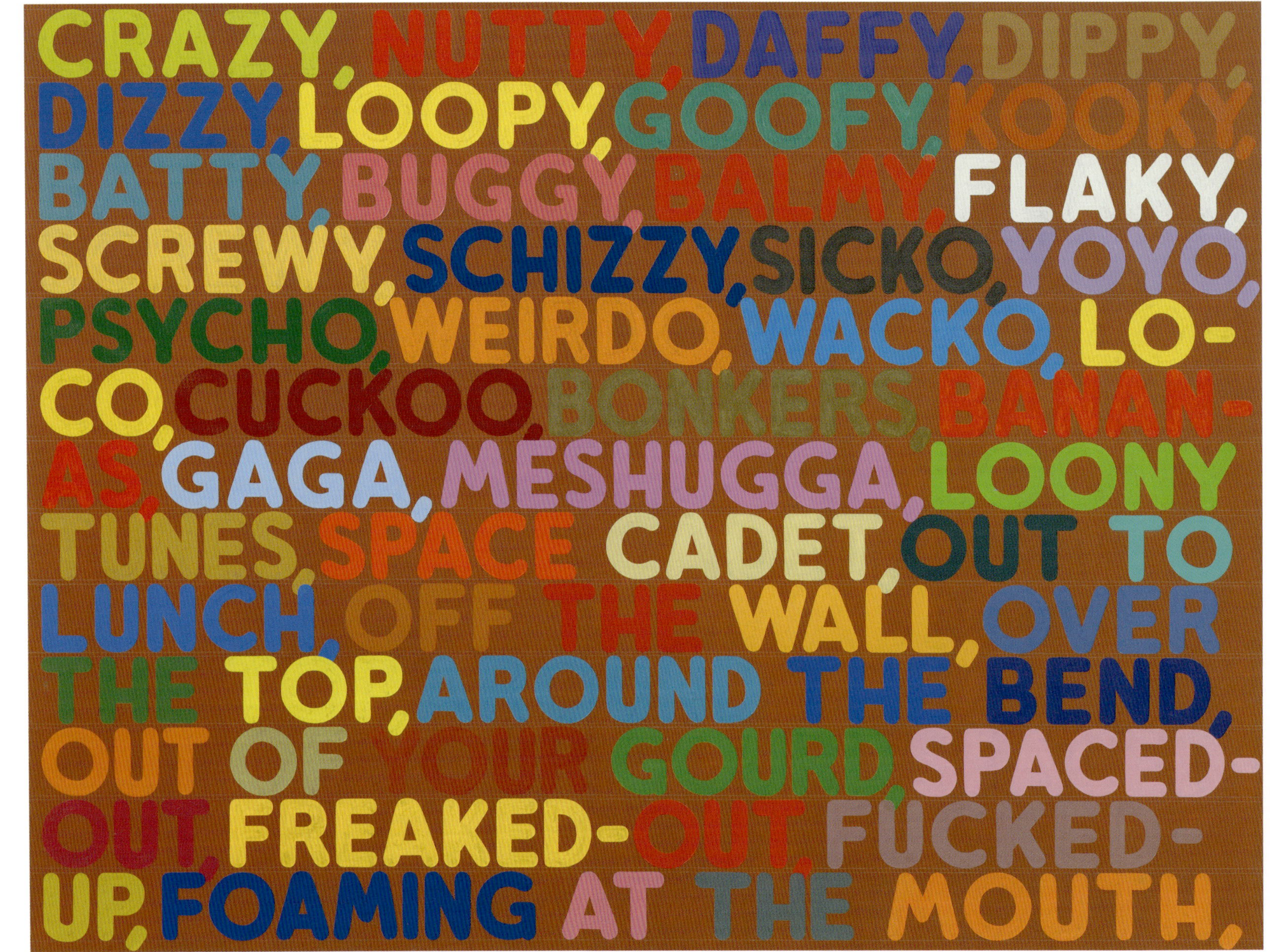


*Crazy,* 2005

Oil and acrylic on canvas, 60 × 80 in. (152.4 × 203.2 cm)
Peter Freeman

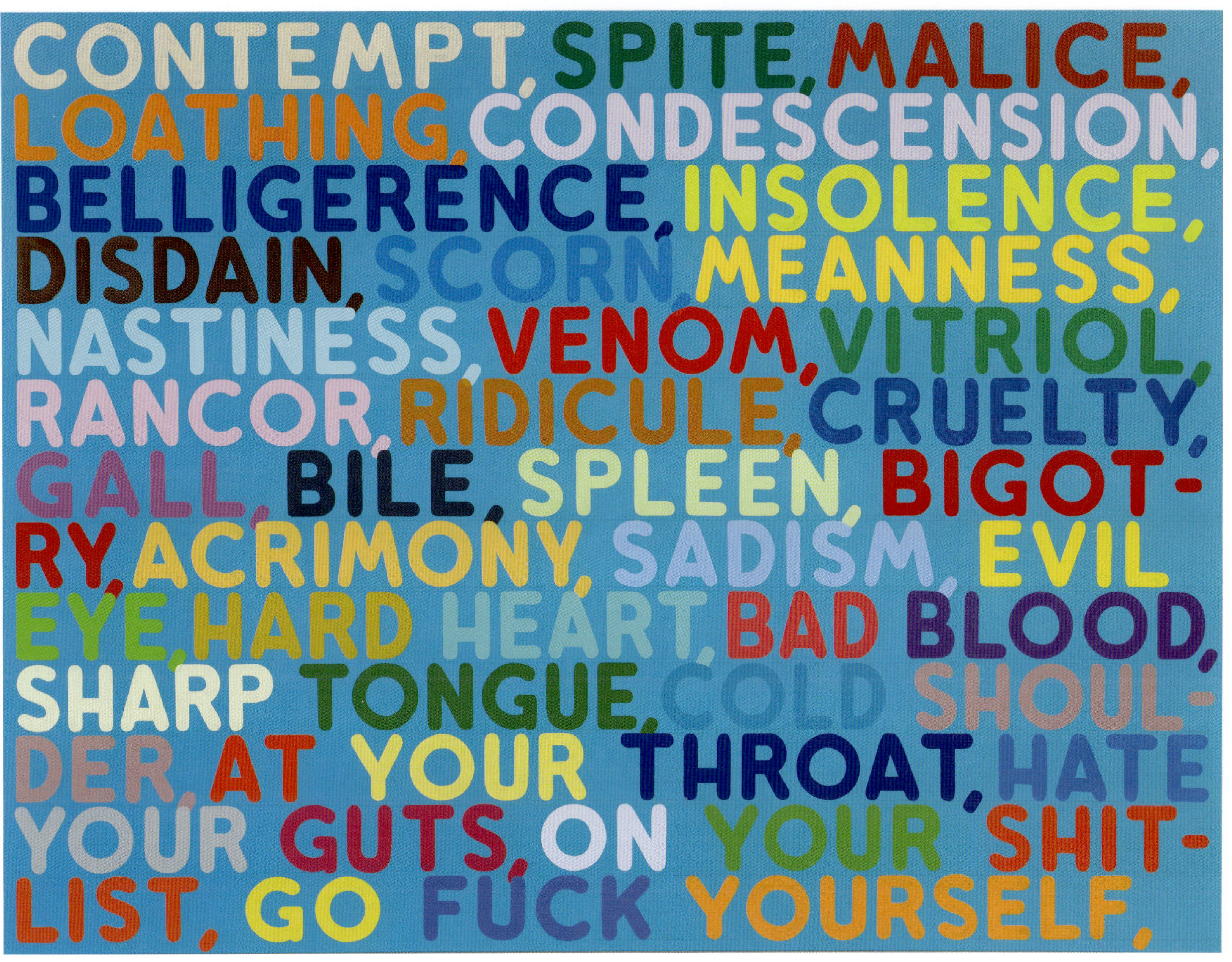



***Contempt,* 2005**

Oil and acrylic on canvas, 60 × 80 in. (152.4 × 203.2 cm)
Suzanne F. Cohen, Baltimore

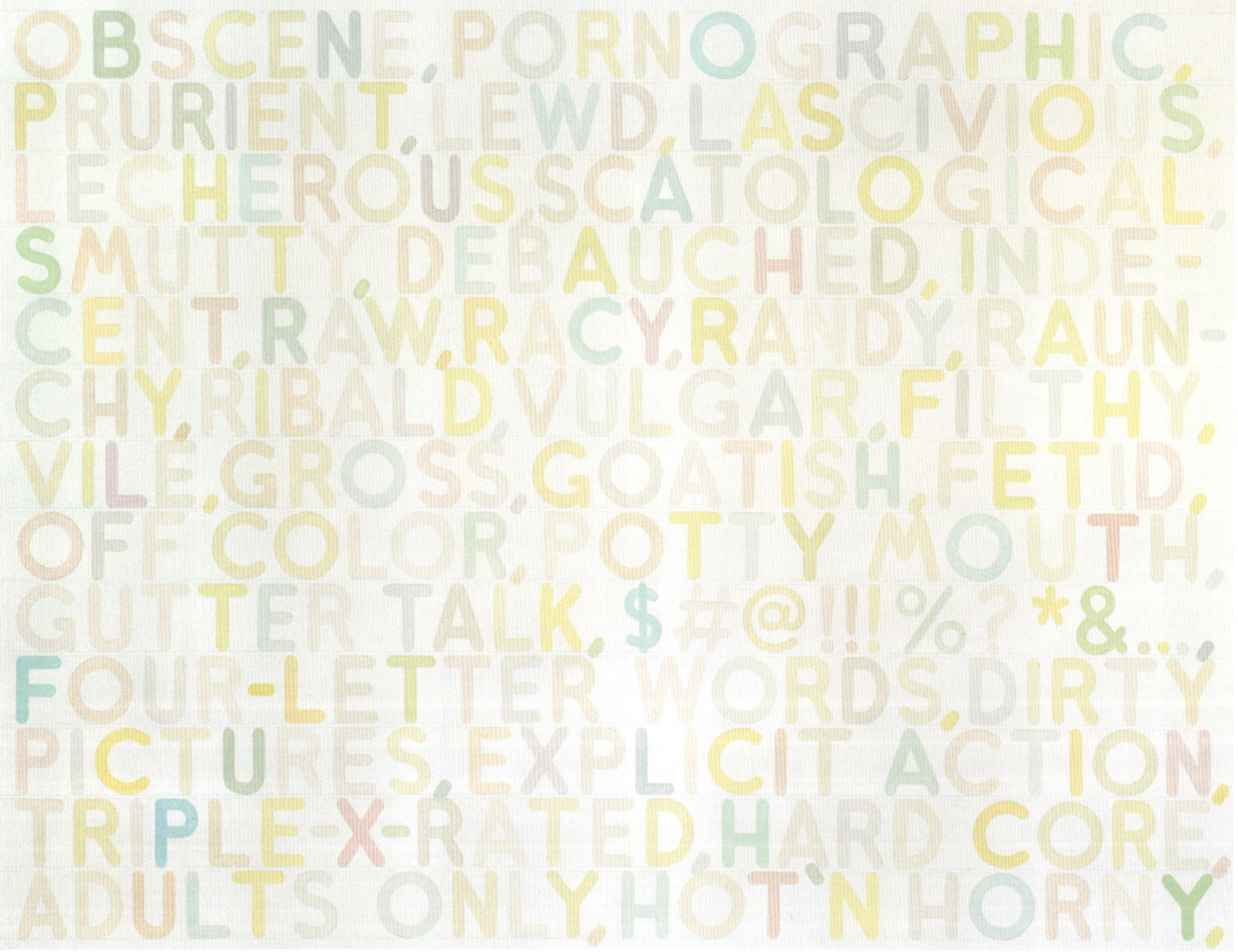

***Obscene*, 2006**

Oil and acrylic on canvas, 60 × 80 in. (152.4 × 203.2 cm)
Private collection

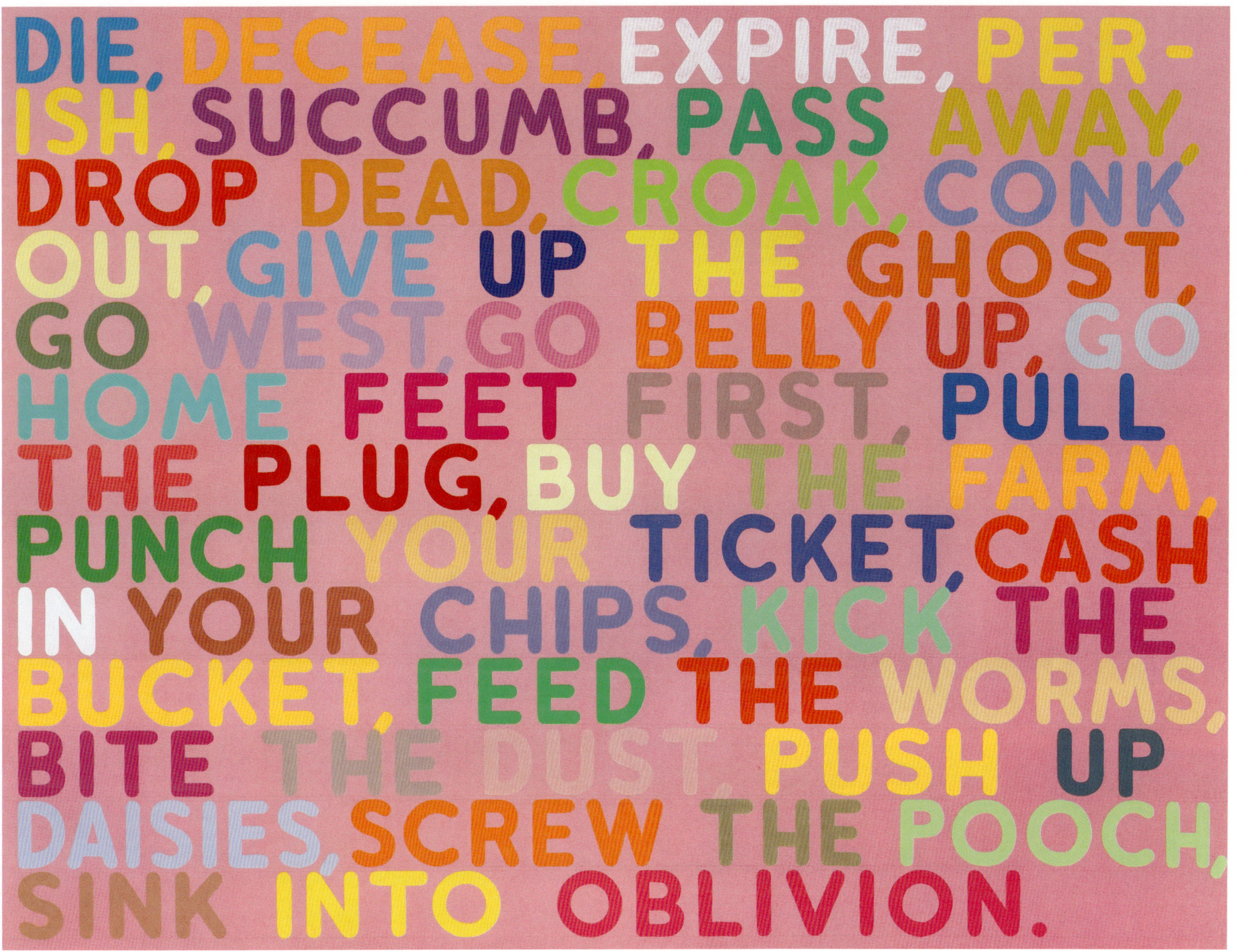


*Die*, 2005

Oil and acrylic on canvas, 60 × 80 in. (152.4 × 203.2 cm)
Peter Freeman, Inc.

*Ridicule,* 2009

Oil on canvas, 80 × 60 in. (203.2 × 152.4 cm)
Randall Kaplan, Los Angeles

RIDICULE, RE-VILE, SLANDER, SMEAR, SNEER, SCOLD, SCOFF, RAZZ, RAG, RANK, JACK UP PUT DOWN, KISS OFF, CUT DEAD, RE-DUCE TO TEARS, DUMP ON, CHEW OUT, REAM ASS.

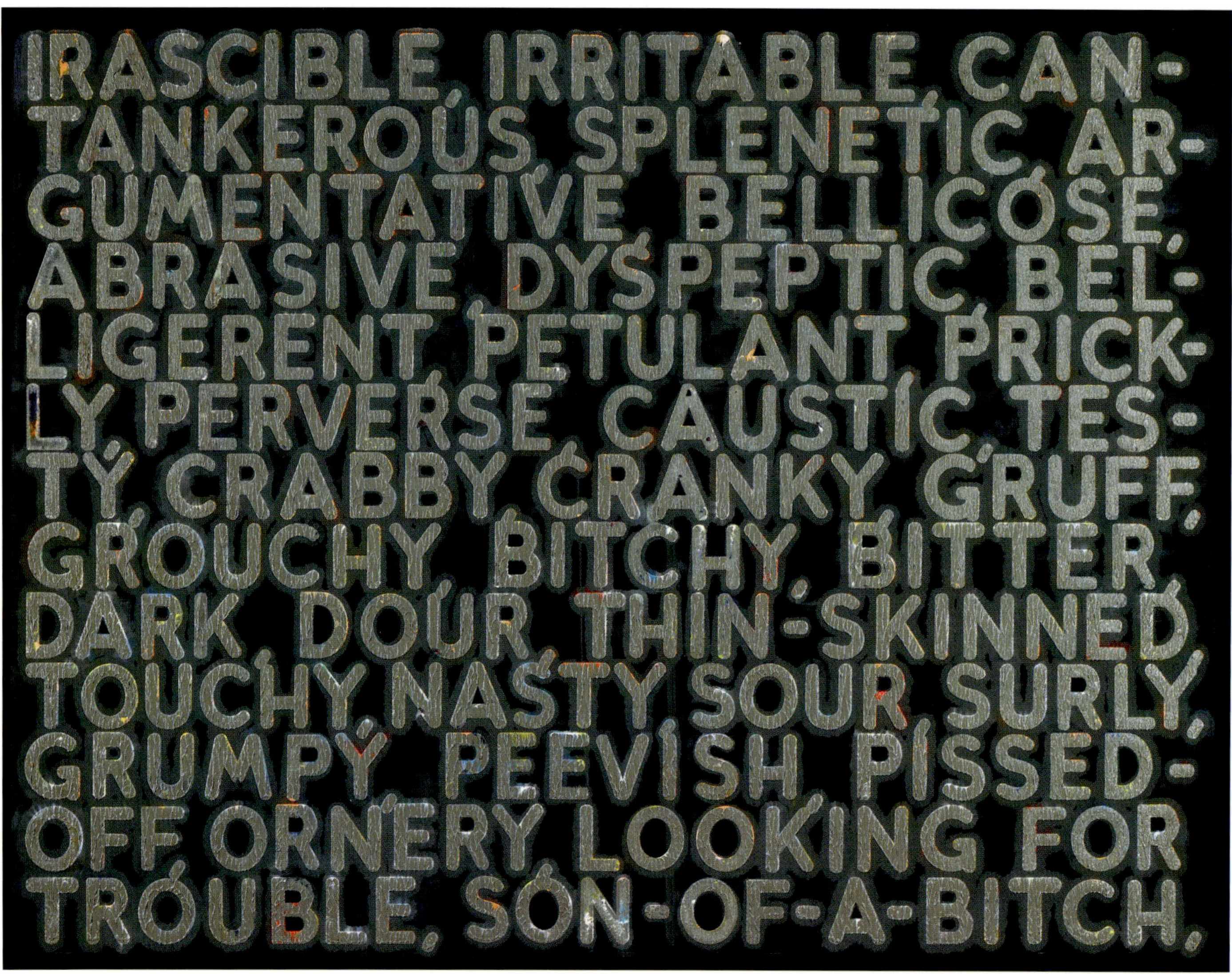

*Irascible*, 2006

Oil on velvet, 36½ × 47½ in. (92.7 × 120.6 cm)
Mr. and Mrs. Werner Kramarsky, New York

*Fucked-Up*, 2009

Oil on canvas, 60 × 45 in. (152.4 × 114.3 cm)
Erik and Heidi Murkoff, Los Angeles

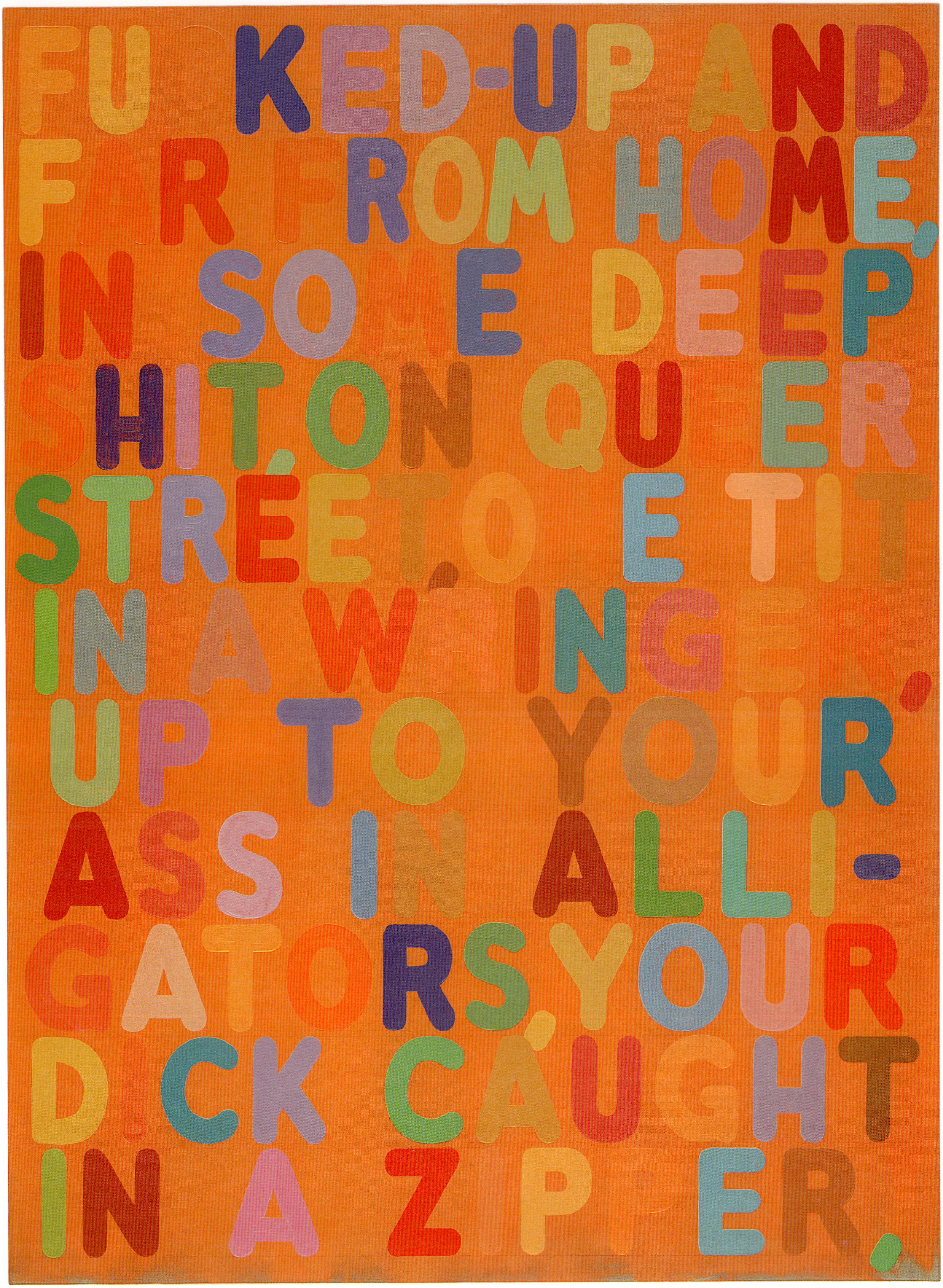

FUCKED-UP AND FAR FROM HOME, IN SOME DEEP SHIT, ON QUEER STREET, ONE TIT IN A WRINGER, UP TO YOUR ASS IN ALLIGATORS, YOUR DICK CAUGHT IN A ZIPPER.

***Amazing*, 2010**

Oil and acrylic on two canvases, 100 × 75 in. (254 × 190.5 cm)
Midwest private collection

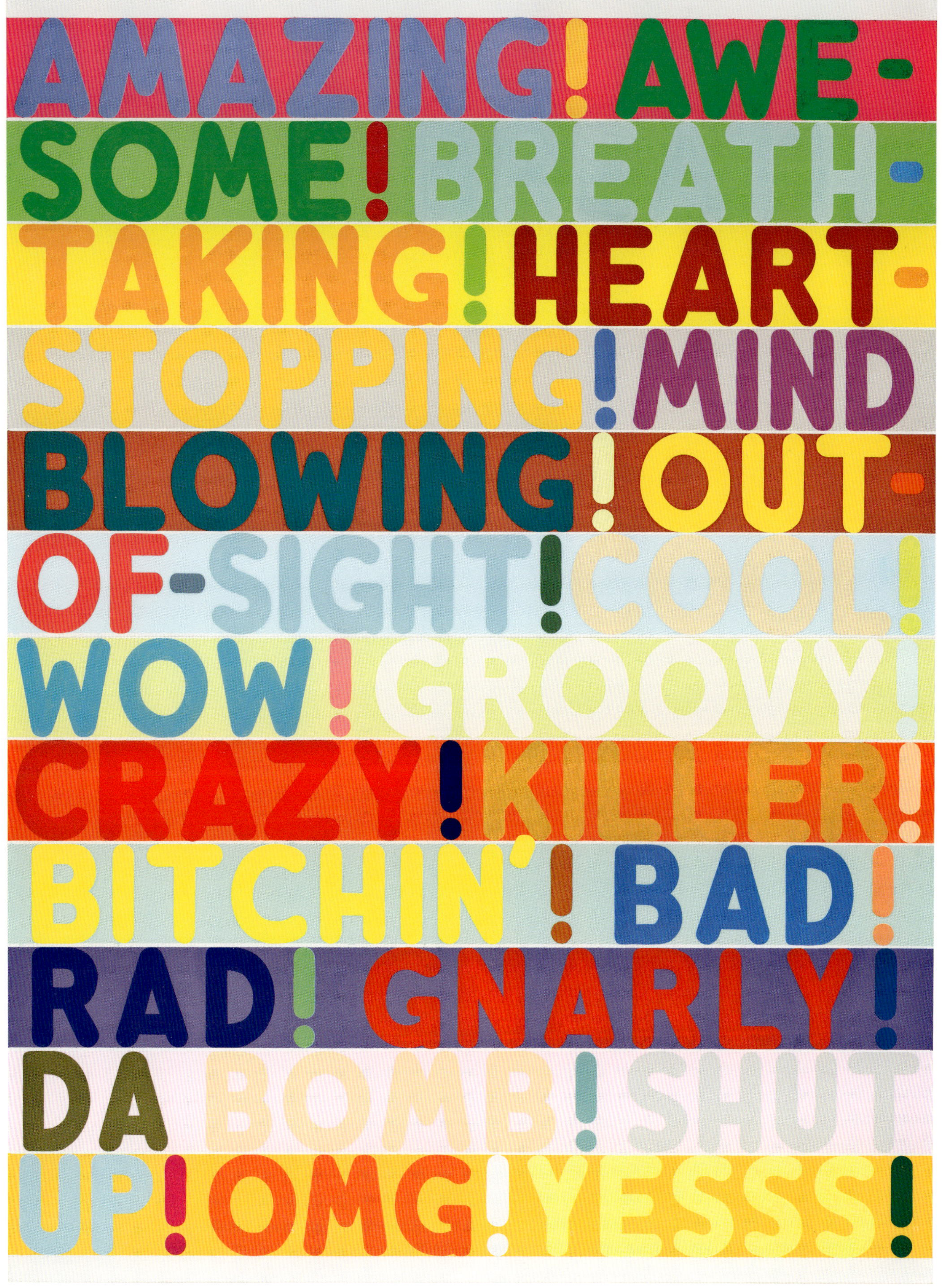

AMAZING! AWE-SOME! BREATH-TAKING! HEART-STOPPING! MIND BLOWING! OUT-OF-SIGHT! COOL! WOW! GROOVY! CRAZY! KILLER! BITCHIN'! BAD! RAD! GNARLY! DA BOMB! SHUT UP! OMG! YESSS!

*Oh Well,* 2010

Oil and acrylic on two canvases, 100 × 75 in. (254 × 190.5 cm)
Neugebauer Family Collection, Munich

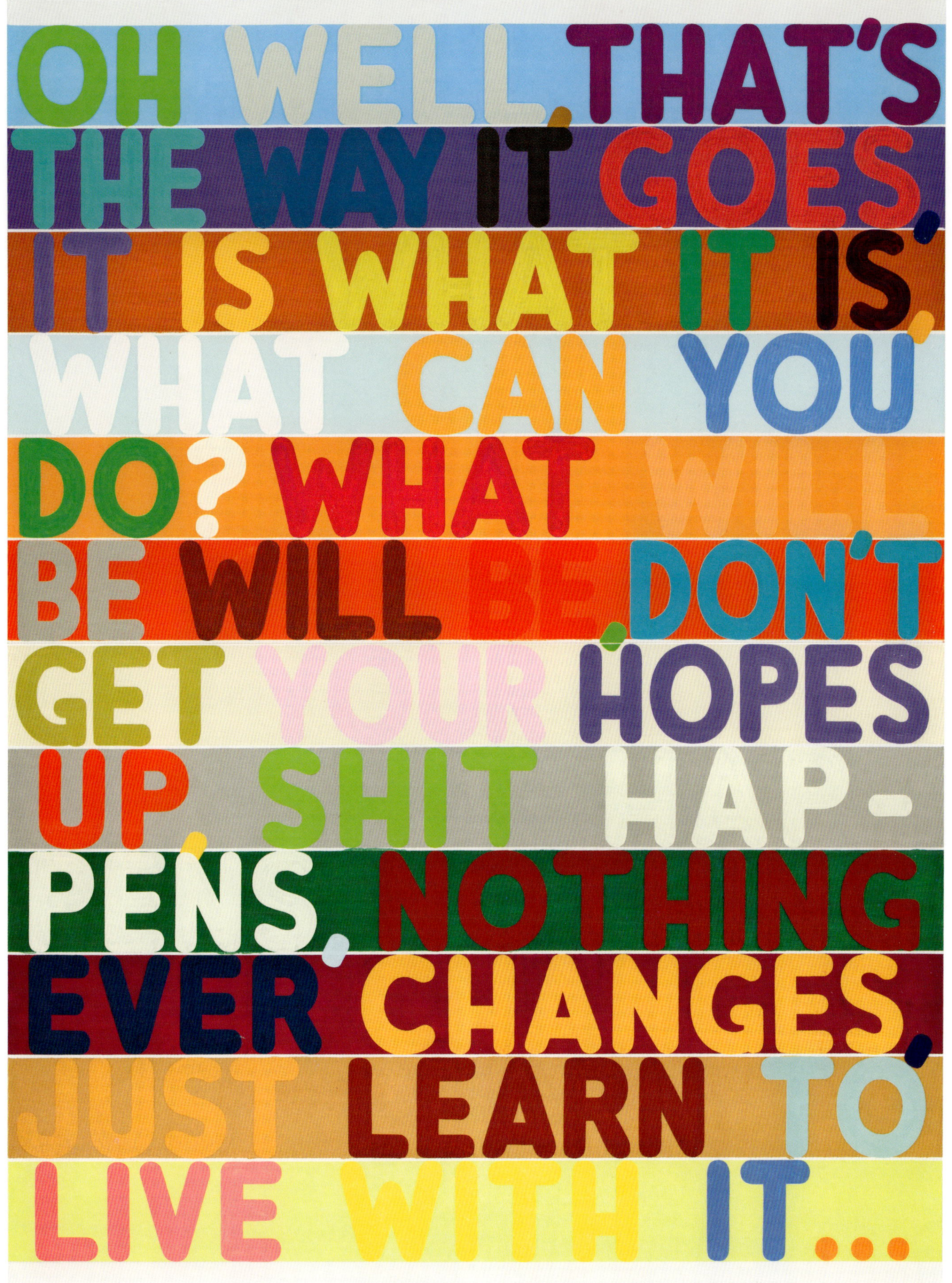

OH WELL, THAT'S THE WAY IT GOES, IT IS WHAT IT IS, WHAT CAN YOU DO? WHAT WILL BE WILL BE, DON'T GET YOUR HOPES UP, SHIT HAP-PENS, NOTHING EVER CHANGES, JUST LEARN TO LIVE WITH IT...

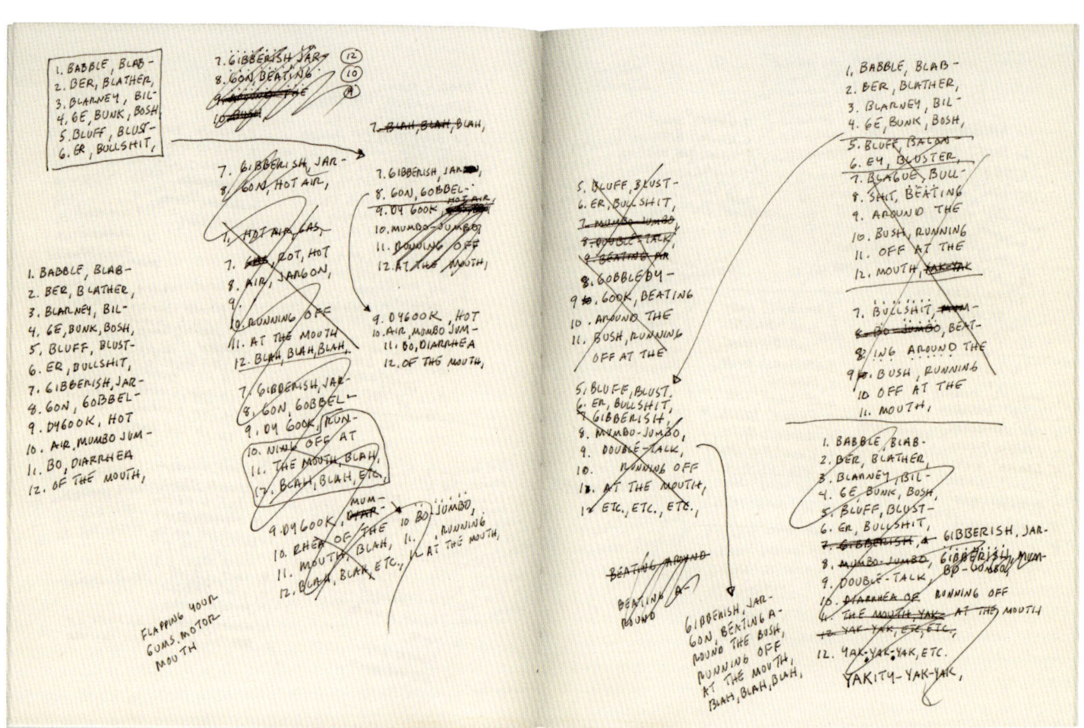

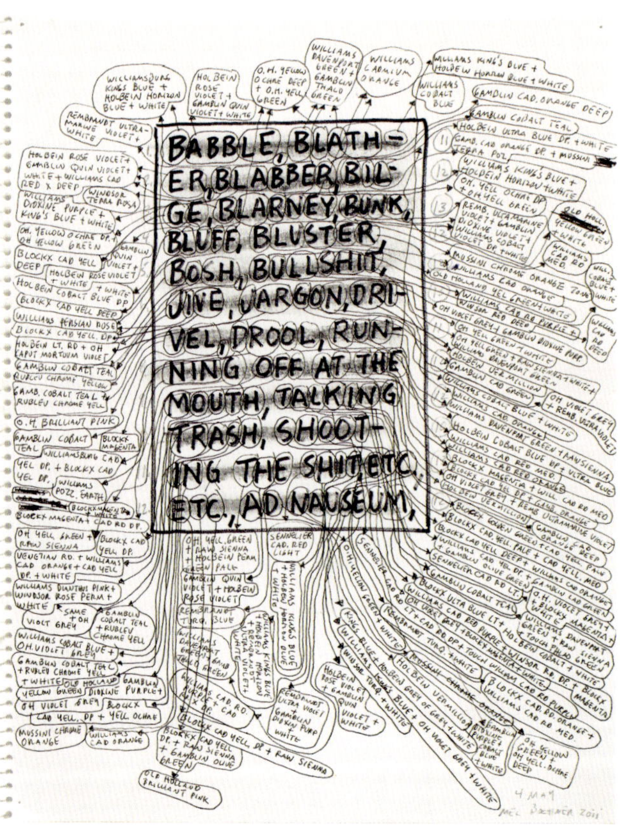

**Preparatory notebook drawings for *Babble*, 2011**

Ink on paper, 10⅝ × 16⅞ in. (27 × 42.9 cm)
Collection of the artist

***Babble*, 2011**

Ink and charcoal on paper, 14 × 11 in. (35.6 × 27.9 cm)
Collection of the artist

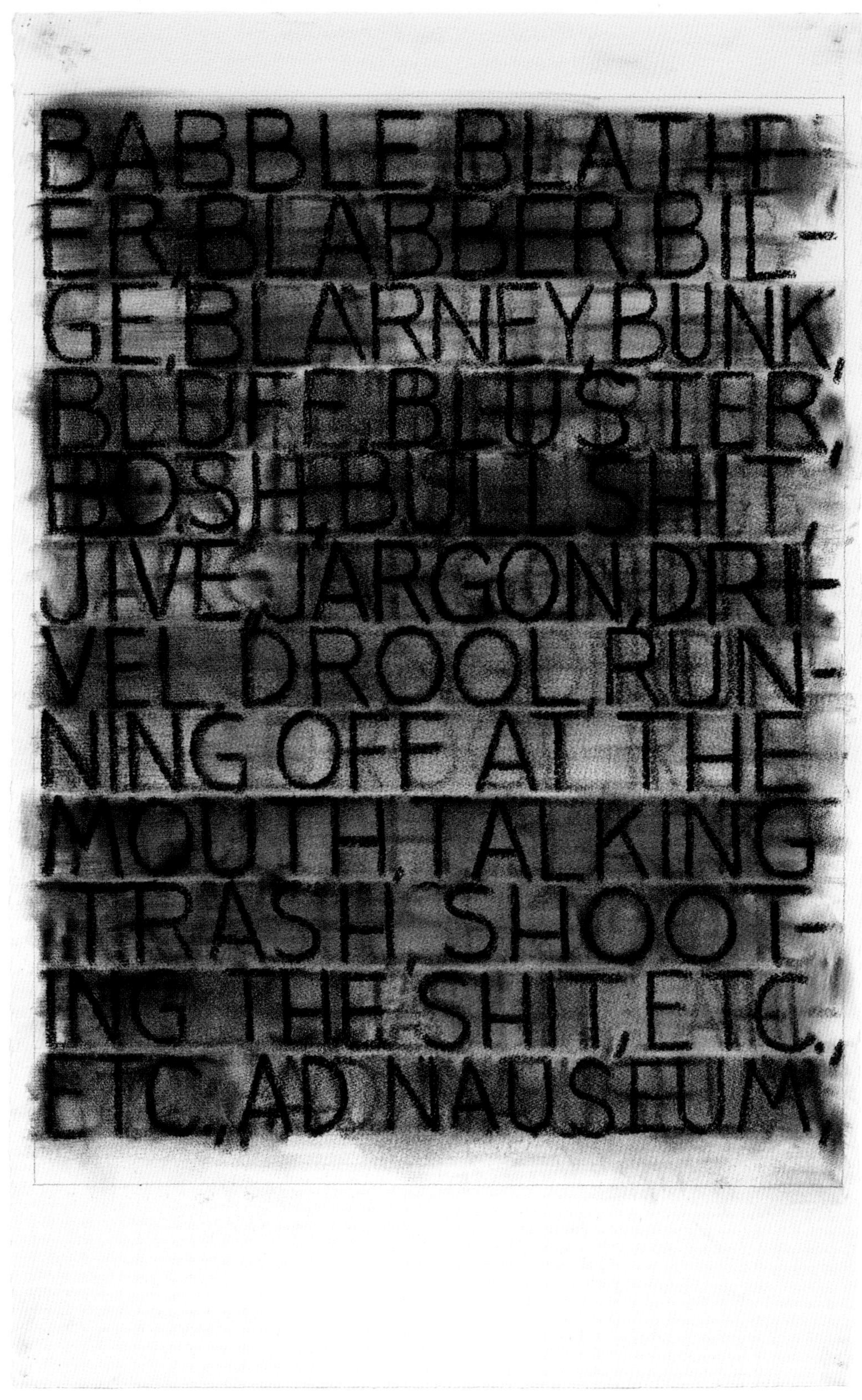



*Babble,* 2011

Charcoal and graphite on paper, 40 × 26 in. (101.6 × 66 cm)
Collection of Wendy Evans Joseph and Jeffrey Ravetch

***Babble,*** 2011

Oil and acrylic on two canvases, 100 × 85 in. (254 × 215.9 cm)
Private collection

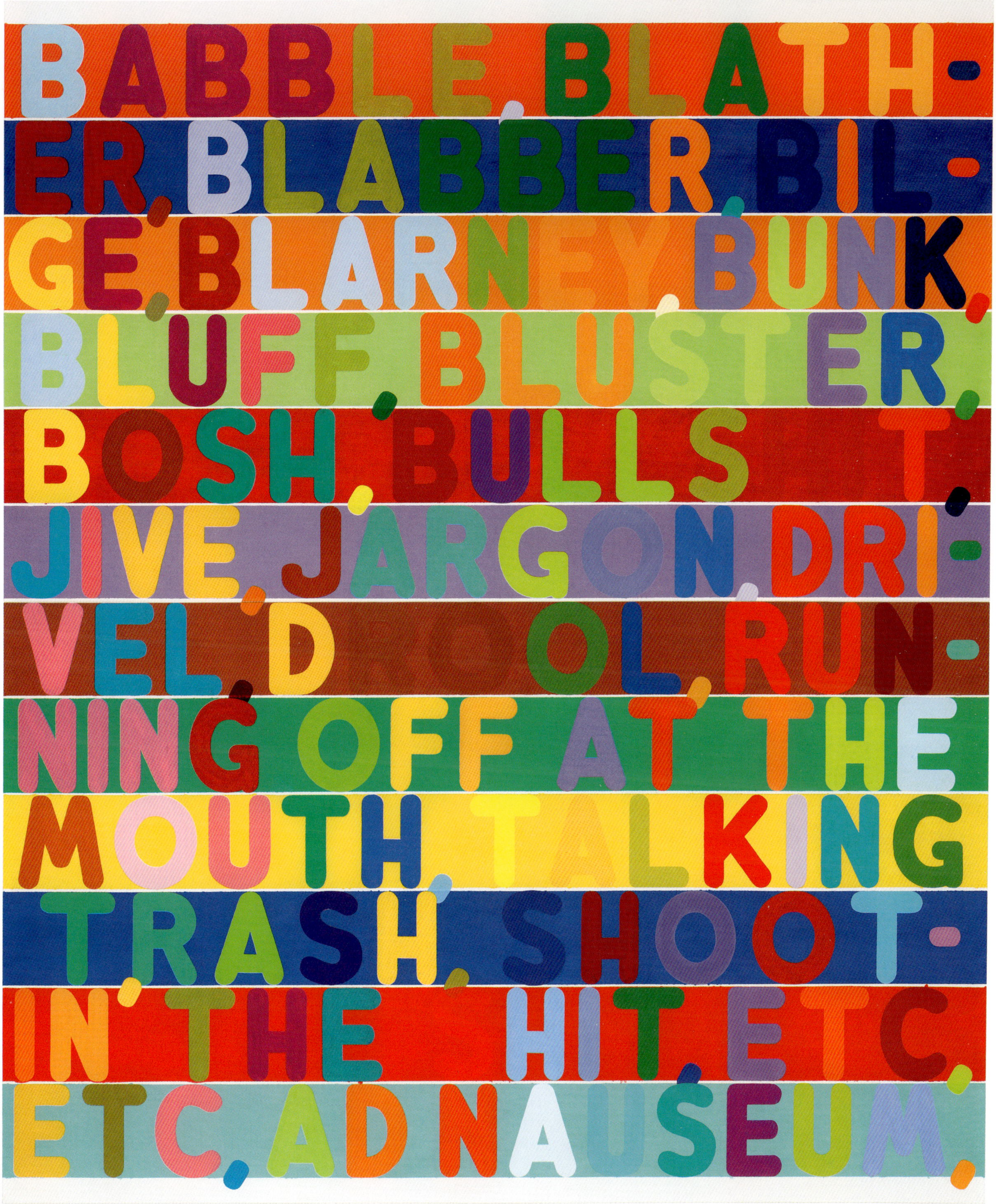

BABBLE BLATHER, BLABBER BILGE, BLARNEY BUNK, BLUFF BLUSTER, BOSH, BULLS T, JIVE JARGON DRIVEL, DROOL, RUNNING OFF AT THE MOUTH, TALKING TRASH, SHOOTIN THE HIT ETC, ETC, AD NAUSEUM,

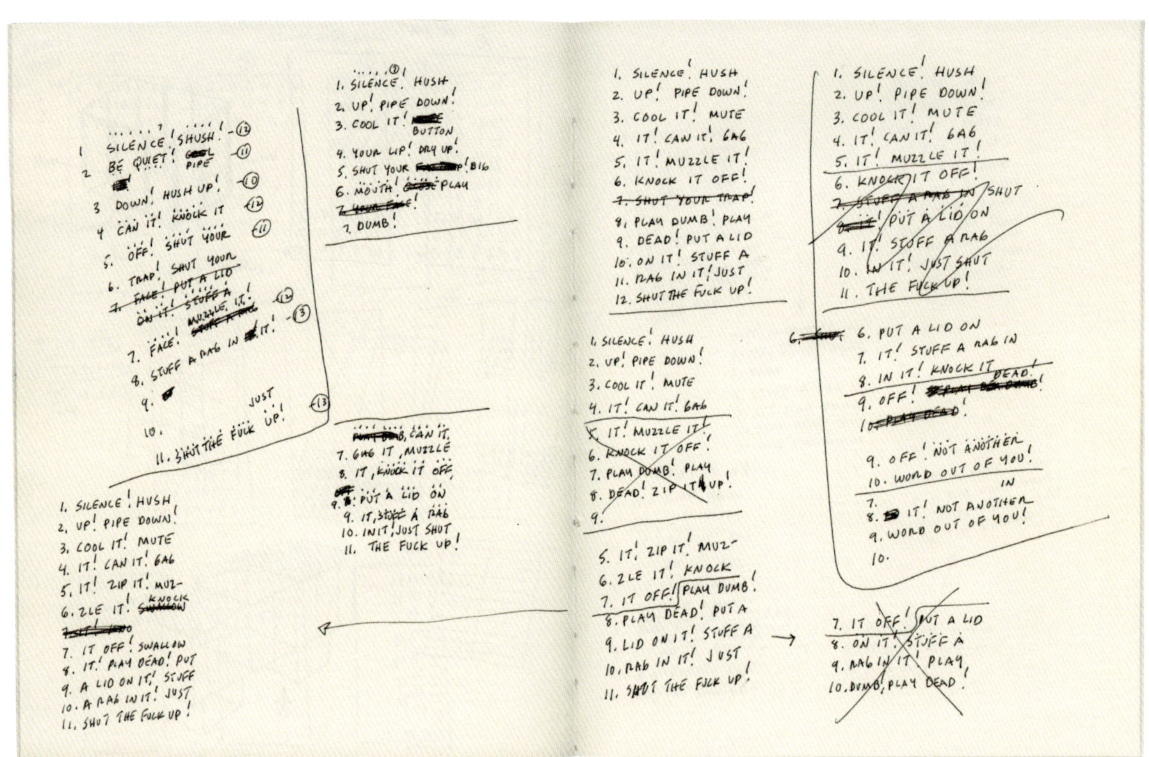

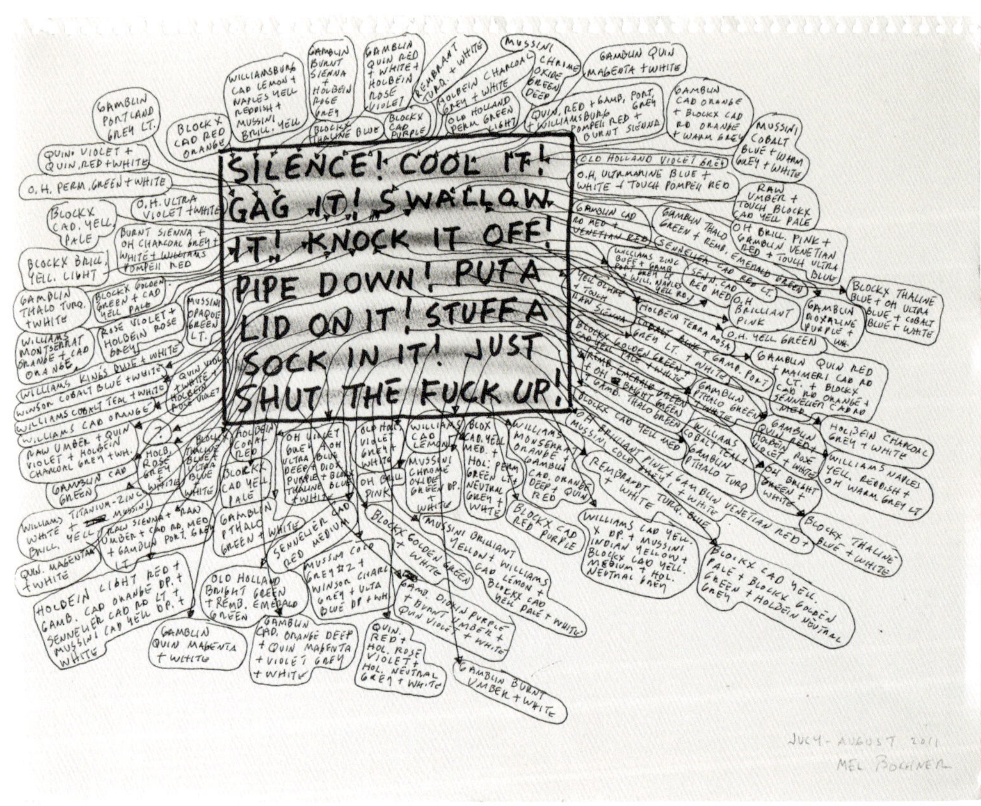



**Preparatory notebook drawings for *Silence!* 2011**

Ink on paper, 10⅝ × 16⅞ in. (26.9 × 42.9 cm)
Collection of the artist

**Working drawing for *Silence!* 2011**

Ink and charcoal on paper, 11 × 14 in. (28 × 35.6 cm)
Lizbeth Marano

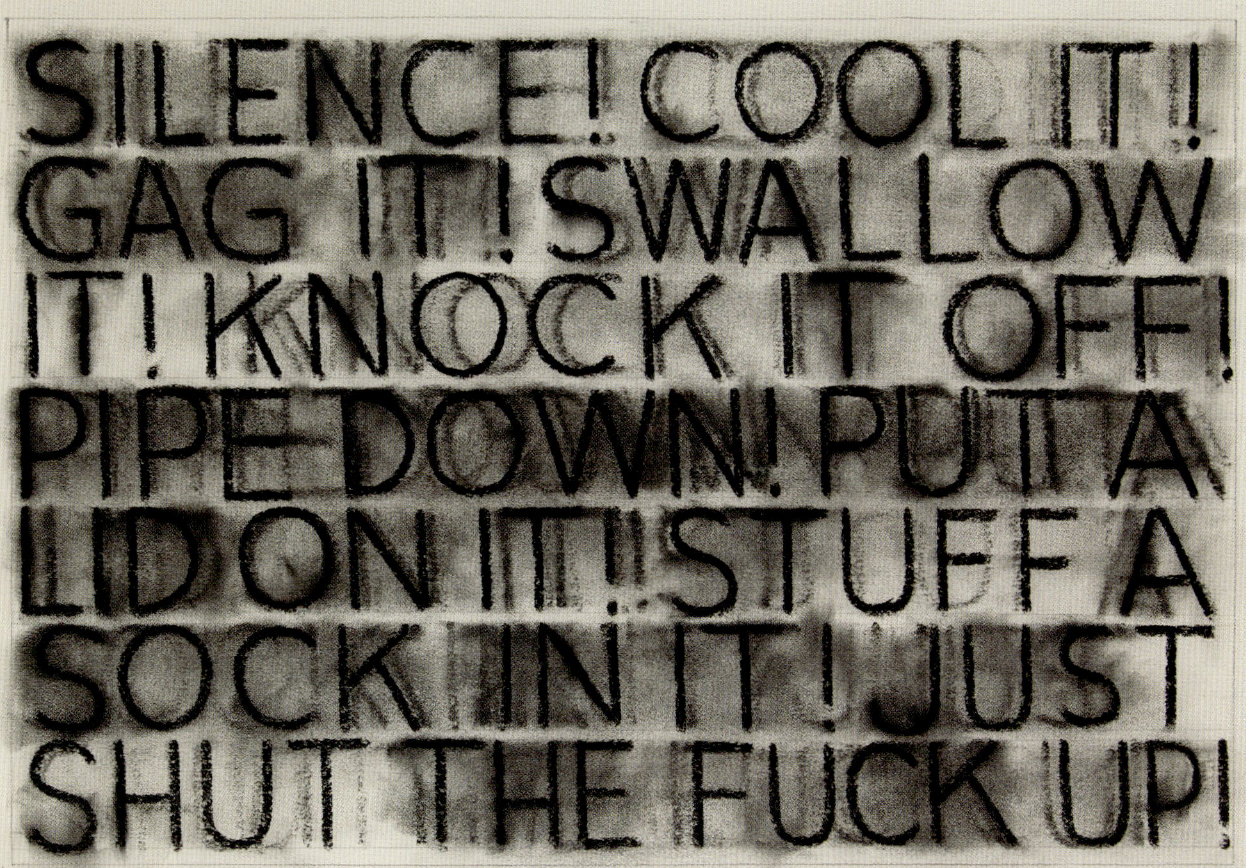



*Silence!* **2011**

Charcoal and graphite on paper, 26 × 37½ in. (66 × 95.3 cm)
Peter Freeman, Inc.

Following pages
*Silence!* **2011**

Oil and acrylic on two canvases, 80 × 120 in.
(203.2 × 304.8 cm)
Courtesy of the Hadley Martin Fisher Collection

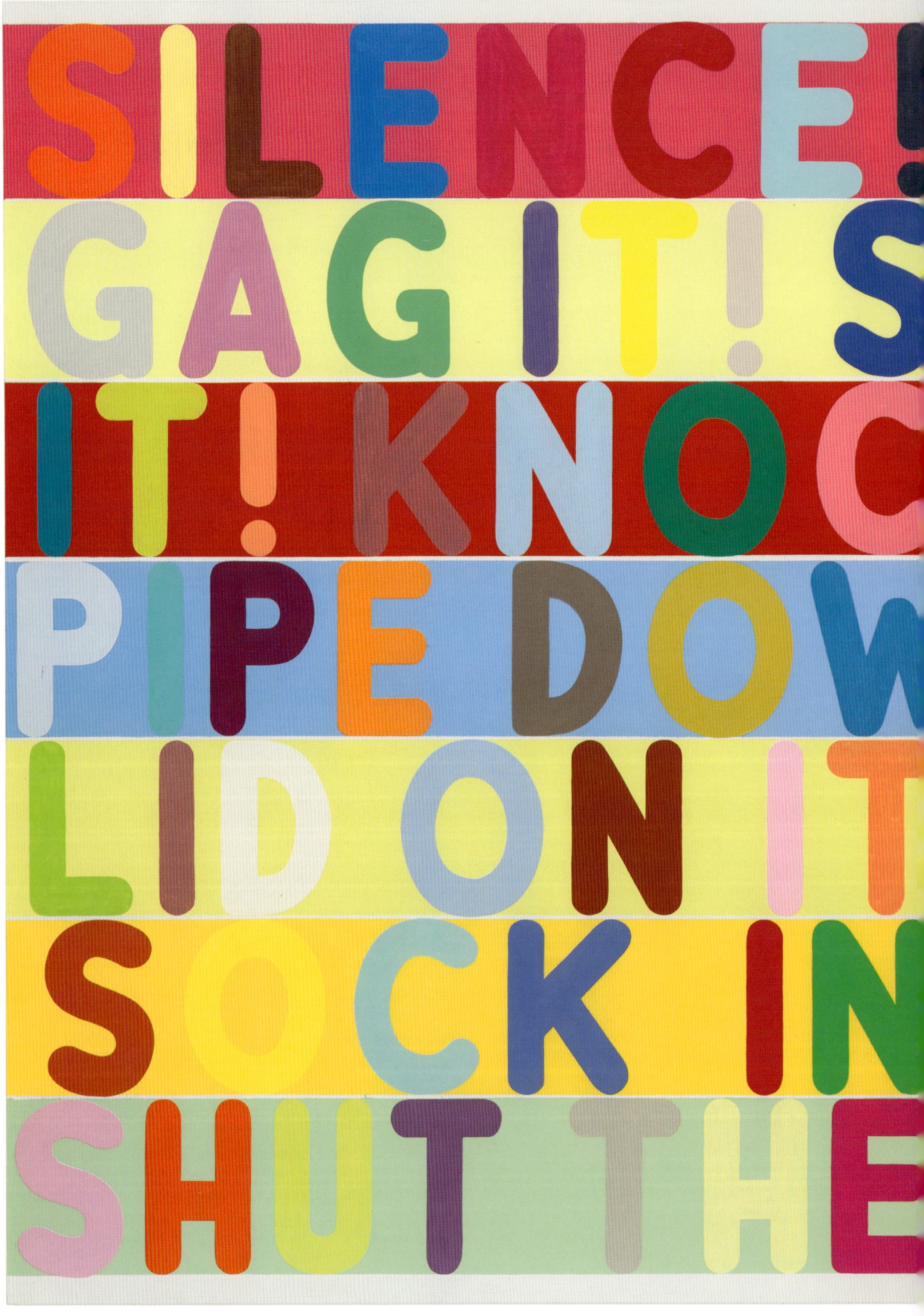

SILENCE!

GAG IT! S

IT! KNOC

PIPE DOW

LID ON IT

SOCK IN

SHUT THE

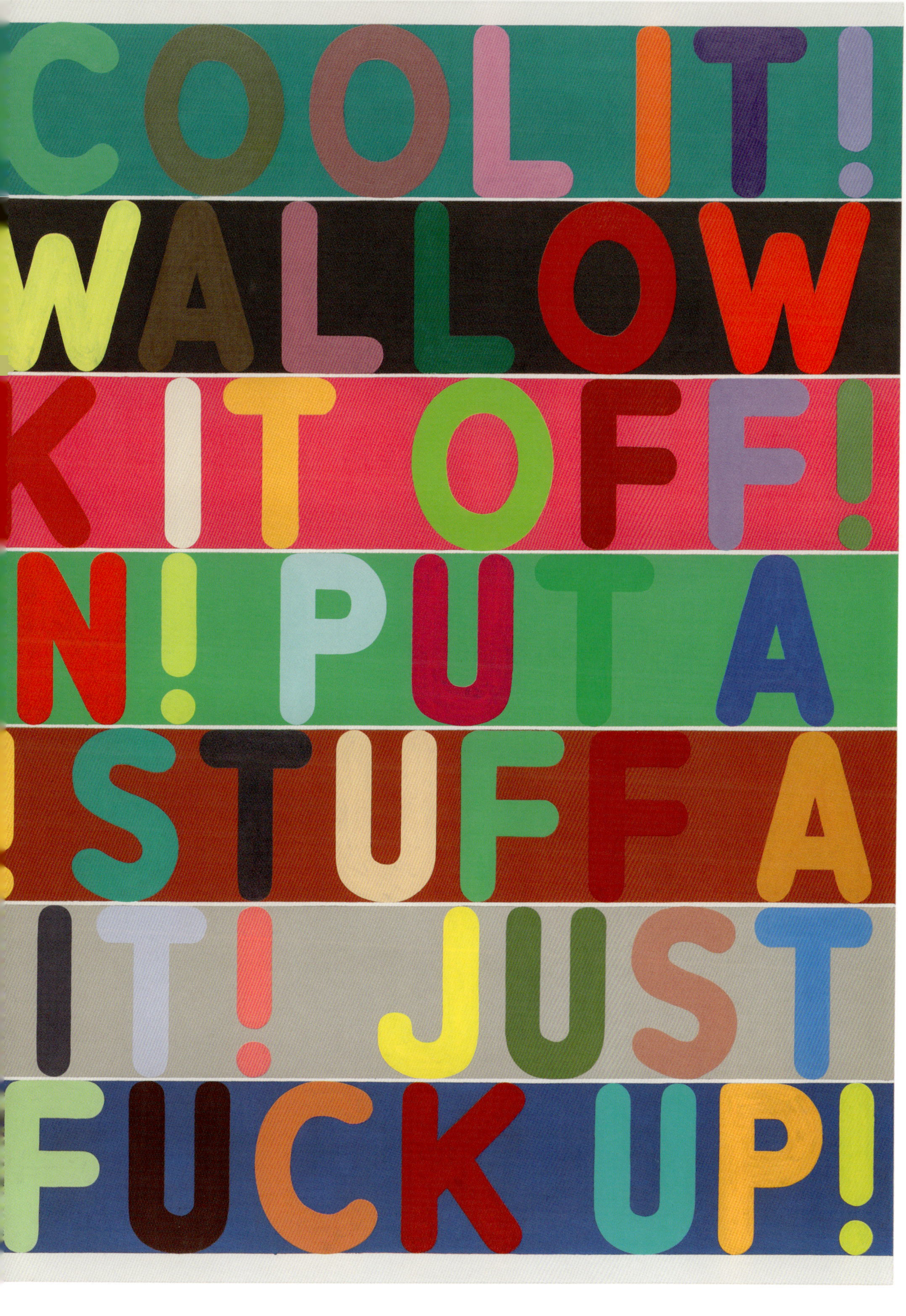

COOL IT! WALLOW KIT OFF! N! PUT A STUFF A IT! JUST FUCK UP!

*All or Nothing,* 2012

Oil and acrylic on two canvases, 100 × 85 in. (254 × 215.9 cm)
Peter Freeman, Inc.

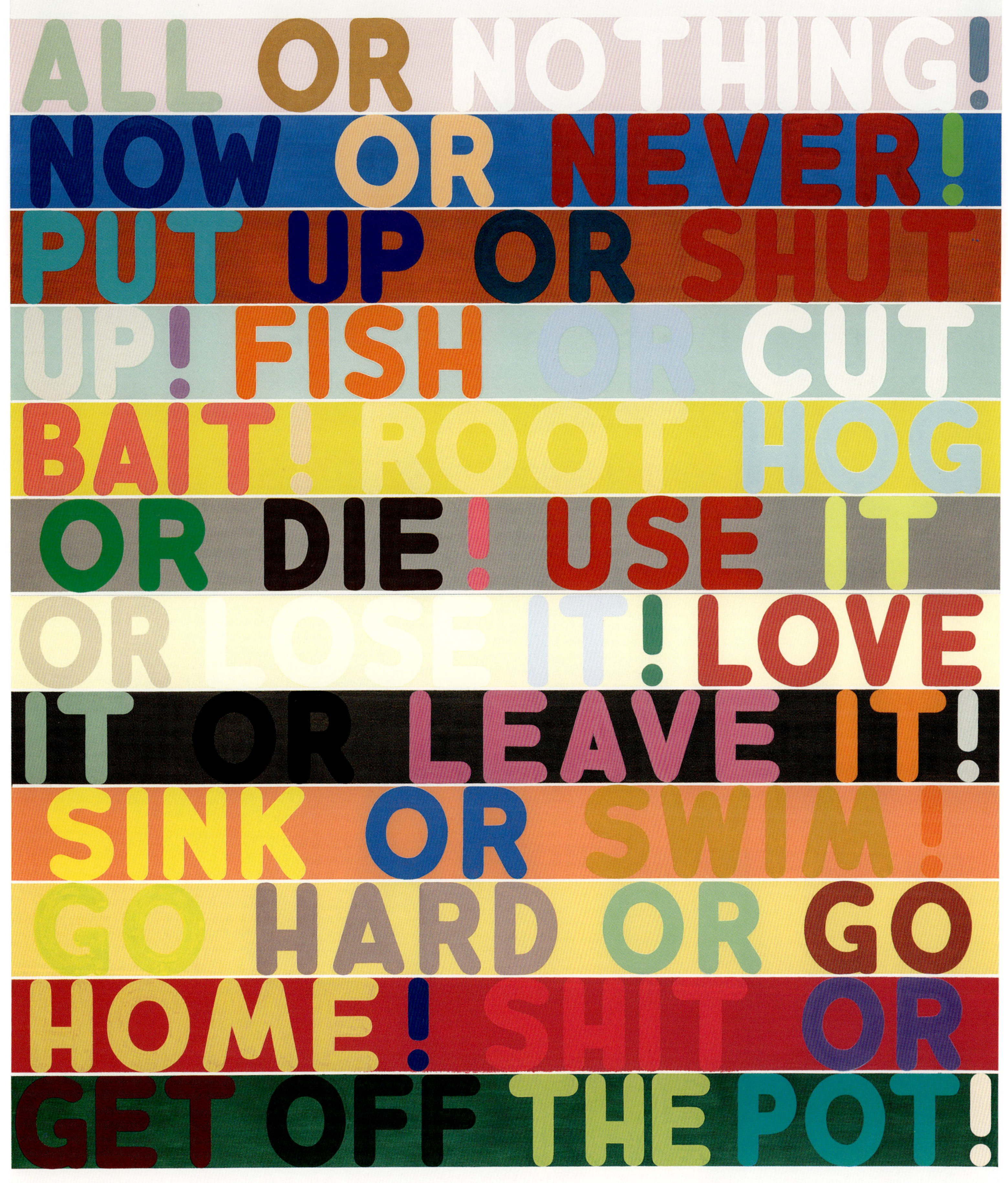

ALL OR NOTHING!
NOW OR NEVER!
PUT UP OR SHUT
UP! FISH OR CUT
BAIT! ROOT HOG
OR DIE! USE IT
OR LOSE IT! LOVE
IT OR LEAVE IT!
SINK OR SWIM!
GO HARD OR GO
HOME! SHIT OR
GET OFF THE POT!

*Going Out of Business,* 2012

Oil on velvet, 93½ × 70¼ in. (237.5 × 178.4 cm)
Private collection, New York

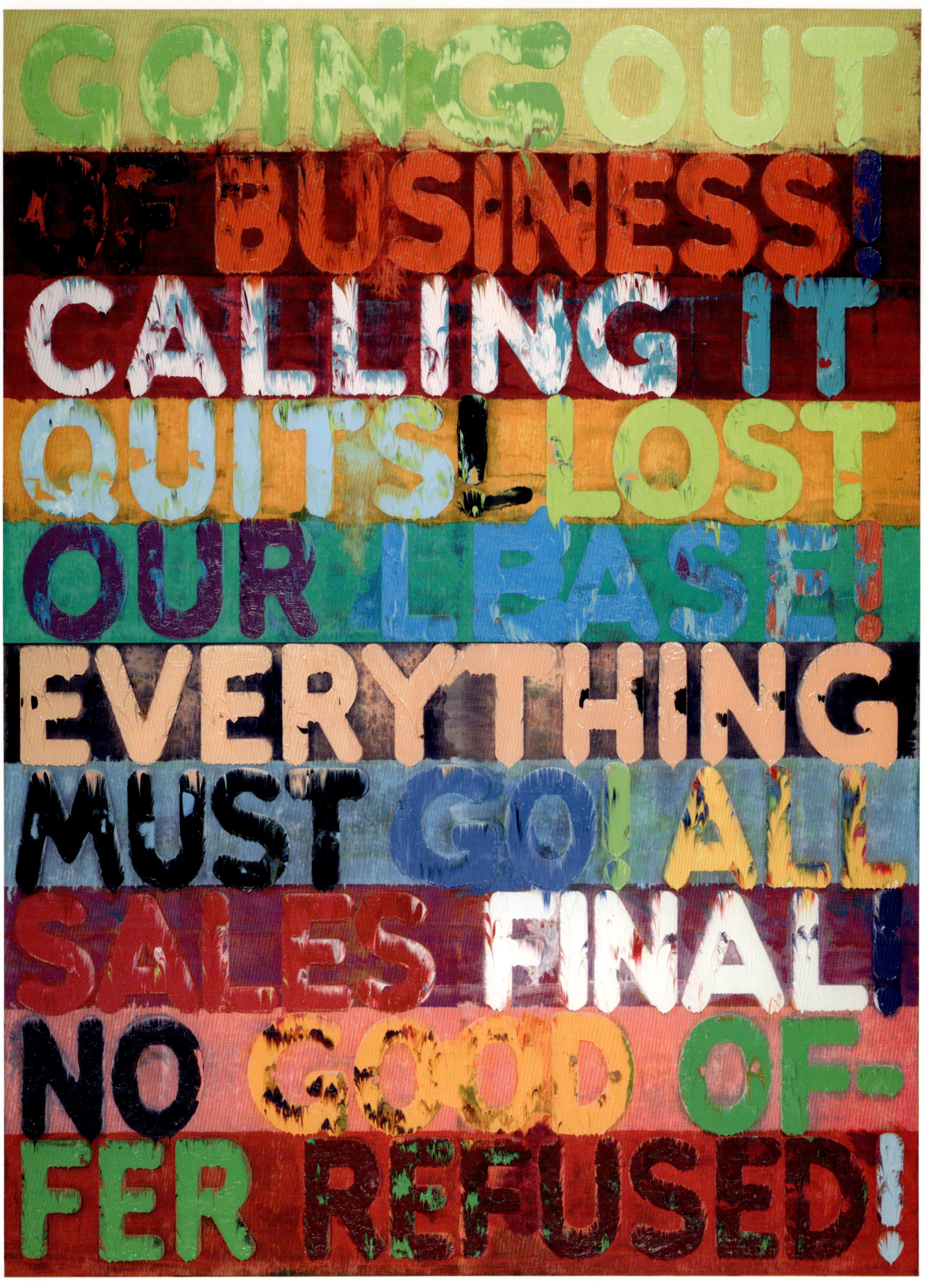
GOING OUT
OF BUSINESS!
CALLING IT
QUITS! LOST
OUR LEASE!
EVERYTHING
MUST GO! ALL
SALES FINAL!
NO GOOD OF-
FER REFUSED!

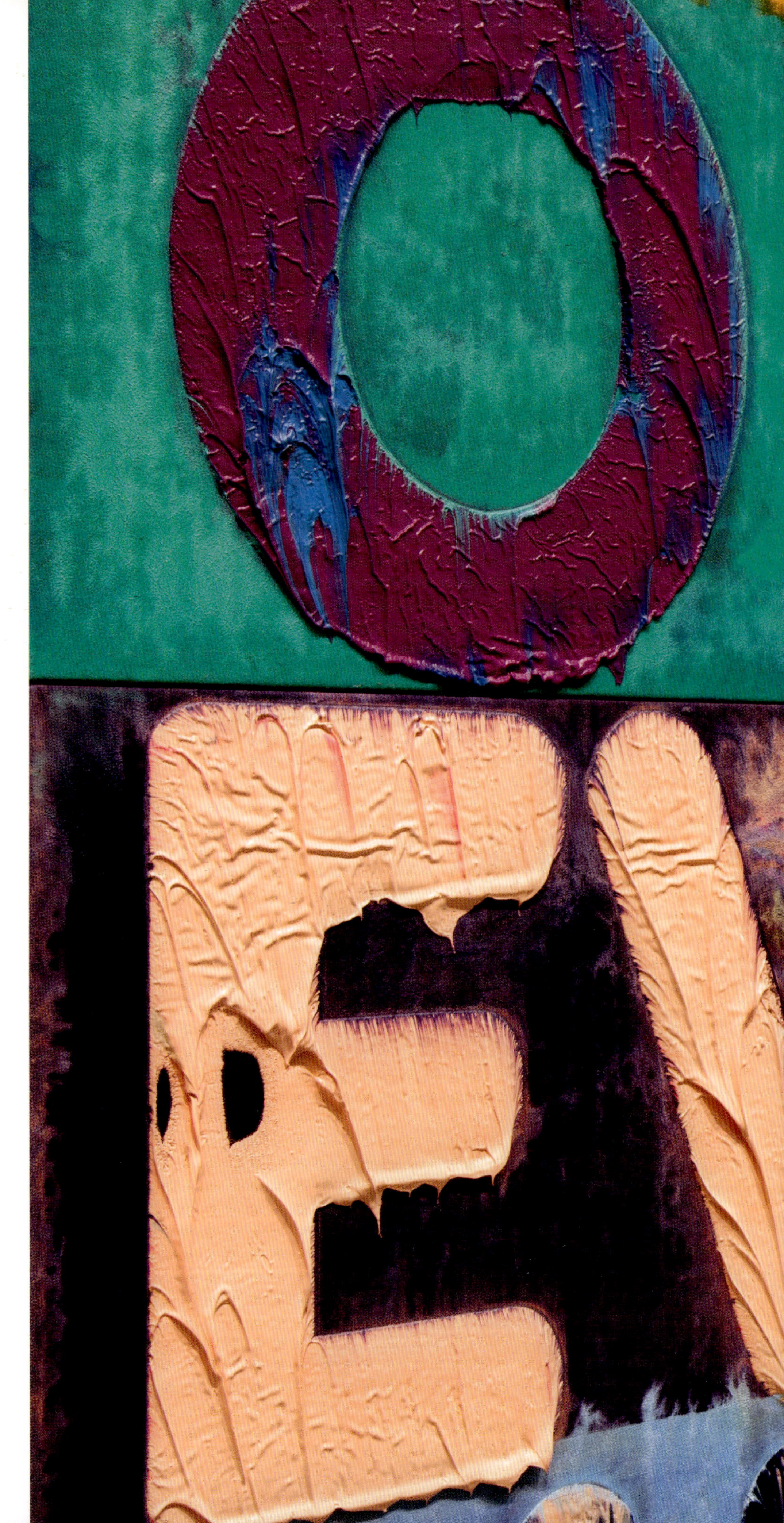

*Going Out of Business*, 2012

Detail

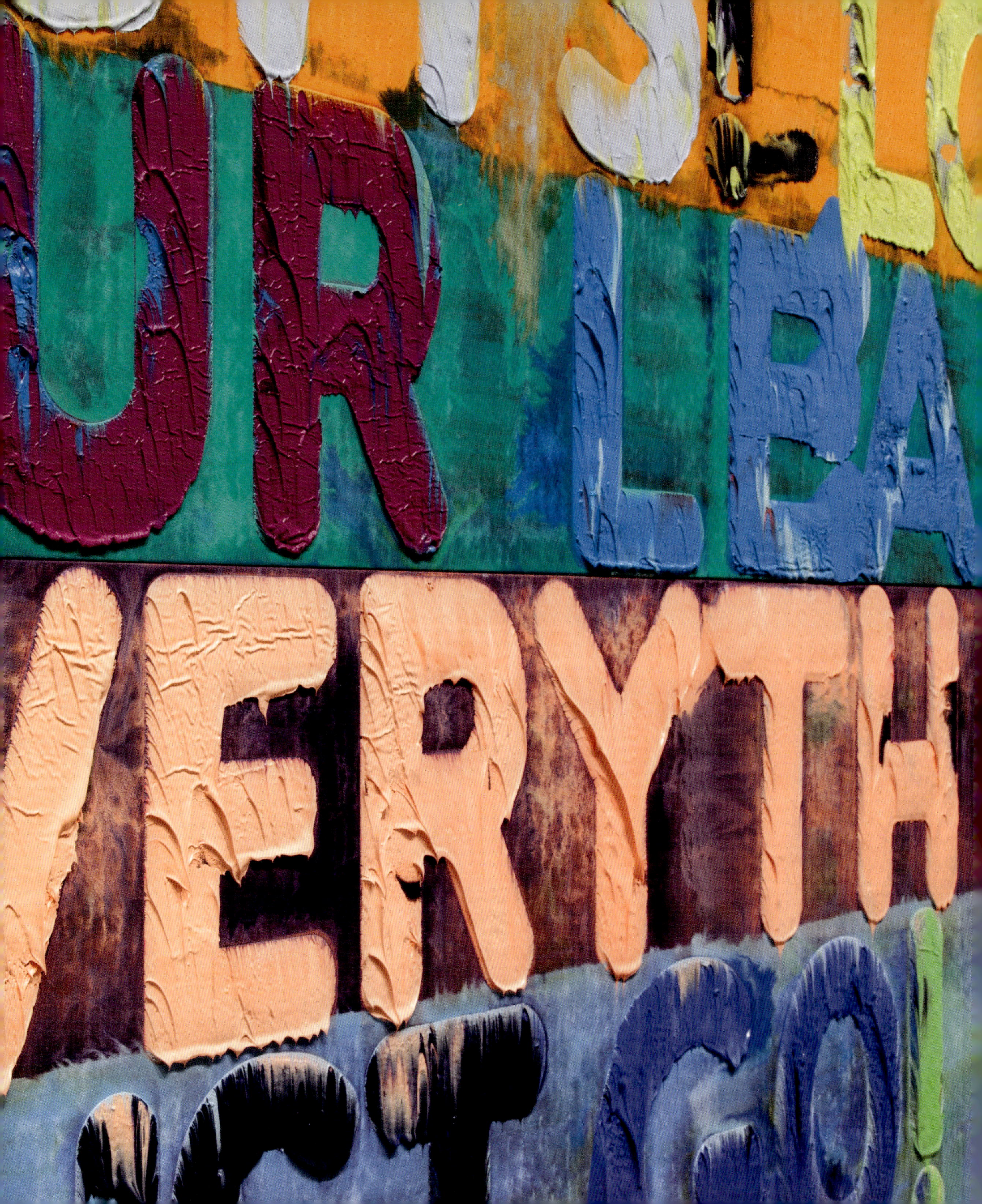
UR LEA
ERYTH

In *Irascible* (page 60) color is minimal: silver-gray words are printed on black velvet. Here the gooey texture of thick oil paint on velvet pile adds complexity and material dimension to the surface.

At around this time Bochner introduced a new element: a different pigment for each letter. In *Obscene* (page 56), chalky pastel letters float on a parchment-pale backdrop. *Ridicule* and *Fucked-Up* present a wild array of colors on simple grounds (pages 59, 61). Since each letter has its own relationship to the background and to other letters, the words become increasingly difficult to read, and new internal patterns emerge. These paintings have an almost musical quality, as if the letters were notes that could be plucked off the canvas in a cadenza of color. There is an element of synesthesia in them, a Baudelairean sense of the interchangeability of sound, color, and language.

Around 2010 Bochner began to further complicate his program by adding striped bands of garish tints to his backgrounds, making the confetti-colored letters appear all the more vivid and varied. The sketches for these paintings are worked out in black and white—pencil or ink, and later charcoal. They show the artist selecting his terms, creating schemes for organizing the sequence of words, and ultimately fitting them into the rectangular limits of the canvas. He chooses his colors intuitively, *alla prima,* and decides as he moves from left to right and top to bottom how closely to match each letter or word with the background.

Meanwhile, Bochner revels in the descent of language into the bawdy and obscene. *Ridicule* begins demurely enough with RIDICULE, REVILE, SLANDER but ends with the rude REAM ASS. *Fucked-Up* is composed of phrases rather than single words, all of them coarsely vernacular: FUCKED-UP AND FAR FROM HOME, IN SOME DEEP SHIT, ON QUEER STREET, ONE TIT IN A WRINGER, UP TO YOUR ASS IN ALLIGATORS, YOUR DICK CAUGHT IN A ZIPPER. As in many of the thesaurus works, the sequence in these paintings often ends with a comma, suggesting that the string of terms is open-ended.

The shock of vulgar language (GOTCHA BY THE BALLS, SHUT THE FUCK UP) is mitigated by Bochner's "delaying mechanism"—the time it takes the viewer to unscramble the colored letters from their backgrounds, to read and comprehend the actual text. As always, the sensual aspects of painting are pitted against the cognitive processes of language, with the viewer caught between the two. Positioning these pictures between the visual and verbal creates what the artist calls "a surplus meaning, a visual meaning . . . that survives the consumption of the narrative."[44]


## JEWISH IDENTITY AFFIRMED AND THREATENED

Yiddishisms pepper the text of many of Bochner's thesaurus pictures. Notable among them are BUBKES in *Nothing,* MAZUMA and GELT in *Money,* MESHUGGA in *Crazy,* KVETCH in *Critic* (see pages 48, 52, 54, 92). Although these words occur in *Roget's Thesaurus,* Bochner is also drawing on his own cultural background: he had grown up in an observant household where Yiddish was in use.

In 2006 he created a temporary site-specific work in Yiddish for the Spertus Museum (now the Spertus Institute for Jewish Learning and Leadership) in Chicago. *The Joys of Yiddish* (page 82) was part of a series of commissioned works by three artists, collectively called *The Language Barrier.* Each artist's work was painted on a literal road barrier in front of a construction site at the institute. In the Bochner project, four rows of bright yellow enameled words are placed on a black ground. Here the source was Leo Rosten's 1968 volume *The Joys of Yiddish,* a compendium of Yiddish words and phrases. In particular, Bochner chose terms that have entered American English, especially—but not exclusively— among Jews. If the thesaurus paintings exhibit a cheeky sense of humor, *The Joys of Yiddish* is about the inherent humor of that language.

In fact, Rosten used Jewish jokes strategically, to trace the way Yiddish terms have entered American discourse. To many Americans, words like KIBITZER, KVETCHER, NUD-NICK, SCHMOOZER, and SCHLEMIEL (all of which appear in Bochner's painting) have become familiar through Jewish comedians of the 1950s and 1960s. Although they are now common, many English-speakers are unaware of what Bochner calls the Yiddish language's "ironic, skeptical, and frequently scatological view of human nature." For Bochner these terms, and the Yiddish language as a whole, also harbor some less lighthearted associations. He calls Yiddish the "original ghetto language, developed . . . to cope with a foreign and often hostile reality."[45]

The palette has a specific symbolism: bright yellow on black refers to the identifying stars that Jews were forced to wear by the Nazis. But the public appearance of *The Joys of Yiddish,* installed on a grand Chicago thoroughfare, celebrates not only the persistence of a culturally complex and culturally specific language but also the survival of a people. The creation of this work has prompted Bochner to reexamine his interest in language as a vehicle of visual expression. He sees his use of language in visual art as deeply rooted in Jewish thought, with its emphasis on text and interpretation.[46]

He has several times revisited *The Joys of Yiddish.* In 2012 he converted the public project into a painting on canvas, using a slightly different set of Yiddish terms to accommodate the dimensions of the canvas (page 85). The following year, during an exhibition of his work at the Haus der Kunst in Munich, he placed a similar text on the building's facade (page 86). The irony embedded in Bochner's Jewish occupation of that building is clear: the museum, now a major venue for contemporary exhibitions, was built by Hitler to house Nazi-approved German art.

In all of these versions, a central thread is the freedom to assert cultural specificity in public and flaunt the recognition and level of comfort Jews have attained within western culture. The paintings are emblems of both Jewish difference and assimilation. Their reiteration in public art and on a more intimate, portable scale once again demonstrates how Bochner's remaking of works yields radically different meanings. A painting meant for an interior domestic or gallery wall has one set of associations. A billboard work outside a Jewish institution under construction in the United States has an entirely different reception from one on the facade of a German institution with a tainted history.

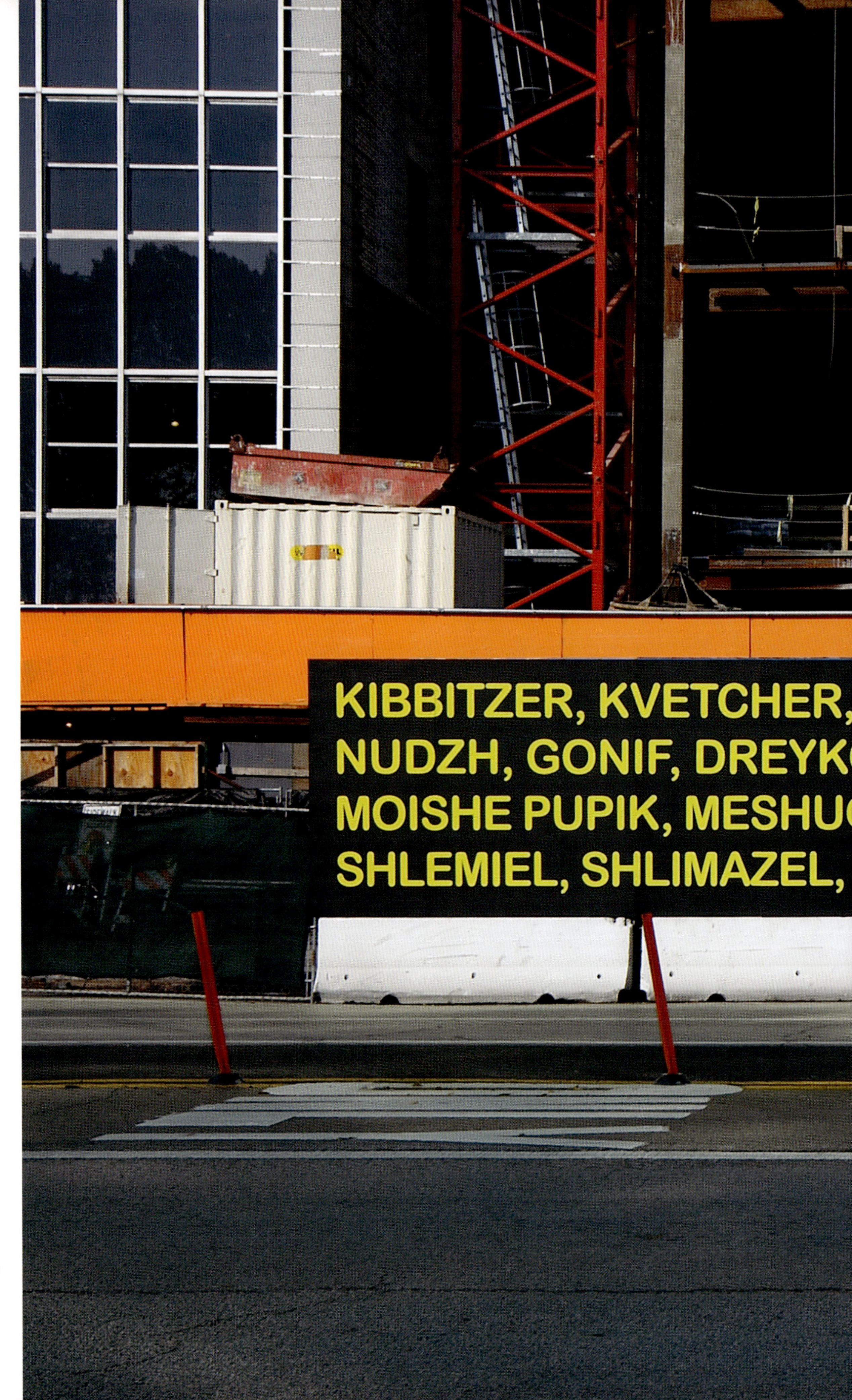


*The Joys of Yiddish*, 2006

Enamel on plywood, 8 × 52 ft.
(2.4 × 15.9 m)
Temporary installation commissioned
by Spertus Institute for Jewish
Learning and Leadership, Chicago, no
longer extant

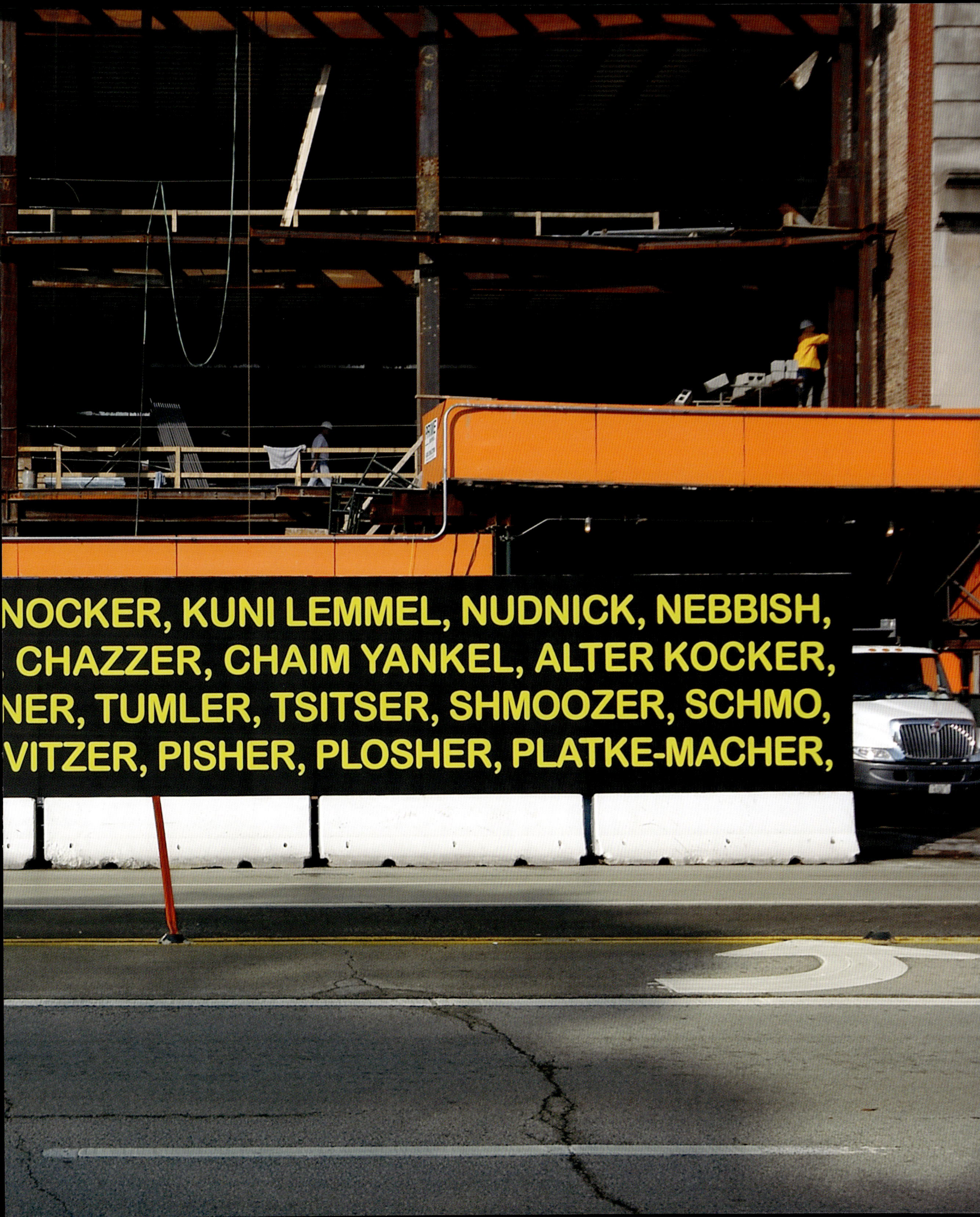
NOCKER, KUNI LEMMEL, NUDNICK, NEBBISH,
CHAZZER, CHAIM YANKEL, ALTER KOCKER,
NER, TUMLER, TSITSER, SHMOOZER, SCHMO,
VITZER, PISHER, PLOSHER, PLATKE-MACHER,

***The Joys of Yiddish*, 2012**

Oil and acrylic on two canvases, 100 × 85 in. (254 × 215.9 cm)
The Jewish Museum, New York

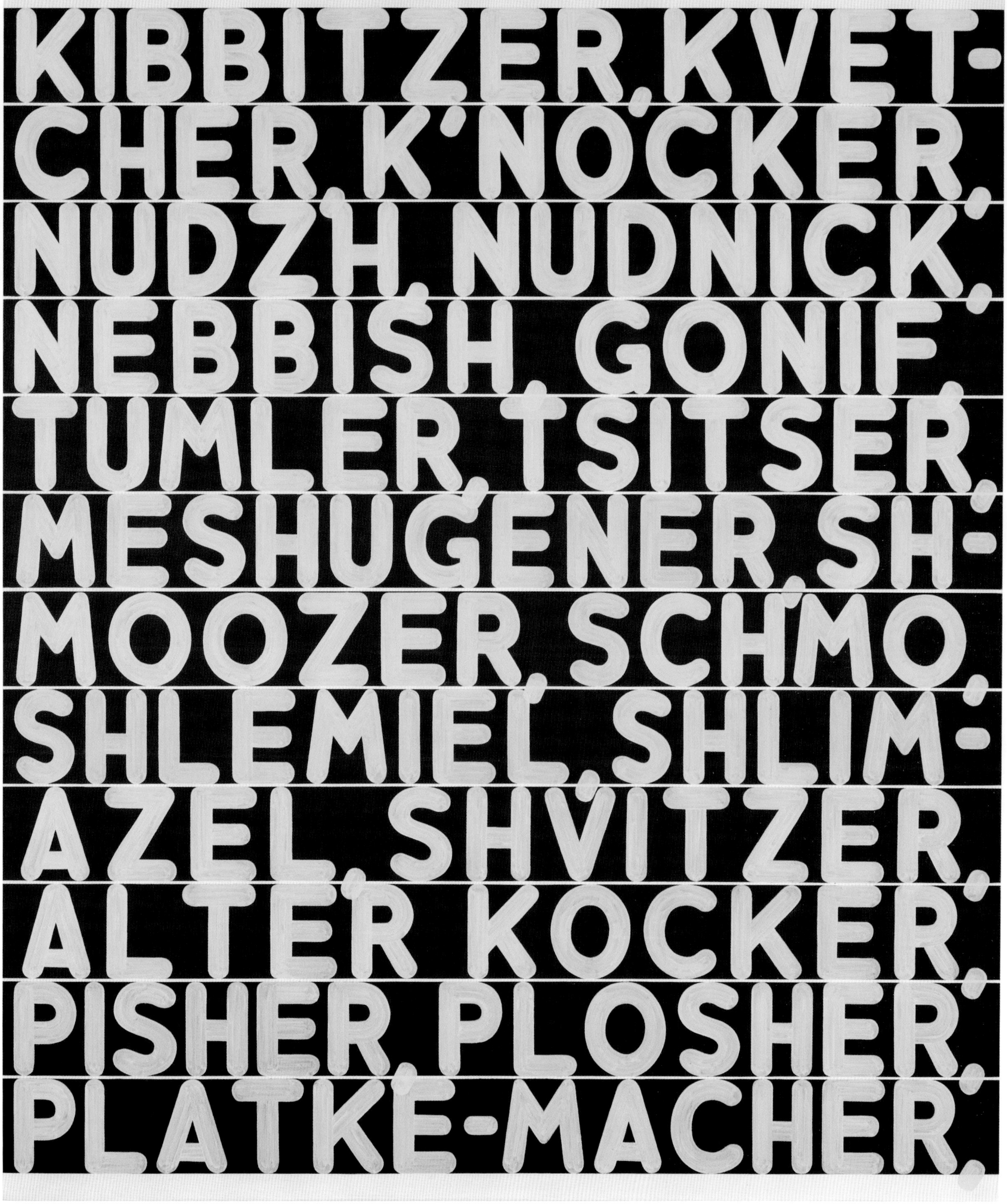

KIBBITZER, KVET-
CHER, K'NOCKER,
NUDZH, NUDNICK,
NEBBISH, GONIF,
TUMLER, TSITSER,
MESHUGENER, SH-
MOOZER, SCHMO,
SHLEMIEL, SHLIM-
AZEL, SHVITZER,
ALTER KOCKER,
PISHER, PLOSHER,
PLATKE-MACHER,

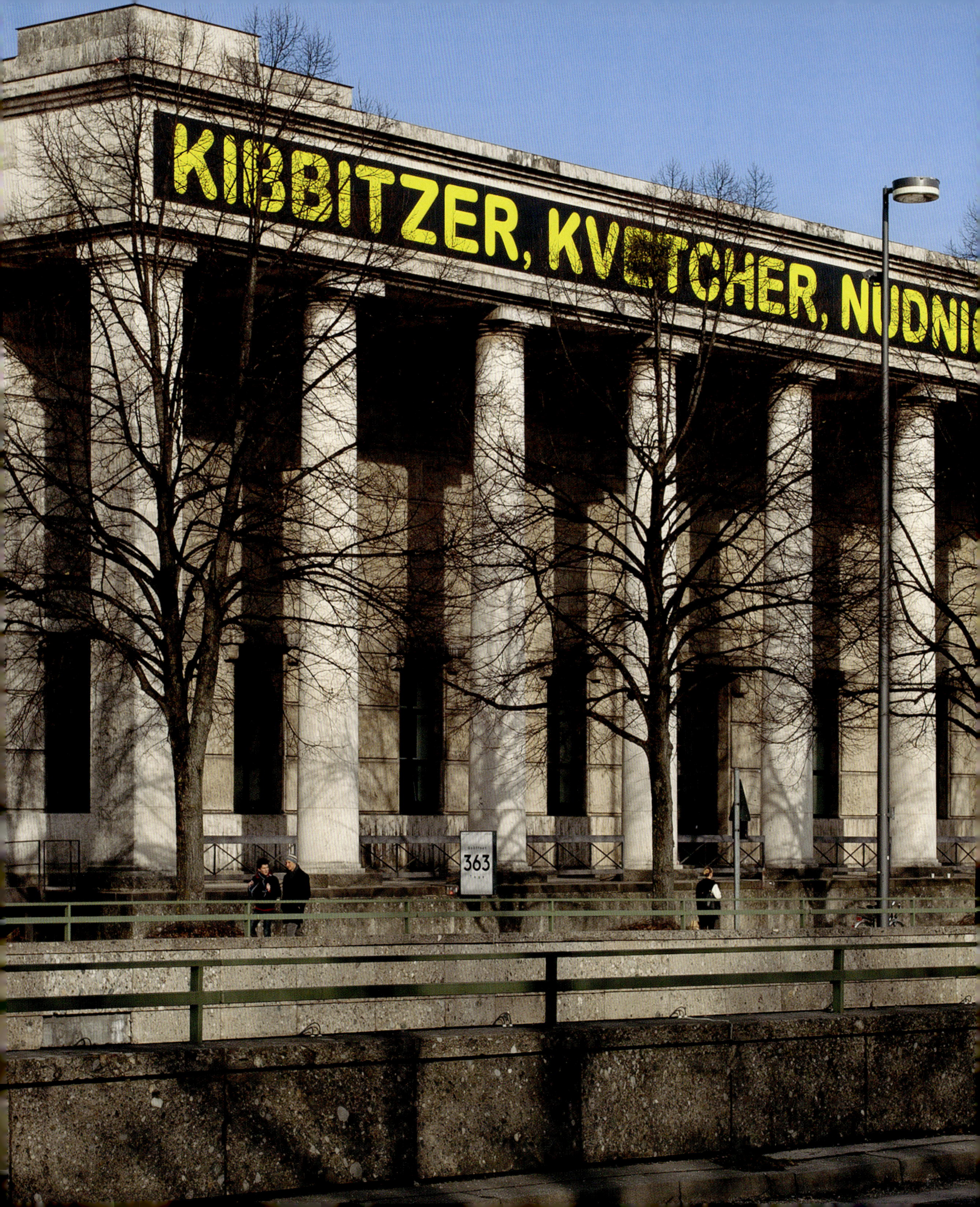

KIBBITZER, KVETCHER, NUDNI
363

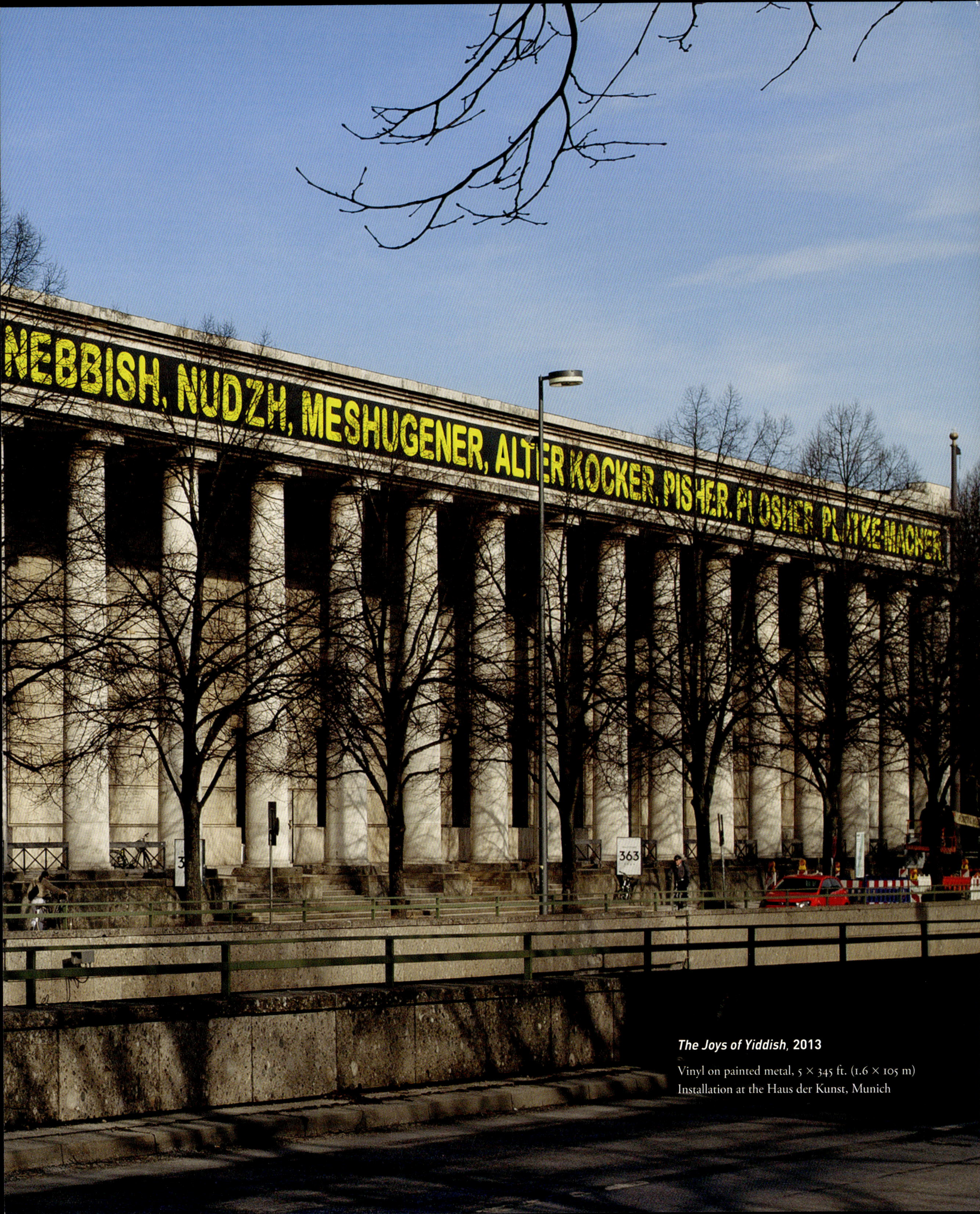


**The Joys of Yiddish**, 2013
Vinyl on painted metal, 5 × 345 ft. (1.6 × 105 m)
Installation at the Haus der Kunst, Munich

*Jew*, 2008

Oil on canvas, 48 × 36 in. (121.9 × 91.4 cm)
Private collection, New York

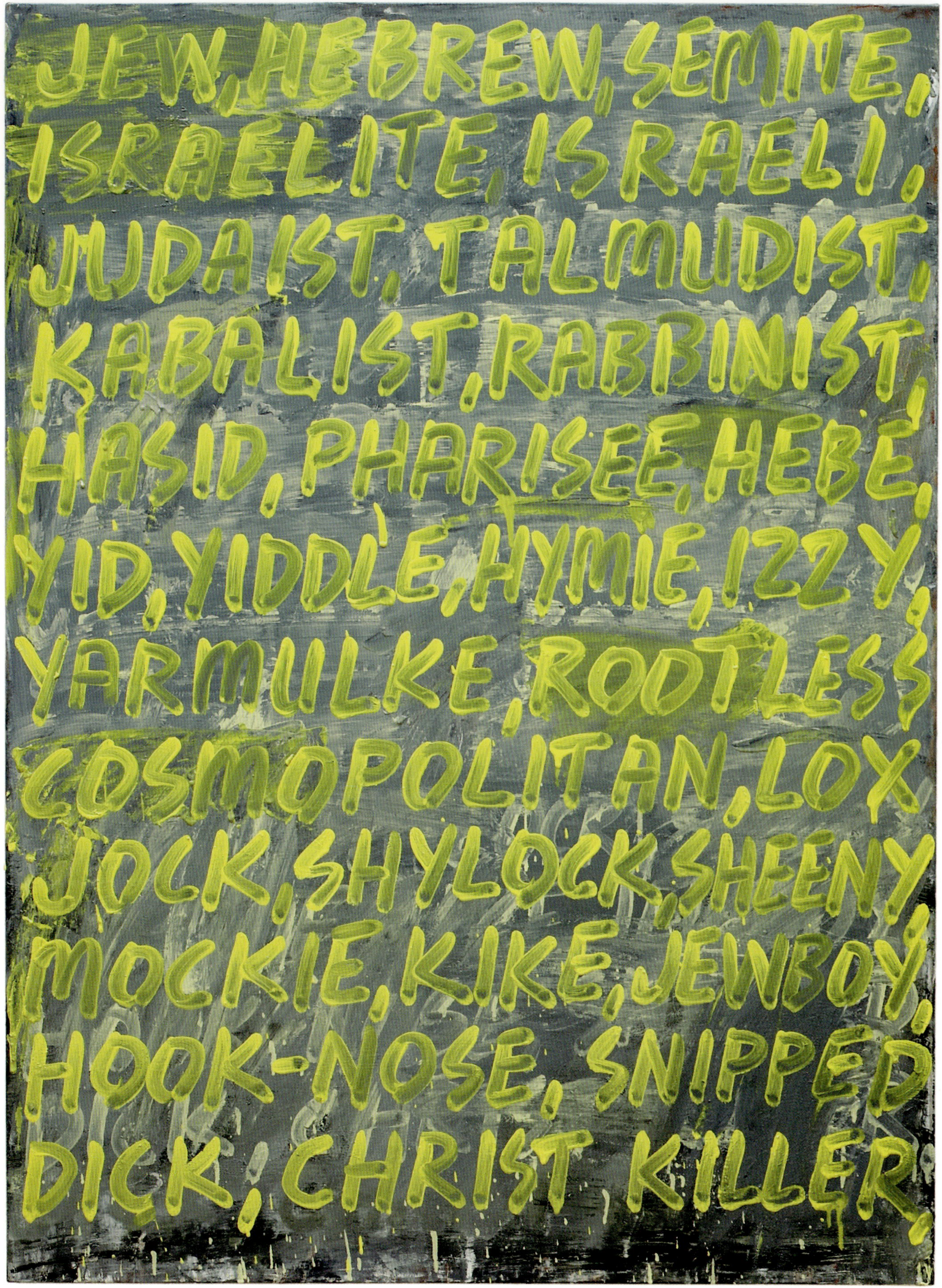

JEW, HEBREW, SEMITE,
ISRAELITE, ISRAELI,
JUDAIST, TALMUDIST,
KABALIST, RABBINIST,
HASID, PHARISEE, HEBE,
YID, YIDDLE, HYMIE, IZZY,
YARMULKE, ROOTLESS
COSMOPOLITAN, LOX
JOCK, SHYLOCK, SHEENY,
MOCKIE, KIKE, JEWBOY,
HOOK-NOSE, SNIPPED
DICK, CHRIST KILLER,

**Working drawing for *Jew*, 2008**

Ink on paper, 13¼ × 9¾ in. (33.6 × 24.8 cm)
Collection of the artist

After *The Joys of Yiddish,* the artist continued to probe the language. In three *Kvetch, Kvetch, Kvetch* canvases the word is repeated without other synonyms (page 111). The word means incessant carping, and these works may be seen as an analogue of sorts to another series, titled *Blah, Blah, Blah* (pages 99–103). The words are crisply rendered in gaudy colors on a painterly backdrop, belying their whiny lament.

Rooting around on the Internet in 2008, Bochner came upon a website with a degrading list of virulent antisemitic synonyms for the word JEW — the grim opposite of Rosten's celebratory tribute. The list shocked and unnerved him, not least because it was formally so similar to those collections of synonyms he had been transforming into art. *Jew* (page 89), the painting that followed this repellent discovery, was a private intellectual and emotional exploration, not initially meant for exhibition.

Disturbing as it is, the painting is politically, visually, and culturally formidable. As in *The Joys of Yiddish,* Bochner used a symbolic acid yellow, this time on a brushy, lead-gray ground. While the language in the thesaurus paintings is often vulgar and embarrassing, in this work it is repugnant and terrifying; the canvas is a direct confrontation with, and appropriation of, a lexicon of hatred. More overtly political than is typical of Bochner, the picture warns against fanaticism. Radiating anxiety, it offers a reminder that racism and antisemitism are not merely relegated to history, and that words are weapons. "As recent history has pain-

The rapidity of communications and increased attention of the mass media have deluded many people as to the real nature of a work of art—except, possibly, when the artist relies on computers to generate art. Then the work is effortlessly digested by the media, without the necessity of seeing it in person.

Art departments in colleges and universities make for broad generalizations about art and artists, which probably compromise originality—except among young people who insist on being artists despite everything. I know there are fine teachers who pass on their understanding of the art process, and make a space for talented young artists. The artistic spirit survives most obstacles. So, yes, an academy continues to function.

The public is used to the idea of an avant-garde. It takes 10 minutes for it to be digested once it presents itself. And another 15 to be gone.

but that for an old fogy like myself, used to the pleasures and absurdity of rendering and polishing shiny objects for consumption, this venue is an unlikely place to end up. The artists of the future will figure out their own way.

**Mel Bochner**

BLAH, BLAH, BLAH, BLAH, BLAH, BLAH, BLAH, BLAH, BLAH, BLAH, BLAH, BLAH, BLAH, BLAH, BLAH,

Mel Bochner: *Blah, Blah, Blah,* 2008, ink on paper, 25½ by 19¾ inches. Courtesy the artist.

**Jim Shaw**

The aughts began with a bubble based on lies, followed by a bust bigger than the recession in the '70s, when I came of age. So we're back to where we began, except that the art world has inflated to encompass the whole world, not just Europe and America.

If there is an avant-garde today, we wouldn't quite recognize it yet, since it wouldn't resemble anything that came before. The art world has realized that the next big thing probably looks unfamiliar, so it invests in the *new* thing, knowing it may well pay off better than something that resembles what we already recognize as art. Thus the avant-garde is deprived of its status as impoverished outsider.

Today we have lots of mini-academic styles, but no overarching academy. We do have a number of art schools that perform the tasks of weeding and tending our garden of hybridized art-star wannabes.

One part of the current economic trap is that most of the artistic communities we congregate in are not the bohemian ghettos of yesteryear but often the most expensive places. Another is that the academic system that has nurtured artists since the '60s has become an assembly line/insider-info track, with an ever-increasing price tag. One might hope that the Internet would allow artists from unknown backwaters, unencumbered by art school connections and debt, to shine. One might also imagine the Internet will come up with an alternate distribution and payment method, and new forms of art. I hope so, but the enormous amount of information surrounding us has so far only reinforced the need to make work that is big and splashy, that can attract attention at a crowded art fair, to stand out in the sea of art product.

We can all join up on the periphery. On YouTube the public is the performer—we only need to have cute cats in our work. I sincerely think that the art of the future will evolve on the electronic front porch that is the Internet,

**Walead Beshty**

I think the flow of information just doesn't seem efficient enough to produce a singular sensibility. There are numerous iterations of the art world operating now, from regional or locus-centric worlds to more diffuse structures, like the academic, museum or gallery systems. Each has its own logic and hierarchies, and each has varying degrees of interest in, and compatibility with, the others. This in itself is positive and, at least in the short run, undermines the truism that globalization necessarily creates homogeneity and integration. The different centers tend to presume that their worldviews are global and inclusive, and to exhibit a general unfriendliness to or ignorance of other systems of valuation, as though each locus were pretending to a singularly dominant role. So I would say that if there is a sensibility I've become more conscious of, it's a kind



SENSIBILITY OF THE TIMES

---

*Art in America,* December 2012, page 170, with Mel Bochner's *Blah, Blah, Blah,* ink on paper, 25½ × 19¾ in. (64.8 × 50.2 cm)

fully taught us," the artist notes, "all abuses of power begin with the abuse of language."[47] If it is to be comprehensive, the study of the mechanisms of language must include even the vilest language.

In purely formal terms, *Jew* belongs less to the Yiddish paintings than to another group of thesaurus works, executed in monochrome with bravura gestures and chalkboard effects. Darker in tonality, these canvases offer sharp stylistic contrasts with the more hard-edged and brightly colored thesaurus pictures. They are sullen in both hue and message.[48] But while the palette has grown dimmer and the brushwork more painterly, the texts of these works remain acerbic and wry. *Critic, Liar,* and *Obsolete* (pages 92, 95, 97) all spring from art-related terminology; as such, they hark back to the artist's early art criticism, with its waterfalls of descriptive words. If the painter is critiquing the art world, he is also holding himself up to judgment.

When asked to comment on the contemporary zeitgeist for a 2012 issue of *Art in America,* Bochner simply submitted one of his recent *Blah, Blah, Blah* works—another series of word-based pictures.[49] In this context it reads as a site-specific work of art and, like his *Domain of the Great Bear,* subverts the vehicle in which it is reproduced.

This colloquial expression first appeared in a small monochromatic gray canvas in 2000, then reappeared at the end of the 2003 painting *Meaningless* (page 51). Since then

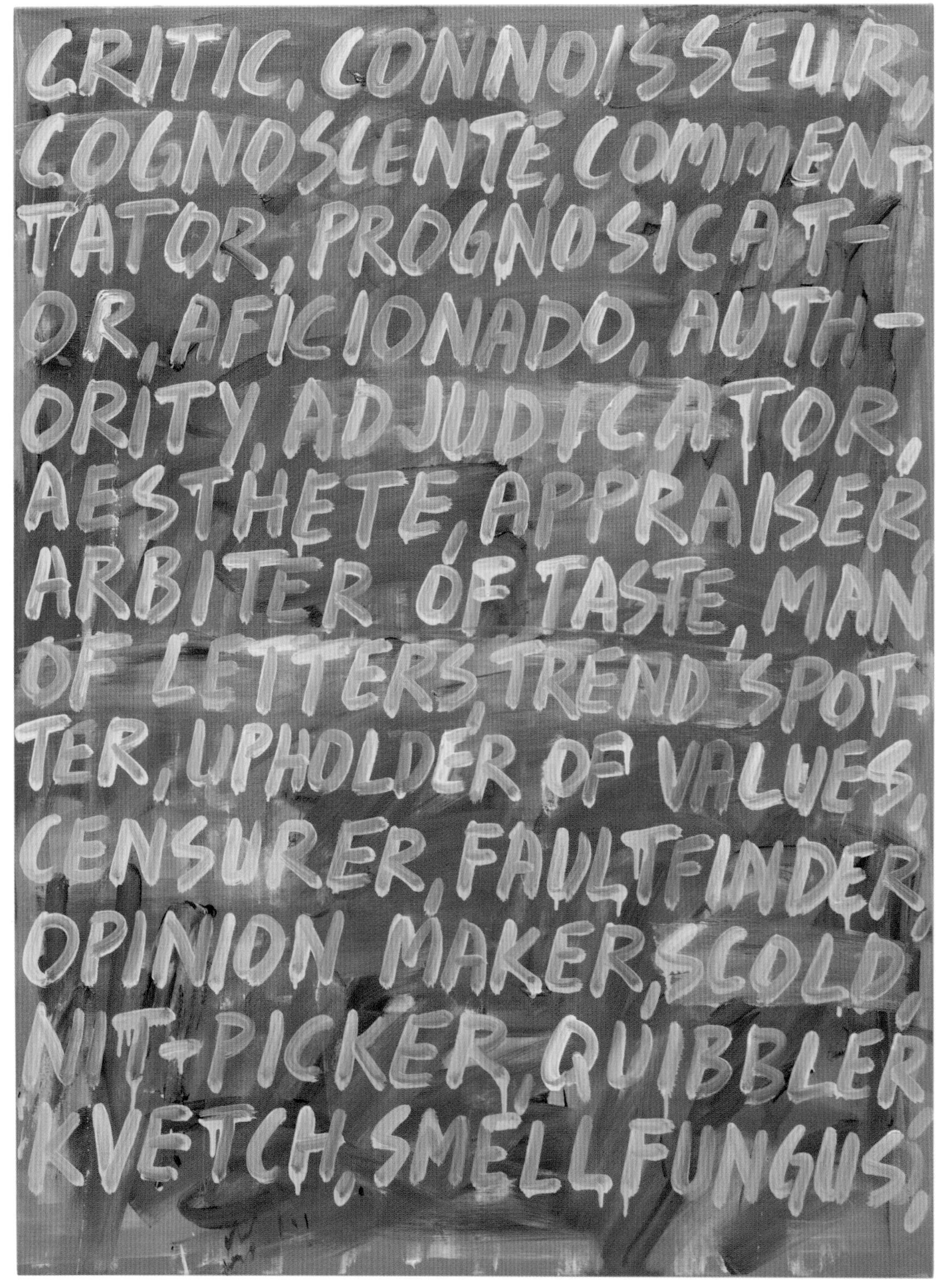


*Critic*, 2007

Oil on canvas, 40 × 30 in. (101.6 × 76.2 cm)
Private collection

*No*, 2007

Oil on canvas, 80 × 60 in. (203.2 × 152.4 cm)
Andrea and Jim Gordon, Chicago

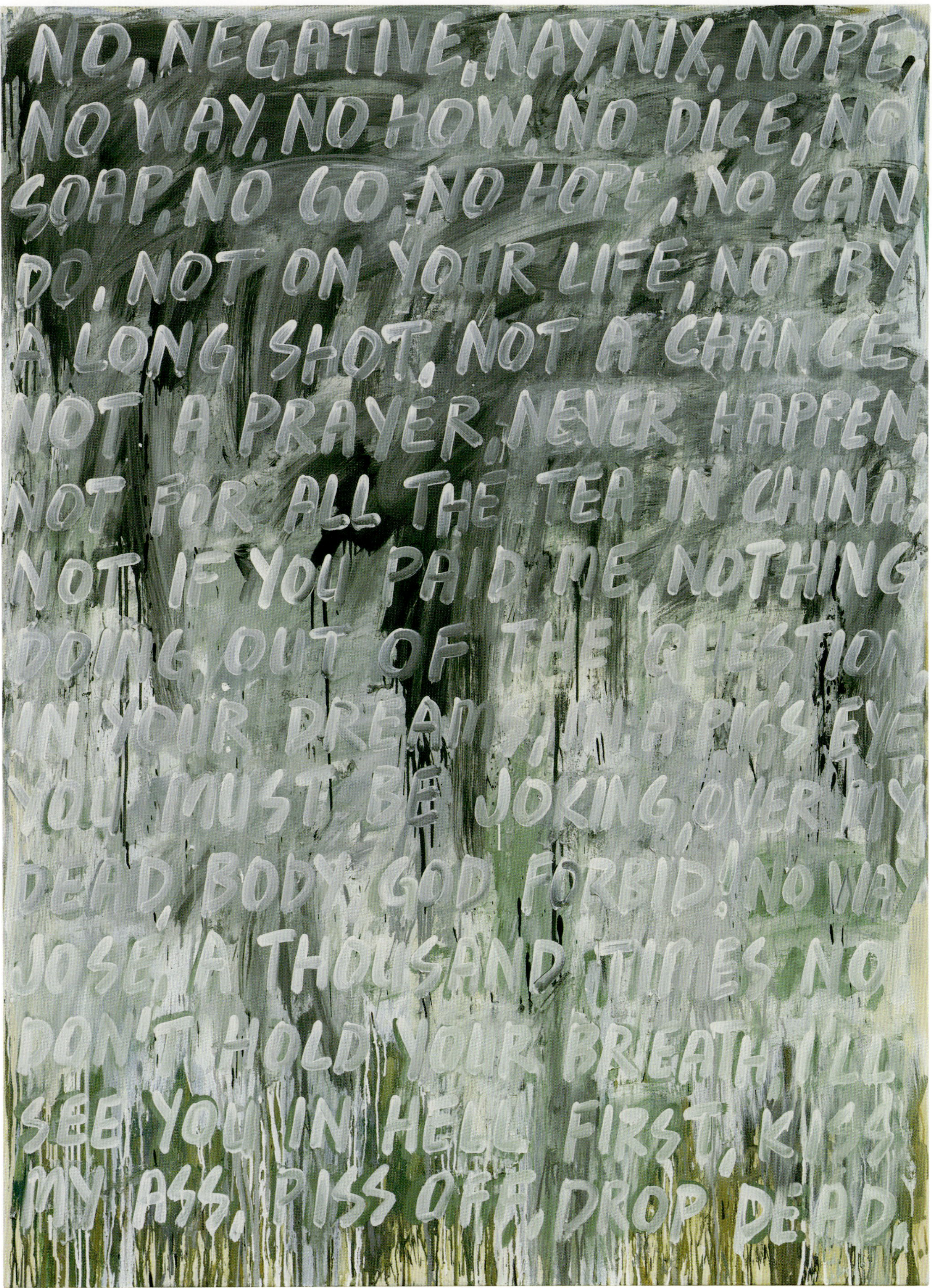

NO, NEGATIVE, NAY NIX, NOPE,
NO WAY, NO HOW, NO DICE, NO
SOAP, NO GO, NO HOPE, NO CAN
DO, NOT ON YOUR LIFE, NOT BY
A LONG SHOT, NOT A CHANCE,
NOT A PRAYER, NEVER HAPPEN,
NOT FOR ALL THE TEA IN CHINA,
NOT IF YOU PAID ME, NOTHING
DOING, OUT OF THE QUESTION,
IN YOUR DREAMS, IN A PIG'S EYE,
YOU MUST BE JOKING, OVER MY
DEAD BODY, GOD FORBID! NO WAY
JOSE, A THOUSAND TIMES NO,
DON'T HOLD YOUR BREATH, I'LL
SEE YOU IN HELL FIRST, KISS
MY ASS, PISS OFF, DROP DEAD.

***Liar,* 2007**

Oil on canvas, 80 × 60 in. (203.2 × 152.4 cm)
Melva Bucksbaum and Raymond Learsy, New York

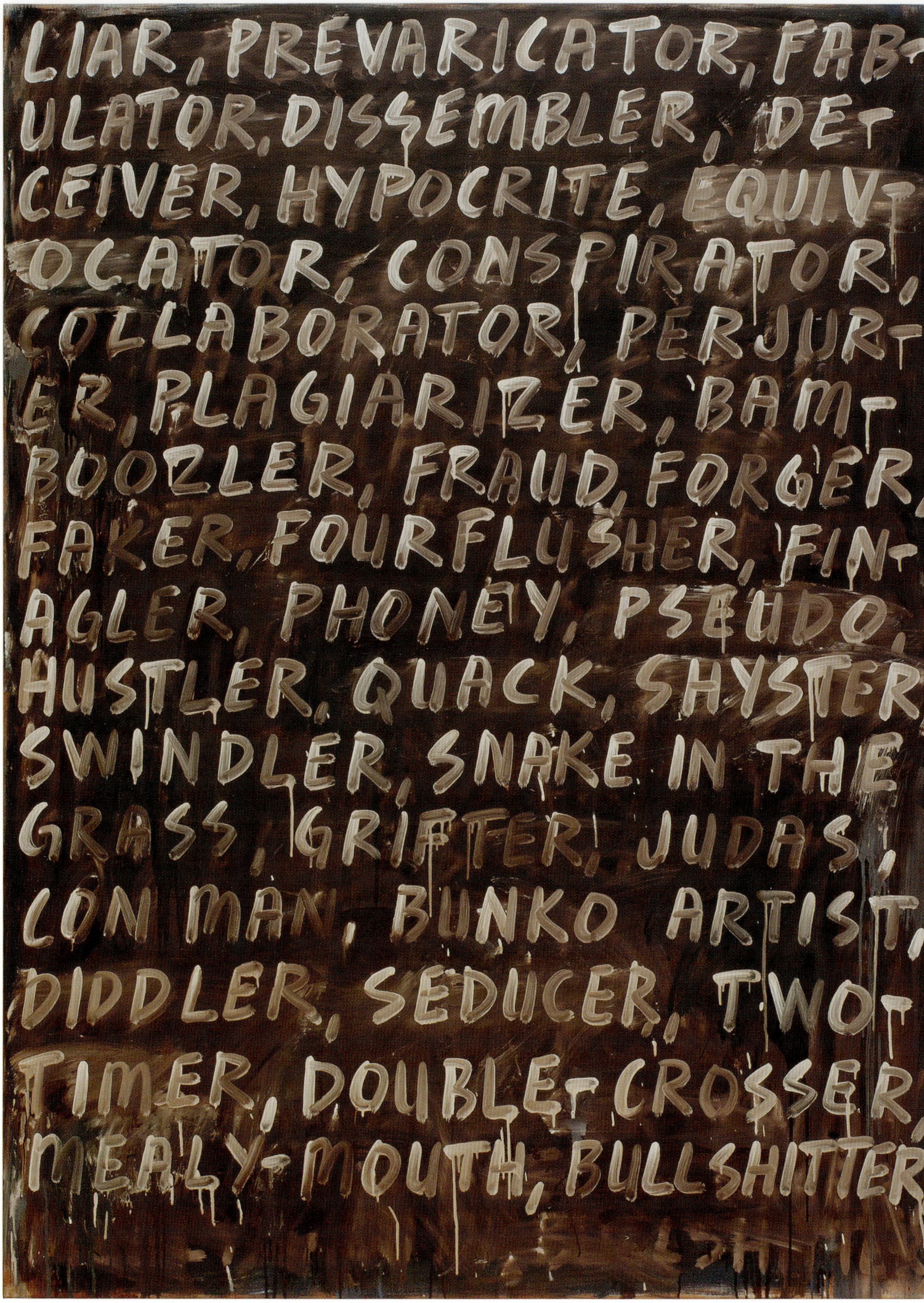

LIAR, PREVARICATOR, FAB-
ULATOR, DISSEMBLER, DE-
CEIVER, HYPOCRITE, EQUIV-
OCATOR, CONSPIRATOR,
COLLABORATOR, PERJUR-
ER, PLAGIARIZER, BAM-
BOOZLER, FRAUD, FORGER,
FAKER, FOURFLUSHER, FIN-
AGLER, PHONEY, PSEUDO,
HUSTLER, QUACK, SHYSTER,
SWINDLER, SNAKE IN THE
GRASS, GRIFTER, JUDAS,
CON MAN, BUNKO ARTIST,
DIDDLER, SEDUCER, TWO-
TIMER, DOUBLE-CROSSER,
MEALY-MOUTH, BULLSHITTER,

***Obsolete*, 2007**

Oil on canvas, 89 × 69 in. (226.1 × 175.2 cm)
Glenstone Foundation, Potomac, Maryland

OBSOLETE, PASSÉ, EXTINCT, OLD,
OLD FASHIONED, OLD SCHOOL, OLD
HAT, OUT-MODED, OUT WORN, OUT-OF-
TOUCH, OUT-OF-DATE, OUT-TO-PAS-
TURE, UNFASHIONABLE, BEHIND
THE TIMES, YESTERDAY'S NEWS, BACK
NUMBER, SECONDHAND, SHOPWORN,
PAWED-OVER, HAS BEEN, MOTHEATEN,
MOSSBACK, GONE TO SEED, DISCON-
TINUED, PHASED OUT, ON THE BACK
BURNER, OVER THE HILL, OLD AS TIME,
OLD FOGY, OLD POOP, ALTE KOCKER,
FUDDY DUDDY, FOSSIL, NOSTALGIA
ACT, CORNY, STUFFY, STODGY, FUSTY,
MUSTY, DUSTY, RUSTY, RETRO, LONG
IN THE TOOTH, LONG GONE, DEAD
AS A DOORNAIL, DEAD AS A DODO, CON-
SIGNED TO THE SCRAPHEAP OF HIS-
TORY, SO YESTERDAY, SHIT-CANNED,

Bochner has produced numerous works with the word BLAH repeated in various configurations and color schemes, in luscious oil-based monoprints and virtuoso paintings.

BLAH is scarcely a word at all, but rather a generic vocalization representing exhausted language—the brain's failure to find the correct word or even remember language at all. Its weary repetition conveys a kind of dismissive boredom. This is emphasized in the way the BLAHS melt into or slide off of the canvas. Bochner's energetic handling of paint stands in contrast to this expressive fatigue. Multiple exposures and dazzling facture turn the lethargic monotone into a chorus of voices, an invocation, a rhythmic chant. The more language fails, the more paint succeeds.

A unique and striking work is *Voiceover* (page 105), in which the artist has recycled a monochrome thesaurus painting that did not please him (originally titled *Aggravate*), turning it into a *Blah, Blah, Blah* by superimposing the phrase in violent red on the old work while leaving major parts of the original visible. Here the trickling paint once again appropriates Abstract Expressionist gesture and, as in *Language Is Not Transparent,* the drip as ironic trope of freewheeling artistic genius. The phrase "blah, blah, blah" both depicts the idea of the tedium of meaningless words and acts as the artist's direct critique of his own failed painting—a deliberate self-exposure. As such, it brings together Bochner's double life as artist and critic. In this sense, *Voiceover* echoes the *Art in America* page.

Throughout the thesaurus series, Bochner has been very careful to separate his words with punctuation marks, most often commas, but sometimes exclamation points, question marks, or hyphens. In two paintings words have vanished and only punctuation remains. *Colon Open Parenthesis* (page 106) is a hand-painted emoticon, a typed symbol common in electronic writing, used to convey a simple emotion. The keyboard version of the smiley or frowny face as commentary is a child of digital communication. *Dollar Hash Exclamation Plus* (page 107) uses these symbols both to represent cursing and to spell out the expletive SHIT in characters that can pass a web-based censor: $#!+. Their strident, dopey, even offensive language is delicately rendered, with a draftsman's aplomb, in charcoal on an ethereal white ground. The sublime style contradicts the banality of the symbols. As always, Bochner creates a collision between two disparate modes of communication: painting and text, serious and funny, high and low, banal and transcendent.[50]

The four-part picture *And/If/Or/But* has a similar painterly visual affect (page 108). Here too the tone contrasts with the ordinariness of the words placed at the center of each panel. Unlike the thesaurus paintings, these words are simple conjunctions, almost meaningless, nothing more than the connective tissue of language. Bochner has rejected the cacophony of synonyms in favor of flat statements on the architecture of language. The subtle, iridescent backdrops respond to the changing conditions of light and reverberate with references to romantic landscape painting and Color Field canvases.

The 2011 painting *Silence!* screams its synonyms as commands, in shrill chromatic juxtapositions (page 72). With the pale, nearly white version of *Silence!,* painted a year later (page 113), Bochner demonstrates how palette can transform the meaning of a painting. Here

**Blah, Blah, Blah, 2008**

Oil on canvas, 60 × 45 in. (152.4 × 114.3 cm)
Collection of Danielle and David Ganek

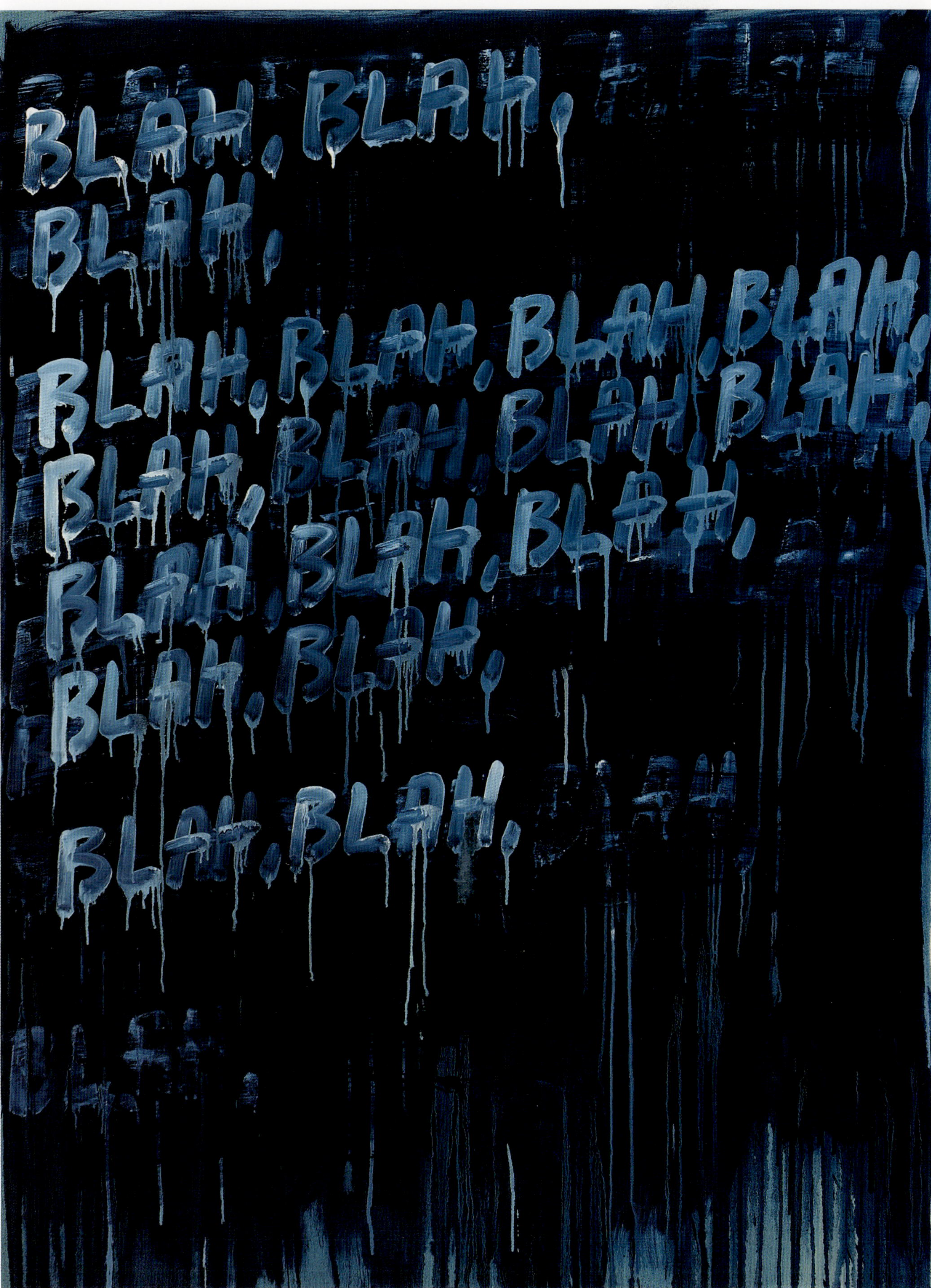

BLAH, BLAH,
BLAH,
BLAH, BLAH, BLAH, BLAH,
BLAH, BLAH, BLAH BLAH,
BLAH, BLAH, BLAH,
BLAH, BLAH,
BLAH, BLAH,

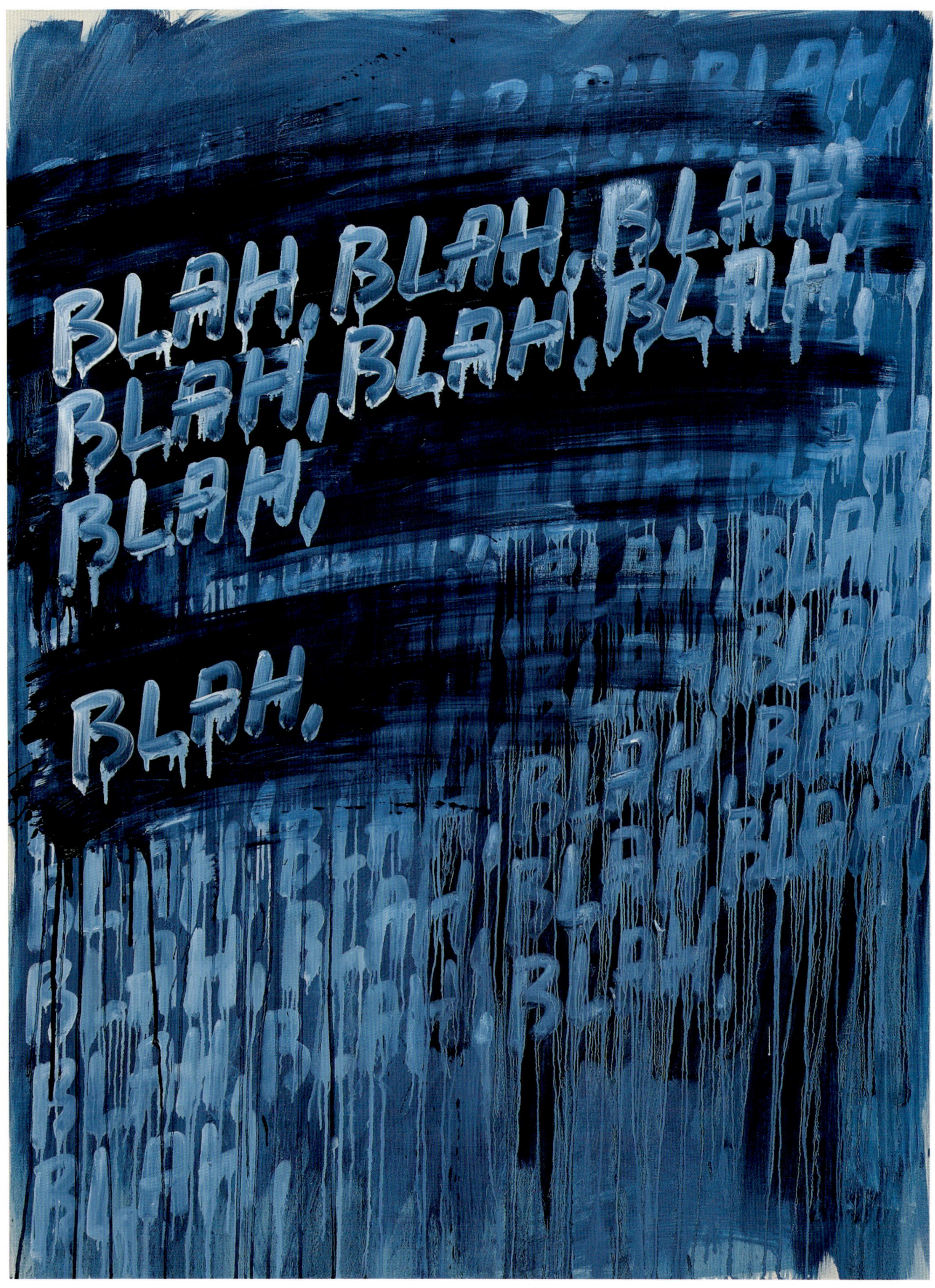

BLAH, BLAH, BLAH,
BLAH, BLAH, BLAH,
BLAH,
BLAH,

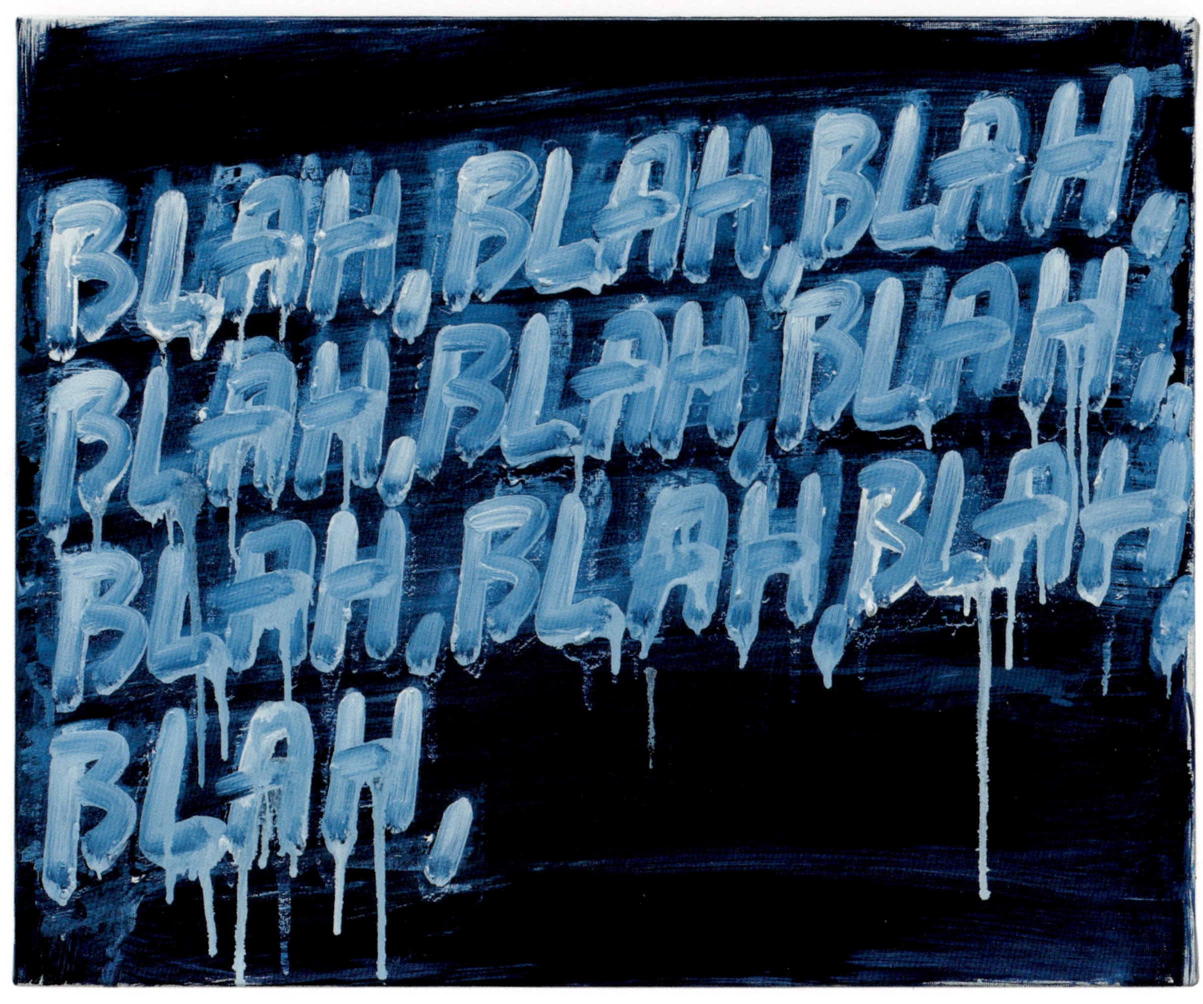

**Blah, Blah, Blah, 2008**

Oil on canvas, 60 × 45 in. (152.4 × 114.3 cm)
Jill and Peter Kraus, New York

**Blah, Blah, Blah, 2008**

Oil on canvas, 16 × 20 in. (40.6 × 50.8 cm)
Evelyn and David Lasry

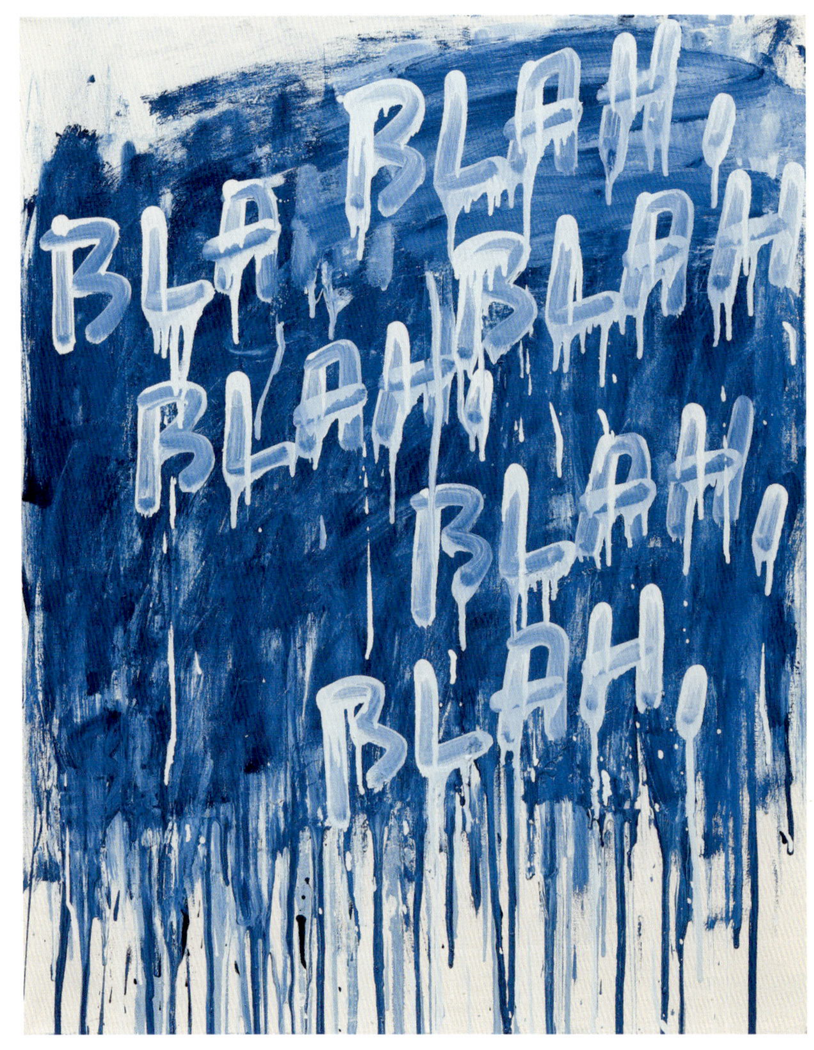



**_Blah, Blah, Blah_, 2009**

Oil on canvas, 30 × 24 in. (76.2 × 61 cm)
Private collection

**_Blah, Blah, Blah_, 2012**

Oil on canvas, 100 × 80 in. (254 × 203.2 cm)
Private collection

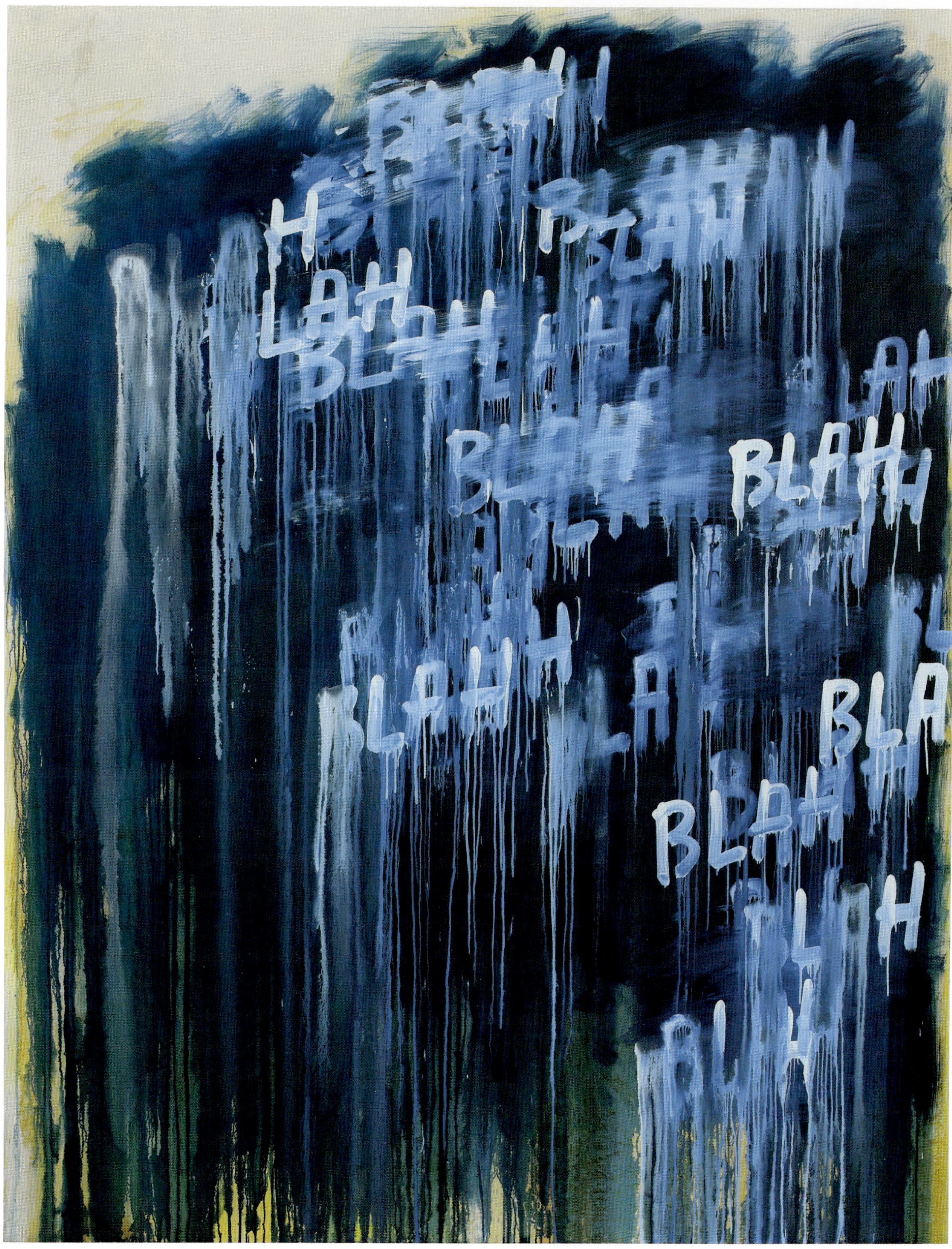

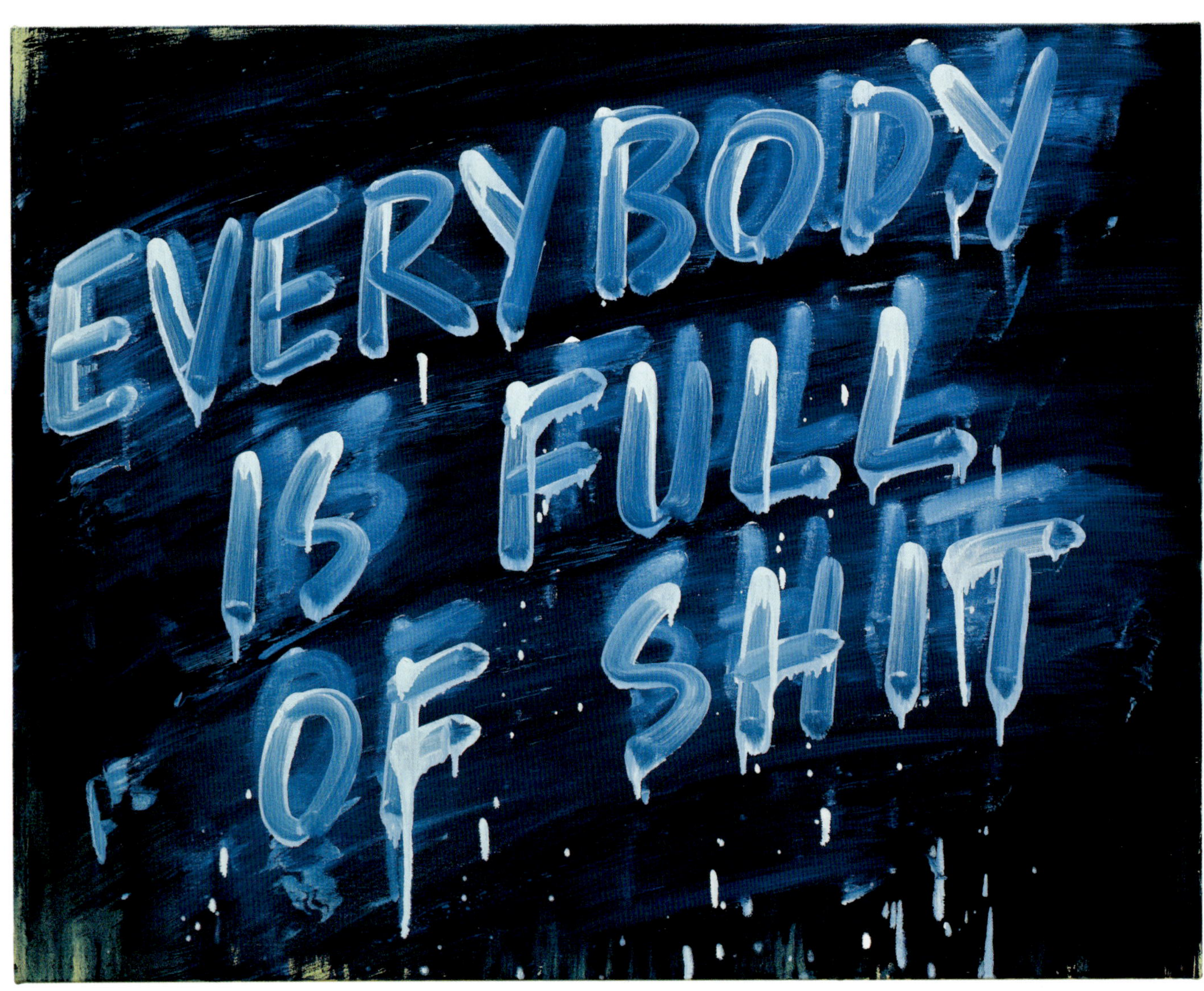


**_Everybody Is Full of Shit_, 2009**

Oil on canvas, 28 × 36 in. (71.1 × 91.4 cm)
Sandro and Fiamma Manzo

**_Voiceover_, 2006/12**

Oil on canvas, 36 × 28 in. (91.4 × 71.1 cm)
Pergamont Collection

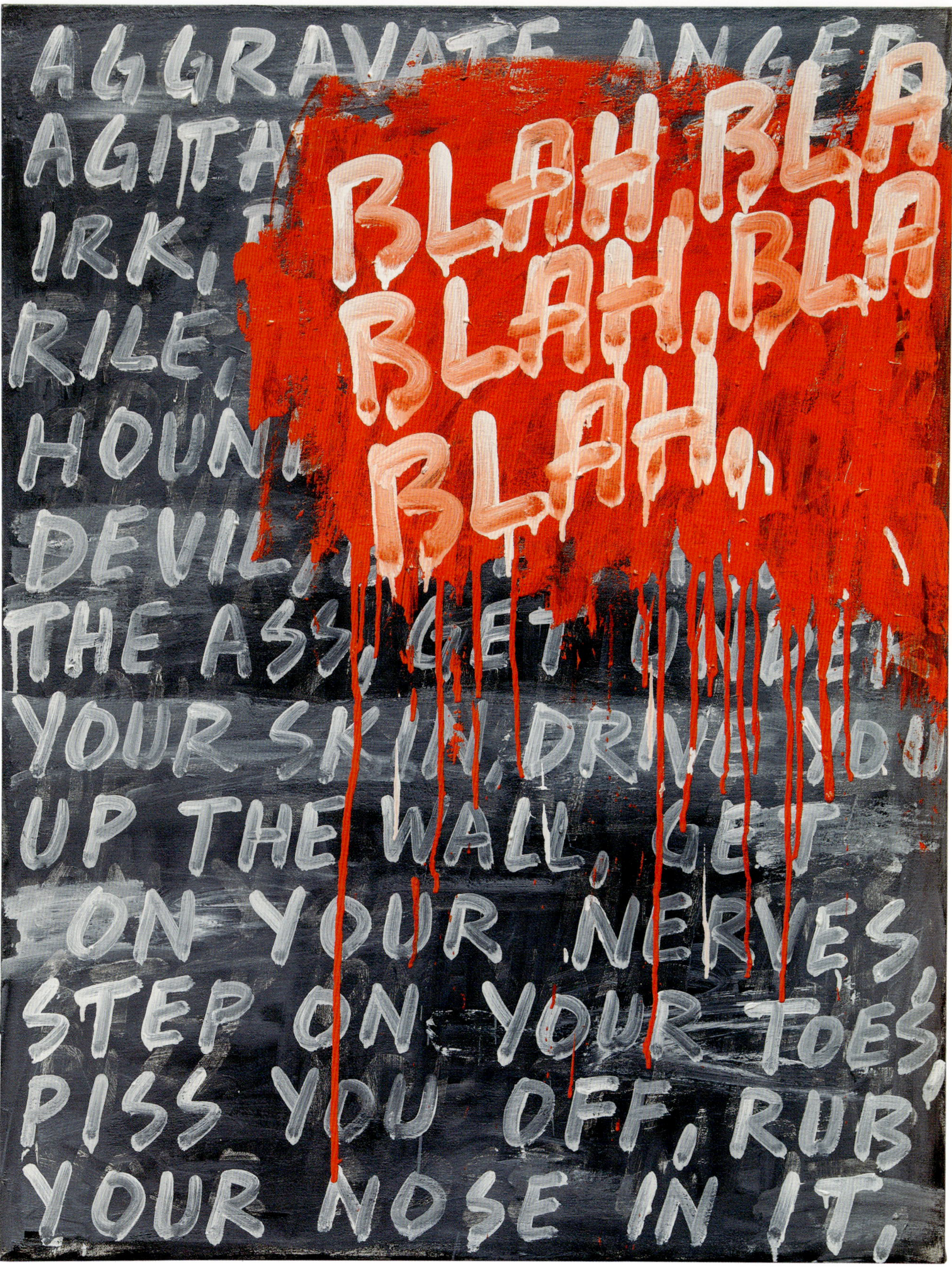
AGGRAVATE, ANGER,
AGITA
IRKI
RILE
HOUN
DEVIL
THE ASS, GET U
YOUR SKIN, DRIVE YOU
UP THE WALL, GET
ON YOUR NERVES,
STEP ON YOUR TOES,
PISS YOU OFF, RUB
YOUR NOSE IN IT.
BLAH BLA
BLAH, BLA
BLAH,

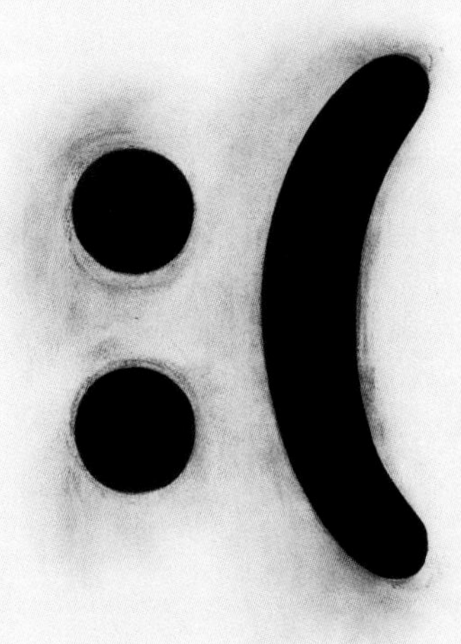

**Colon Open Parenthesis, 2011**

Oil and charcoal on canvas, 45 × 60 in. (114.3 × 152.4 cm)
Peter Freeman, Inc.

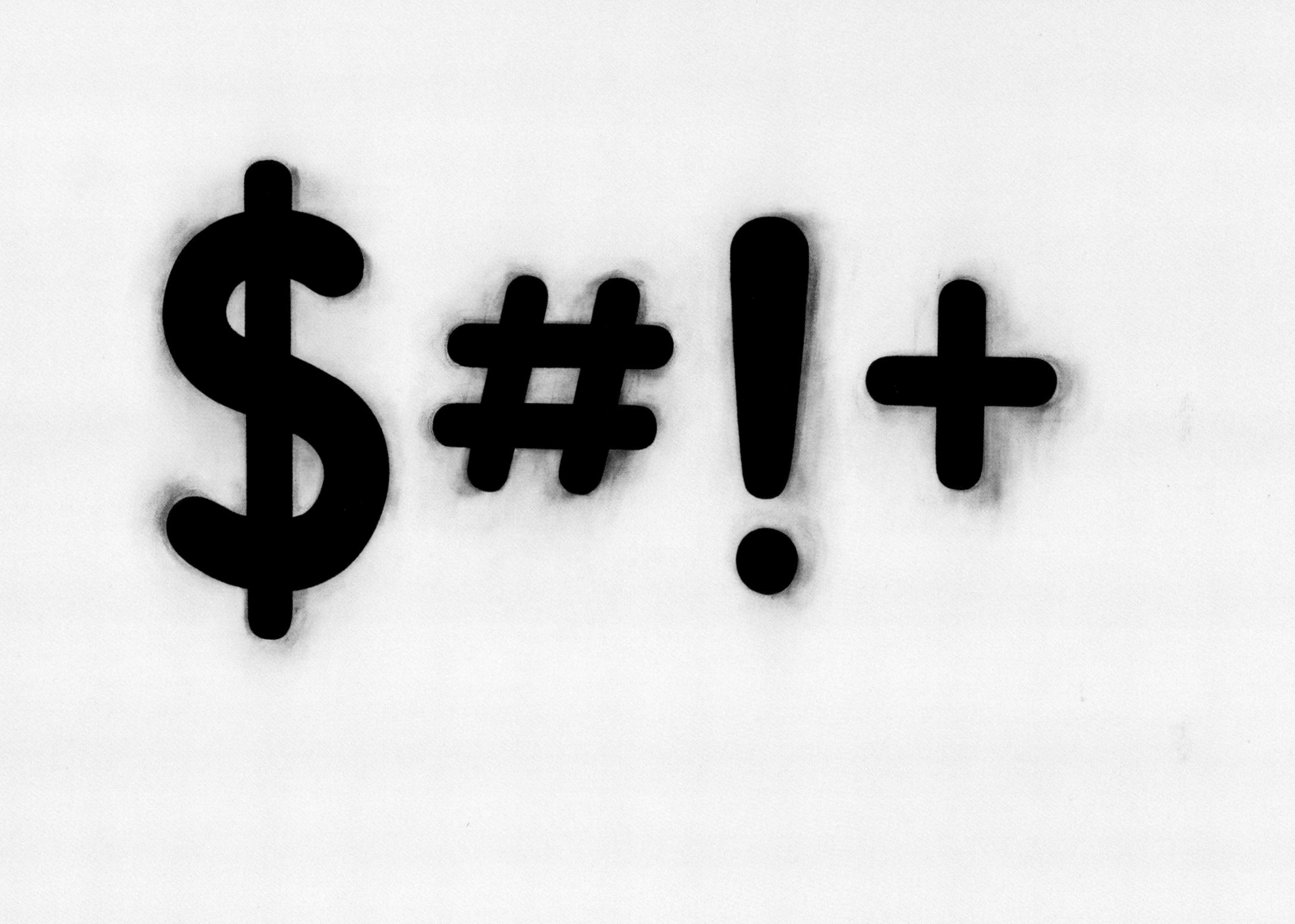

***Dollar Hash Exclamation Plus*, 2011**

Oil and charcoal on canvas, 45 × 60 in. (114.3 × 152.4 cm)
Peter Freeman, Inc.

AND
IF

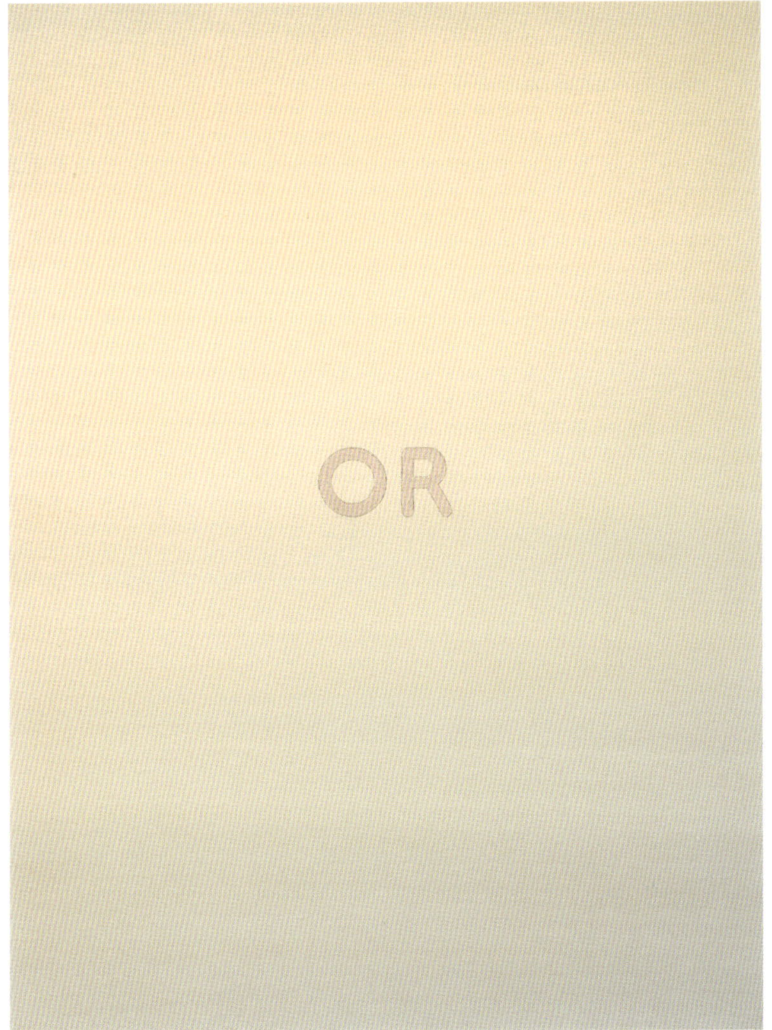

***And/If/Or/But*, 2006**

Acrylic on four canvases, each 40 × 30 in. (101.6 × 76.2 cm)
Irving Stenn, Jr., Chicago

***Kvetch, Kvetch, Kvetch*, 2010**

Oil and acrylic on canvas, 45 × 60 in. (114.3 × 152.4 cm)
Collection of Danielle and David Ganek

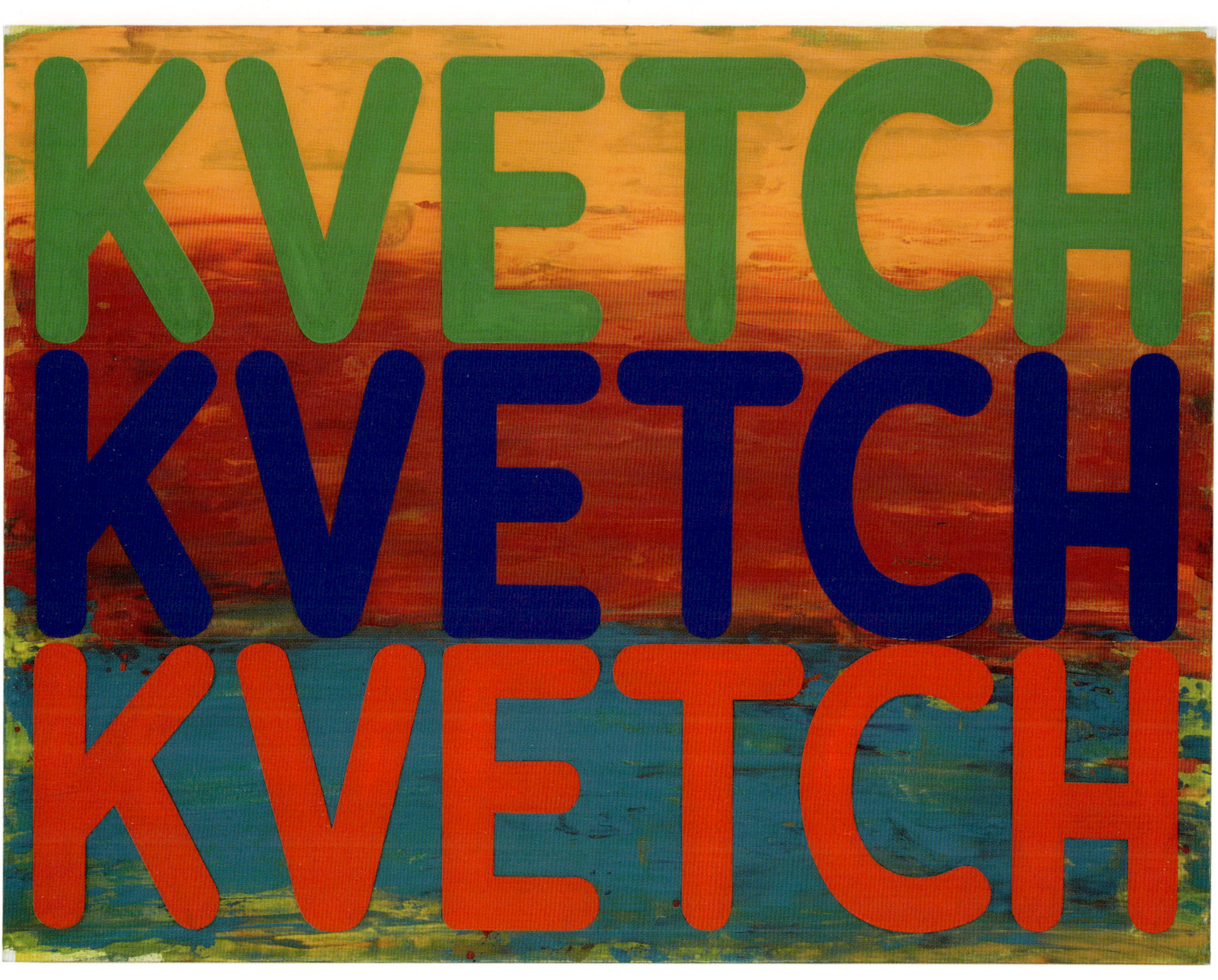

KVETCH
KVETCH
KVETCH

Oil on velvet, 63 × 47 in. (160 × 119.4 cm)
Private collection

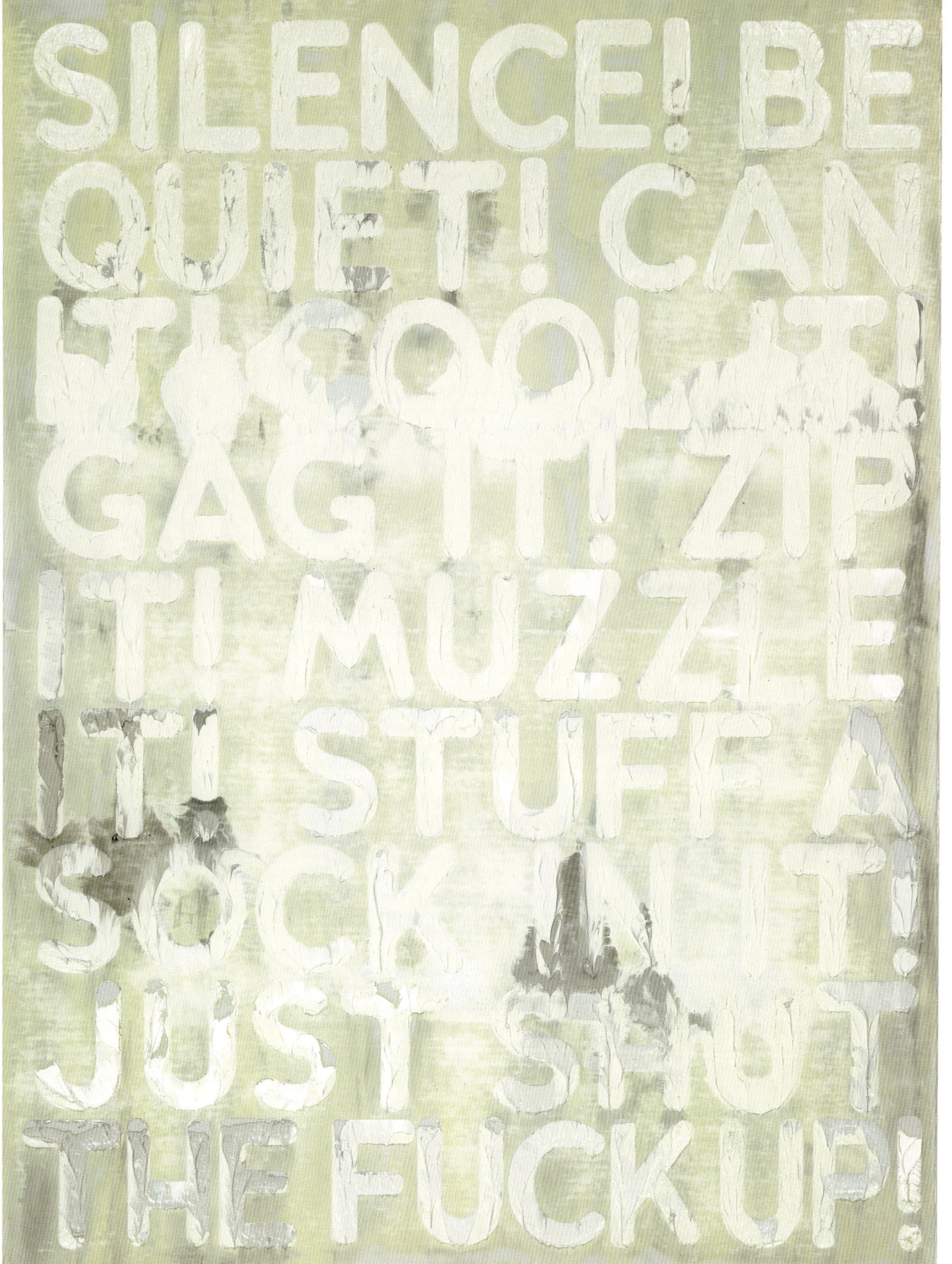

SILENCE! BE
QUIET! CAN
IT! COOL IT!
GAG IT! ZIP
IT! MUZZLE
IT! STUFF A
SOCK IN IT!
JUST SHUT
THE FUCK UP!

the viewer is propelled into a blizzard of whites, entering a spectral visual space, one in which reading the text becomes a challenge. If the multicolor version excites and energizes the viewer, this monochrome imparts a slower and more meditative emotional state.

Bochner is understood as a transformative artist of the mid-twentieth century—one of the originators of Conceptual art. In about 1979 he returned to the historical medium of painting on canvas (though not exclusively), but his pictures are far from traditional. His recent works must be considered within the various strategies of painting in the 2000s, although they often build upon the groundwork of his earlier experiments.

Painting today is a complex hybrid. Artists cite, embrace, and dismantle postwar formalism; play with different means of figuration; and adapt analytic and expressionistic trends from the 1960s through 1980s—all of which Conceptualism had rejected. Painting in the twenty-first century also addresses the longstanding modernist tension between representation and abstraction, and draws more conceptually based approaches into its expressive techniques.

Bochner's art is purposefully slippery; the fissions and fusions endemic to it make it difficult to categorize. His canvases and murals from 1979 on, and particularly his thesaurus paintings, negotiate between painterly and Conceptual concerns. His return to painting at that time occurred within a more general return to painting internationally and may perhaps be seen as a harbinger of what has recently been dubbed Conceptual Expression—an attitude in which Conceptual approaches are embedded within expressive paint handling. Such works "dissolve the classical frontline between supposedly conceptual and expressive practices."[51] But Bochner does not selectively cobble together bits of Conceptualism and passages of painterly facture (see page 78); rather, he maintains the two modes in elastic tension.

Painting is no longer about the sanctity of the picture plane, but more and more about giving the viewer a performative role in the completion of the artwork. In Bochner, that role is deliberately made uncertain. The position of the viewer is dialectical: he or she both reads the text and absorbs the sensuality of paint. As readers we are inside the canvas; as spectators we stand outside it. The observer is never permitted to experience the painting conclusively and wholly.

The viewer's inability to experience the thesaurus paintings in their totality—the tendency of the work of art to pull itself apart—is a fundamental mechanism for Bochner, one that finds numerous echoes in recent painting by younger artists. The vocabularies of the visual and the verbal are in perpetual combat, leaving the viewer torn between the experience of the painterly object and that of the textual content. The viewer is thus the necessary mediator among the warring parts of the artwork; without a viewer, the work cannot cohere. The mental and physical position of the viewer—the conceptual and experiential space he or she inhabits—is itself an aspect of Bochner's observation of the way media and methods simultaneously reveal and conceal. With their tensions and dualities, complexities and contradictions, Bochner's thesaurus paintings hark back to his earlier realization that art exists "in the space where the mental and the physical overlap."[52]

Repetition and reinvention are a consistent strategy in Bochner's art. They turn up in innumerable forms. Thus, the rubber-stamp version of *Language Is Not Transparent* begets the insistent reinstallation of its painted versions. In *Photography Before the Age of Mechanical Reproduction,* the repetitions inherent in photography and printmaking profoundly transform the meaning of the earlier *Misunderstandings (A Theory of Photography),* the work from which it is derived. The reuse of thesaurus word lists leads to the reductive, existentially weary repetition of the meaningless sound BLAH BLAH BLAH or KVETCH KVETCH KVETCH. When the artist returns, in *Voiceover,* to a rejected painting from one series and deftly repurposes it into another, he is acting on the same impulse that has him revisiting the concept of silence in two emotively different palettes. When he invades the pages of *Arts Magazine* with *The Domain of the Great Bear* or the pages of *Art in America* with a recent *Blah* picture he is using the same tactic with a totally different function. Revisiting and repetition are more than a method; the recirculation and transformation of ideas are intrinsic to Bochner's art. His work persistently questions its own premises, restlessly pushing forward while anxiously looking back. Nothing is ever either finished or abandoned. As in his earliest word drawing, *Cause and Effect,* the serpent—the ancient Ouroboros—is constantly devouring itself.


NOTES

1. Bochner's work from the Conceptual period is a staple in shows about the movement; it has received a thorough reexamination in Richard S. Field, *Mel Bochner: Thought Made Visible,* exh. cat. (New Haven: Yale University Press, 1995), and the attendant exhibition. Bochner's installation *Working Drawings and Other Visible Things on Paper Not Necessarily Meant to be Viewed as Art* (1966) is sometimes considered the first Conceptual art installation; see, for example, Tony Godfrey, *Conceptual Art* (London: Phaidon, 1998, repr. 2011), 116, 429. A classic characterization of the period is Lucy Lippard's pioneering observation about the "dematerialization of art"; see Lippard, *Six Years: The Dematerialization of the Art Object from 1966 to 1972* (New York: Praeger, 1973), esp. pages 166–77 on Bochner. However, Bochner tends not to consider this term applicable to his work. He has often expressed dislike of the term "Conceptual art" and skepticism about the existence of any cohesive movement of that name—or about his own placement within such a rubric. That said, in 1969 he wrote to the curator Harald Szeemann, "Let me say that I have for some time been deeply involved in moving away from the tangible 'Object of Art,' into a more conceptual notion of art as a procedure"; letter, Bochner to Szeemann, January 17, 1969, on display in the exhibition "When Attitudes Become Form: Bern 1969/ Venice 2013," Fondazione Prada, Venice, 2013.

2. "How Can You Defend Making Paintings Now? A Conversation Between Mel Bochner and James Meyer," in Philip Armstrong et al., *As Painting: Division and Displacement,* exh. cat. (Columbus: Wexner Center for the Arts, Ohio State University, and Cambridge, MA: MIT Press, 2001), 74–79, 199–204; repr. in Mel Bochner, *Solar System & Rest Rooms: Writings and Interviews* (Cambridge, MA: MIT Press, 2008), 158–66. Also see his discussion of his work as a "continuous investigation" into painting in the same volume.

3. See Johanna Burton et al., *Mel Bochner: Language, 1966–2006,* exh. cat. (Chicago: Art Institute of Chicago, 2007), 16, 22, 23; and Elaine King, *Mel Bochner, 1973–1985* (Pittsburgh: Carnegie Mellon University Press, 1985), 9. Like Burton, other writers often use the term "contradiction" or the concept of opposition in describing Bochner's practice. Burton's section headings—Conceptual/Material, Reductive/ Additive, Internal/External—are examples. Many references to such dichotomies exist in the extensive literature on Bochner; for instance, Richard S. Field: "It is always the play between counting and order, concept and demonstration, mental and visual apprehension, that is at the center of his work"; "structure . . . would persist beneath Bochner's sensuosity"; "Bochner has situated himself between and at the edges," in *Mel Bochner: Thought Made Visible,* 54, 62, 63. Bochner speaks of his "way of working through contradictions"; see Mel Bochner, "Art in Conversation: Mel Bochner with Phong Bui," *Brooklyn Rail* (May 2006): 16–17, cited in Burton, *Mel Bochner: Language,* 36 n. 35. See also Frédéric Paul, "Mel Bochner: Experience and Its Paradoxes," in *Mel*

*Bochner,* trans. Simon Pleasance, exh. cat. (Bignan, France: Centre d'Art Contemporain—Centre Culturel de Rencontre, Domaine de Kerguéhennec, 2009), 30.

4. Bochner's personal biography rarely gets much discussion in the literature on his work. Such references tend to be brief and sketchy; see Achim Borchardt-Hume et al., *Mel Bochner: If the Colour Changes,* exh. cat. (London: Ram, 2013), in which the artist's biography is five lines long; and Ulrich Wilmes, in "Between Reading and Seeing," in Borchardt-Hume et al., *Mel Bochner: If the Colour Changes,* 33; "Art in Conversation: Mel Bochner with Phong Bui," *Brooklyn Rail* (May 2006).

5. Conversation with the author, March 18, 2013.

6. Field, *Mel Bochner: Thought Made Visible,* 46, emphasis added.

7. See Rosalind E. Krauss, *Line as Language: Six Artists Draw* (Princeton, NJ: Princeton University Art Museum, 1974), 13. Occasionally, Bochner uses simple dictionary definitions rather than strings of synonyms; in *Portrait of Marcel Duchamp* he aptly applies a cryptogram.

8. James Meyer notes that the smears and erasures in the new versions make them palimpsests, appropriate to their new role as memorials; see *Mel Bochner: Colorful Language,* exh. brochure (Washington, DC: National Gallery of Art, 2011), n.p. [5].

9. In micrography, words are positioned to form letters, abstract shapes, or images. In Jewish visual tradition it is a response to an aniconic interpretation of scripture. Bochner may have seen such texts on display at The Jewish Museum when he was a guard in the Judaica galleries in 1963–64, although he does not recall having done so. On micrography, see Katrin Kogman-Appel, "Jewish Art and Non-Jewish Culture: The Dynamics of Artistic Borrowings in Medieval Hebrew Manuscript Illumination," *Jewish History* 15, no. 3 (2001), esp. illustrations on 190–91.

10. Bochner confirms this order, email to the author, March 29, 2013. For a useful extended discussion of the Reinhardt portrait, see Briony Fer, "Abstraction/Corruption," in Borchardt-Hume et al., *Mel Bochner: If the Colour Changes,* 25–30.

11. The movement of the words mirrors itself, as is suggested by the symmetrical shape of the piece: The first and the eighth (last) panels are easily read from left to right. The second and seventh are read in a snakelike zigzag pattern. The third and sixth run from right to left. The two smallest strips, at center, are read together in an up-and-down "s" pattern. The resulting complete text reads: "The discovery that both light and matter have wave and particle characteristics has made it easier to understand how these

properties can exist together in either light or matter. This understanding is set out in the new description of nature, perfected in 1920, known as quantum mechanics. The basic objects described by the quantum mechanics are particles that are localized in." The passage is slightly modified from Gerald Feinberg, "Light," *Scientific American* 219, no. 3 (September 1968): 54.

12. Field, *Mel Bochner: Thought Made Visible,* 55.

13. Charles Boultenhouse, "Poems in the Shapes of Things: A Survey 300 B.C. to A.D. 1958," *Art News Annual* 28 (1959): 65–83. In such works, the relationship of a poem's shape to its content may be literal, as in the Renaissance poet George Herbert's wing-shaped poem "Easter Wings" or Guillaume Apollinaire's calligrams; or it may be more abstract and impressionistic, as in Stéphane Mallarmé's *Un Coup de Dés.*

14. In Simone Martini's *Annunciation,* 1333, for example, the angel's words appear in gold, running from his mouth to the Virgin Mary's ear. In Rembrandt's 1636 *Belshazzar's Feast,* the "writing on the wall" appears as literal writing in the canvas. See Achim Borchardt-Hume, in Borchardt-Hume et al., *Mel Bochner: If the Colour Changes,* 14–15. Borchardt-Hume points out that the struggle between word and image is very old, and that Greek Orthodox icons are "written," not painted. Johns is frequently cited as an influence on Bochner in the literature, along with Jackson Pollock and Reinhardt; Briony Fer probes this connection persuasively in "Abstraction/Corruption," in Borchardt-Hume et al., *Mel Bochner: If the Colour Changes,* 25–30.

15. "Delaunay-Terk and Cendrars called their work the first 'simultaneous book,' referring to the way that the combination of text, images, and color energize the optical experience. . . . A new kind of modern vision, . . . where contrasts of color train the eye to read in one glance the whole of a poem." Ann Temkin and Leah Dickerman, audio commentary for *Inventing Abstraction, 1910–1925: How a Radical Idea Changed Modern Art,* on the website of the Museum of Modern Art, www.moma.org/explore/multimedia/audios/339/4328, accessed May 10, 2013.

16. Letter, Blaise Cendrars and Sonia Delaunay-Terk to André Salmon, October 12, 1913, cited in Matthew Affron, "Contrasts of Colors, Contrasts of Words," in Leah Dickerman, *Inventing Abstraction, 1910–1925: How a Radical Idea Changed Modern Art,* exh. cat. (New York: Museum of Modern Art, 2102), 82–83, 85 n. 6 (emphasis in original).

17. Joseph Kosuth and Lawrence Wiener use this more sober approach.

18. Bochner did not discover Andre's concrete poetry until much later. On Andre's poems, see Liz Kotz,

*Words to Be Looked At: Language in 1960s Art* (Cambridge, MA: MIT Press, 2007), 139f.

19. Serra describes the drawing this way: "In 1967 and 1968, I wrote down a verb list as a way of applying various activities to unspecified materials. To roll, to fold, to bend, to shorten, to shave, to tear, to chip, to split, to cut, to sever. . . . The language structured my activities in relation to materials which had the same function as transitive verbs. . . . [For example,] I took a rectilinear sheet of lead 18' by 36' and rolled it. The interval between the thickness of the concentric circles, how many and how large, defined the form. Drawing was implied in the activity. The making of the form itself . . . was implied in the drawing within the physical transformation of material from one state to another. . . . Forming with molds in molten lead (the juncture of the wall and the floor) and cutting were other modes of drawing contained in the sculpture. . . . It's how we do what we do that confers a meaning on what we've done." In Clara Weyergraf, ed., *Richard Serra: Interviews, Etc., 1970–1980,* exh. cat. (Yonkers, NY: Hudson River Museum, 1980), 78.

20. As Robert Pincus-Witten noted at the time, in "Anglo-American Standard Reference Works: Acute Conceptualism," *Artforum* (October 1971): 83.

21. Mel Bochner, "Primary Structures," *Arts Magazine* (June 1966): 33. Yve-Alain Bois has discussed Bochner's focus on vocabulary in his early criticism: "What is absolutely striking in these early yet amazingly authoritative texts is both their taxonomic drive and the request for a new vocabulary, two aspects that are intimately linked"; Foreword, in Bochner, *Solar System,* xiii.

22. Bochner, "Eccentric Abstraction," *Arts Magazine* (November 1966): 16.

23. Mel Bochner, "Review: Sol LeWitt," *Arts Magazine* (September–October 1966): 61. On the relation to Bochner's own work, see Joanna Burton, "The Weight of the Word: Mel Bochner's Material Language," in Burton, *Mel Bochner: Language,* 20.

24. Mel Bochner, in Bochner, *Solar System,* xvii.

25. See Bois, Foreword, in Bochner, *Solar System,* xii. The artist points out that the first part of the text, which deals with phenomenological issues, is his, and the references to science fiction are Smithson's; conversation with the author, June 11, 2013.

26. Collapsing the borders between reality and fiction, *The Domain of the Great Bear* has been noted as a precursor of contemporary projects by artists like Pierre Huyghe; see Mel Bochner, with an introduction by Tim Griffin, "Secrets of the Domes: Mel Bochner on 'The Domain of the Great Bear,'" *Artforum* 45, no. 1 (September 2006): 340–45. The

dated, nearly kitsch appearance of the imagery may be related to Surrealist collage and montage. The idea of camp as an aesthetic practice was current at the time; Susan Sontag had published her influential *Notes on "Camp"* in 1964.

27. Sasha M. Newman, "The Photo Pieces," in Field, *Mel Bochner: Thought Made Visible,* 116.

28. Mel Bochner, in the press release for *Photography Before the Age of Mechanical Reproduction,* Two Palms, New York, 2011.

29. Abstract Expressionism reached the height of its influence around 1958 with the Museum of Modern Art's traveling exhibition of new American painting, just when Bochner was a student at Carnegie Institute of Technology (later Carnegie Mellon University) in Pittsburgh. Virtually all the new movements of the 1960s, including Pop, Fluxus, Minimalism, and Conceptualism, sought ways to attack the personal mythologies embedded in gestural painting.

30. "Mel Bochner and Ludwig Wittgenstein," *Print Collector's Newsletter* 22 (July–August 1991): 98. See also Jessica Prinz, "Language Is Not Transparent," in Field, *Mel Bochner: Thought Made Visible,* 192–95.

31. Prinz, "Language Is Not Transparent," 194.

32. Most of the thesaurus paintings, for example, use words that are abstract in nature—SILENCE, DIE, MONEY, etc. On this issue in Wittgenstein, see Ray Monk, "Looking for Wittgenstein," *New York Review of Books* (June 6, 2013): 58.

33. The full passage in the artwork reads: "Nothing we do can be defended absolutely and finally. But only by reference to something else that is not questioned. I.e. no reason can be given why you should act (or should have acted) *like this,* except that by doing so you bring about such and such a situation, which again has to be an aim you *accept.*" Ludwig Wittgenstein, *Vermischte Bemerkungen* (1977), *Culture and Value,* trans. Peter Winch (Chicago: University of Chicago Press, 1980), 16e.

34. Marie McGinn describes Wittgenstein's goal as a "philosophically more enlightened conception of the relation between the subject and the world"; "Wittgenstein's *Remarks on Colour,*" *Philosophy* 66, no. 258 (October 1991): 453.

35. Ludwig Wittgenstein, *Remarks on Colour* (1950), trans. Linda McAlister and Margarete Schättle (Berkeley: University of California Press, 1977), 61, paragraph 326. On this series, see esp. Borchardt-Hume, "Colour My Mind," in Borchardt-Hume et al., *Mel Bochner: If the Colour Changes,* 19–21.

36. Mel Bochner, "Institute of Fine Arts Lecture" (2007), repr. in Borchardt-Hume et al., *Mel Bochner: If the Colour Changes,* 179. Bochner uses the same

phrase to describe Wittgenstein's *Remarks on Colour;* see "Mel Bochner in Conversation with James Meyer," in Burton, *Mel Bochner: Language,* 141. Gauging the connection between these paintings and Bochner's earlier Conceptual interests, James Meyer notes, "Strategies of simultaneity, complementarity, duration, and repetition—hallmarks of the artist's early work—return in a credible new form." James Meyer, "Best of 2000: 13 Top Tens. Mel Bochner, 'If the Color Changes,'" *Artforum* 39, no. 4 (December 2000): 114.

37. In using the term "painterly Readymade" I distinguish it from a Readymade painting or a painted Readymade. Gerhard Richter, Jasper Johns, and Ed Ruscha have created work in a similar manner. On various sources of contemporary hybrid Readymades, see Benjamin H. D. Buchloh, "Readymade, Photography, and Painting in the Painting of Gerhard Richter," in *Neo-Avantgarde and Culture Industry: Essays on European and American Art from 1955 to 1975* (Cambridge, MA: MIT Press, 2003), 365ff. I am grateful to David Joselit for a fruitful discussion of this phenomenon.

38. James Meyer briefly suggests that an American realist tradition (whether philosophical or artistic) may be in the background of Bochner's formation: "Bochner represents the way we speak now, the chatter of the cell phone and the street. An insistently American realism enters conceptualism through its back door"; James Meyer, *Mel Bochner: Colorful Language,* n.p. [5]. Briony Fer takes an opposing view. "James Meyer has recently called Bochner an American realist, and what is most insightful about this observation is that it does not preclude him from being at the same time an artist almost entirely fuelled by pictorial models drawn from abstract painting"; "Abstraction/Corruption," in Borchardt-Hume et al., *Mel Bochner: If the Colour Changes,* 25.

39. Bochner in "Mel Bochner, Frédéric Paul, a Conversation, December 3, 2007–February 13, 2008," in *Mel Bochner,* exh. cat. (Bignan, Domaine de Kerguéhennec), 12, cited in Borchardt-Hume et al., *Mel Bochner: If the Colour Changes,* 43. Bochner has also expressed the duality in less confrontational terms: "By being both experiential and linguistic, the color collapses the space between seeing and reading"; see Burton, *Mel Bochner: Language,* 141. Achim Borchardt-Hume succinctly notes that in this series "colour both eschews and challenges language," Borchardt-Hume, "Colour My Mind," 14.

40. See David Markus, "Mel Bochner," *Brooklyn Rail* (June 7, 2008), online at www.brooklynrail. org/2008/06/artseen/mel-bochner, accessed May 10, 2013. Bochner and Rosalind Krauss also discuss the importance of the figure/ground relationship to his

oeuvre over the decades; see Krauss, "Theory of Painting," in Field, *Mel Bochner: Thought Made Visible,* 217–22.

41. Conversation with the author, April 19, 2013.

42. See Mel Bochner, "The Serial Attitude" and "Seriality and Photography," 1967, repr. in Bochner, *Solar System,* 42–48; see also Bois, Foreword, in Bochner, *Solar System,* xvi.

43. Bochner, "Institute of Fine Arts Lecture" (2007), 180.

44. Burton, *Mel Bochner: Language,* 141.

45. Bochner, "Institute of Fine Arts Lecture" (2007), 181.

46. Conversation with the author, May 1, 2012.

47. Bochner, "Institute of Fine Arts Lecture" (2007), 181.

48. "Bochner seems to be rendering his version of the dour Modernist monochrome as an entropic field of language." Roberta Smith, "Mel Bochner: Art in Review," *New York Times,* May 2, 2008.

49. *Art in America* (December 2012): 170. In the image the word BLAH in block capitals is overprinted seventeen or eighteen times in black ink on white paper, with the words running off the edge at bottom. The effect is of a voice intoning "blah, blah, blah" intrusively in the middle of a conversation among the surrounding contributors. Bochner uses *Art in America*'s real estate to reproduce a work of his own, and in using a reproduction of his own artwork to deliver a commentary on the state of the art world in a widely circulated magazine he has created a new work.

50. As Judith Flanders notes, "Bochner has taken art-historical dichotomies—the tensions between perspective and the picture plane, between figurative and abstract art—and transformed them into threads of language and colour, meaning and emotion." "Joyous, Pointless Information," *TLS,* November 9, 2012, online at http://issuu.com/haus_der_kunst/docs/meld.bochner, accessed May 10, 2013.

51. David Salle, Markus Lüpertz, and Martin Kippenberger are three examples. The term Conceptual Expression is Isabelle Graw's; see her "Conceptual Expression: *On Conceptual Gestures in Allegedly Expressive Painting, Traces of Expression in Proto-Conceptual Works, and the Significance of Artistic Procedures,*" in Alexander Alberro and Sabeth Buchmann, eds., *Art After Conceptual Art* (Cambridge, MA: MIT Press, 2006), 119–33, here 121.

52. Field, *Mel Bochner: Thought Made Visible,* 55.

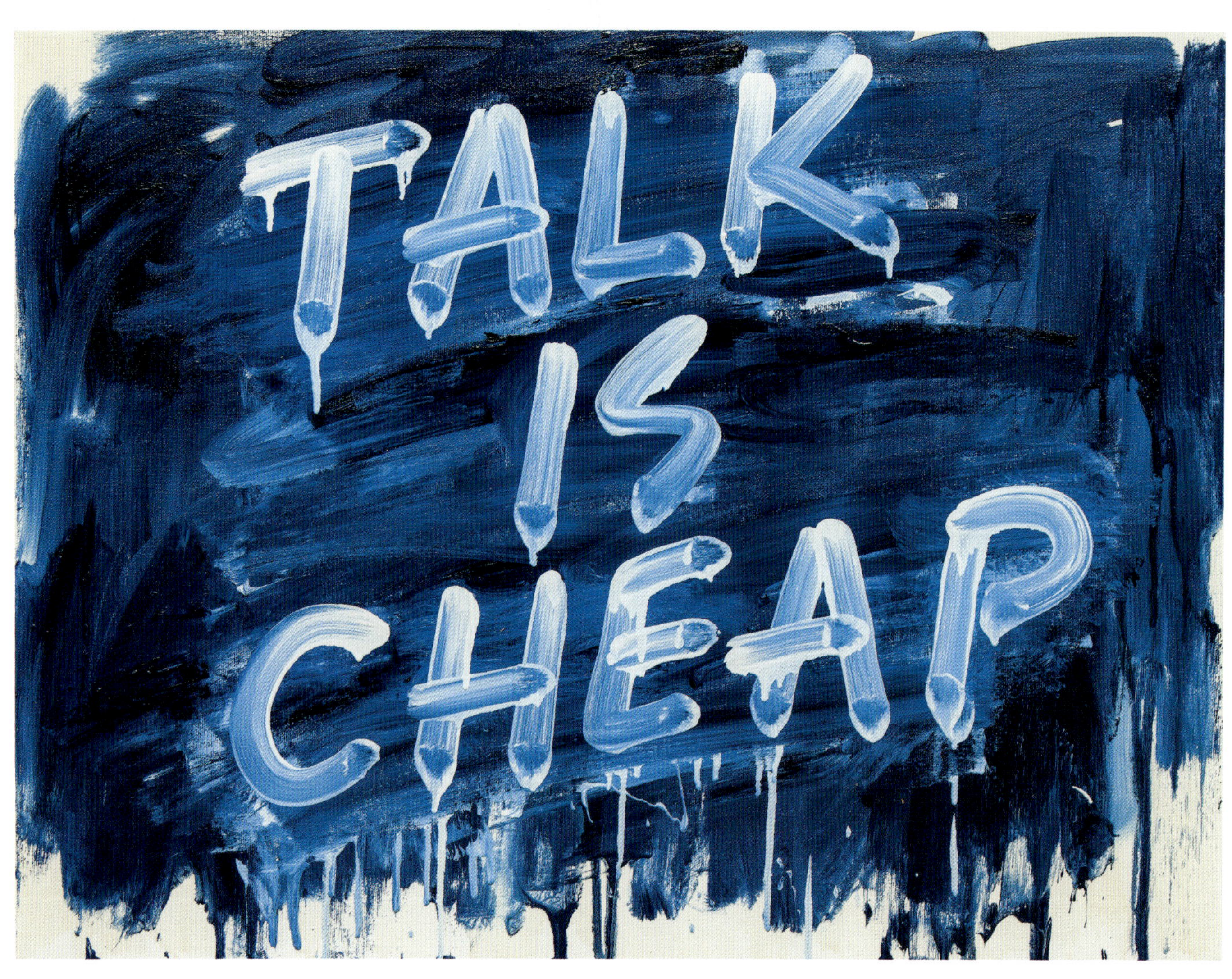

TALK
IS
CHEAP

# Some Thoughts on Color, Language, Painting, and *Blah, Blah, Blah*

**MEL BOCHNER**, 2007/2013

**Talk Is Cheap**, 2011
Oil on canvas, 18 × 24 in. (45.7 × 61 cm)
Collection of the artist

*Theory, like mist on eyeglasses, obscures facts.*
CHARLIE CHAN

In 1672 Newton discovered that passing white light through a prism divides it into red, orange, yellow, green, blue and violet. Of equal if not greater importance was his discovery that passing it through the prism again turned the colors back into white. Goethe, writing 100 years later, railed against Newton. "That all colors mixed together produce white is an absurdity which people have credulously repeated for a century, in opposition to the evidence of their senses." Of course Newton was talking about the physical properties of color, while Goethe was talking about his subjective experience.

In the last year of his life, inspired by Goethe, Wittgenstein attempted to address these two antithetical ways of thinking about color. He tried to shift the debate away from theory to what he called our usage of color terms, i.e., their role in "the language game." (For example, within the rules of grammar, we may speak of an "orangish-blue," but, in reality, no such color exists.) As he states, "Goethe's theory is not an unsatisfactory theory of color, rather it's not really a theory at all. Nothing can be predicted with it." The closest to a conclusion Wittgenstein arrived at was this: "We do not want to find a theory of color (neither a physiological nor a psychological one), but rather the logic of our color concepts." However, in trying to discover the logic of our "color concepts" he kept bumping into the problem of other minds. (When I say "red," does it match the image of "red" in your mind? I'll never know.) So instead of what he called "fumbling around with words," Wittgenstein kept returning to this maxim: "Practices give words their meaning." Or (as every painter knows) . . . color is what color does.

*To observe is not the same thing as to look at or view. "Look at this color and say what it reminds you of." If the color changes you are no longer looking at the one I meant. One observes in order to see what one would not see if one did not observe.*
LUDWIG WITTGENSTEIN, *REMARKS ON COLOUR*

In 1997, while reading *Remarks on Colour,* I became fascinated by the opacity and ambiguity of this statement. The harder one tries to unpack it the more baffling it becomes. When he says, "If the color changes you are no longer looking at the one I meant," the ground suddenly drops out from under "you." How did the color change? Was the change perceptual or grammatical? And, more mysteriously, who or what caused the change?

Using this quotation as a pretext, I began a series of paintings collectively titled *If the Color Changes.* One of the underlying themes of these paintings is the question of translation, not only from one language to another, but also from the textual to the visual. Superimposing the English translation over the original German, a slippage is created; a space opens up inside the text. In this palimpsest of languages, German shadowing English, English obscuring German, the text is frequently reduced to illegibility. By later paintings in the series, the words often dissolve into little more than a fog of color, diverting the text from any duty to meaning.

In addition, the optical antagonism makes it a struggle to decipher the text, reenacting the very situation described in the quotation. Decoupling the eye from the mind raises an even thornier question: Is it possible to *look* at the painting and *read* the text simultaneously? Or is it an either/or situation . . . a kind of duck/rabbit dilemma in which an image can be read as either a duck or a rabbit but not both at once?

From Aristotle, who thought of color as a drug, to Derrida, who thought of it as a poison, color has always represented excess and danger. It creates a surplus meaning, one independent of my intentions, which survives the reading of the text, and continues to engage viewers long after they get the idea.

*Yes, I'm the guy who put "masturbation" into Roget's Thesaurus.*
GEORGE DAVIDSON, EDITOR, *ROGET'S THESAURUS*

In 2002 I came across a new edition of *Roget's Thesaurus.* I was surprised to discover it included not only very up-to-date vernacular and slang, but outright obscenity as well. Because children, beginning in grade school, use the thesaurus, this signaled to me a dramatic change in what is considered "ordinary" language. I wanted to explore what had happened to the boundaries of public discourse—both linguistically and politically.

Peter Mark Roget (1779–1869) compiled the first systematic thesaurus. He conceived of it as an "aid to writers." Roget was an Enlightenment man; a medical doctor; the inventor of the slide rule; as well as the discoverer of the persistence of vision phenomenon that eventually led to the invention of motion pictures. A stickler for round numbers, Roget dreamed of forcing all language into precisely 1000 categories, by imposing on it grand, rationalistic classifications, like "Mind and Ideas," or "Behavior and the Will." However, it turned out that this was impossible since no place exists outside of language from which to impose them. One of the greatest disappointments of his life was that he was unable to whittle the number of categories down to less than 1002 (the most recent edition has ballooned up to 1075).

*I craved certainty the same way other people craved religious faith.*
BERTRAND RUSSELL

In the early twentieth century language itself became the subject of a hotly contested philosophical debate. The belief was that everyday language was crippled by ambiguity and must be recast along the lines of logic. Analytic philosophy, as it came to be known, rested on the premise that the definition of a word must establish the necessary and sufficient conditions for its usage. However, ambiguity refused to disappear from language. By the 1930s Ludwig Wittgenstein had repudiated his earlier views about definitions and necessary conditions. He came to believe that there was nothing wrong with ordinary language as it stands, and that if close attention were paid to the everyday use of words all philosophical problems would dissolve. It was at this point that he introduced the concept of language games, a more use-oriented concept that viewed language as "a way of life." However, just as there is no single thread uniting all games, the variety of activities that constitute language also have little in common, except for what he termed "family resemblances." This concept describes perfectly the way that the thesaurus is structured: every word occupies a unique spot on an endlessly branching tree of family resemblances.

*There is something at once uplifting and terrifying in the fact that nothing in the world is so unique that it can't be entered on a list.*
GEORGES PEREC

As Roget himself noted, there is no such thing as a synonym, as no two words can ever mean exactly the same thing. The thesaurus is a Pandora's box of language. Its lists offer an overview of the communal uses of a word, as well as an implicit archaeology of those uses, since as new editions are published, words are constantly added but rarely dropped. For this reason the *Thesaurus Paintings* spark personal associations across a wide, generational cross-section of viewers. The art historian and critic Mark Godfrey watched how visitors to the 2004 Whitney Biennale expressed these personal responses: "I tried to pay attention to what people were saying in front of these paintings. The whole room became a kind of social space. Viewers were reminded of people they know. One person said 'oh, your father uses that word a lot.' They were wandering around, looking at them and saying things like 'that must be an English phrase,' or 'I think that comes from such-and-such place.' People recalled a lot of personal memories when they looked at them."

*It is estimated that English has more than eight hundred expressions for copulation, a thousand for penis, twelve hundred for vagina, and two thousand for wanton woman (making one wonder why people make such a fuss about the number of Eskimo words for snow).*
STEVEN PINKER

There is no program governing my choice of words in my paintings. It has been pointed out that I have a penchant for the suffix "less"—as in *Meaningless* or *Useless*. But beyond acknowledging a taste for the more downbeat side of language, I prefer not to engage in interpretations of meaning or intention. The key word for a painting may come to me from anywhere and everywhere: my reading; thinking about the state of the world; a conversation overheard on the subway; my kids (living with teenagers is like living in a language factory); or sometimes they just seem to pop into my head from nowhere. I stockpile words in notebooks that I constantly refer to. But I usually don't know, beyond the painting I'm currently working on, what the next word is going to be. Combing through the thesaurus is like going on a fishing trip; you might catch something, you might not. When I do come across a word that intrigues me I begin by copying out the entries. As the words proliferate and the list grows, I gradually eliminate and rearrange them, paying close attention to both sense and sound. I'm trying to evolve a narrative that leads from the first word to the last . . . but one that zigzags through conceptual detours and psychological potholes. Although I do not think of my word lists as poetry, there

are certain formal constraints involved. The size, proportion, and orientation of the canvas, as
well as the number of lines of text, impose certain boundary conditions. The number of words
and of letters per line governs many decisions. While some lists come together quickly, others
take months or years, or are still waiting further work somewhere in a stack of notebooks.

*A black, E white, I red,*
*U green, O blue: vowels*
*I shall tell, one day,*
*Of your mysterious origins.*
ARTHUR RIMBAUD

In the *Thesaurus Paintings*, there is no preceding plan or color study. Every word, in some
cases every letter, is painted a different color, no matter how similar some may appear.
Choices are made sequentially, one at a time, in a process I think of as improvisational. I have
no idea what the painting will look like until the final punctuation mark is painted. I do not
use stencils or masking tape. Every letter is painted freehand.

  The color of certain words is so close to that of the background that they virtually
disappear, while others *sizzle,* popping right off the surface. These optical effects undermine
the horizontal architecture of the text. As the eye involuntarily focuses and refocuses to perceive
the color, one absent-mindedly begins to rearrange the words. Liberated from the convention of
left-to-right reading, the words freely reorder themselves along vertical, diagonal, and other
nonlinear axes. These recombinations, in which the subconscious seems to take the initiative,
can produce unpredictable, startling new meanings. The text, by remaining open to a new reading by every viewer, is thus never "finished." I see this as analogous to what Jorge Luis Borges
called "a labyrinth which is a straight line . . . along whose length many have lost their way."

*A painting is made of paint—of fluids and ground-up stones.*
JAMES ELKINS

There are countless ways to apply paint to a surface, and no delivery system is superior to
any other. Thick or thin, matte or glossy, neat or sloppy, they all come hardwired with historical meanings. But those meanings can be reframed, treated ironically, or adapted to self-
contradictory ends. I have never felt obligated to develop a signature style, process, or medium.
For me everything works in a cycle of use and necessity. At a certain point in time a medium
becomes necessary for the expression of an idea, so I use it. The thing is to never get locked
into any particular framework. Every medium has its own way of revealing something—and
simultaneously concealing something else. A change of mediums offers one the possibility of
stepping outside the frame and discovering what's being concealed. At the same time, the
immediate and particular physicality of the medium is essential to the meaning of a work.

  I began making paintings on velvet in 2005. The initial impulse came from a book on
incunabula (printing before the invention of movable type). In most cases these books and

broadsheets were woodblocks printed on paper, but a few were printed on cloth. That gave me the idea of trying to print directly on various kinds of unprimed textiles—linen, cotton, silk, etc. Unfortunately, without primer, paint was absorbed into their porous surfaces. Velvet, much to my surprise, was the only material that kept the paint up. And while it wasn't my intention, the kitschy aura of paintings-on-velvet (*Elvis!*) was an unexpected but not unwelcome bonus.

Since Jackson Pollock, one of the directions painting has taken has been to exploit the expressiveness of paint itself. But while Pollock proclaimed "no chaos, damn it!" it is the surrender of control that frees the paint to express its *paintness*. In the velvet paintings the paint is delivered to the surface indirectly. First a computer-controlled laser engraves the text into a thick acrylic sheet, which will serve as a printing matrix. Then, letter by letter, the words are hand-filled with pure oil paint, sometimes up to a pound per letter. Finally, the velvet is laid face down on the plate, placed in a hydraulic press, and subjected to 750 tons of vertical pressure. With so many uncontrollable variables (temperature, humidity, viscosity, and pressure) there is no predicting what the paint will do. The paint's chemistry, its "fluids and ground-up stones," determines, beyond any dictates of good or bad taste, what the final painting will look like. Under pressure the paint, with nothing to prevent it, bleeds freely into weirdly marbleized puddles. The more viscous colors spurt out of the letters, while the densely pigmented ones emerge in wrinkled globs. The random smudging and smearing render some words unreadable, obliterate others, and further estrange them from any "necessary and sufficient" meaning. When the velvet is pulled off the plate, the result is always a surprise, sometimes a jolt.


*Go fuck yourself!*
VICE PRESIDENT DICK CHENEY TO SENATOR PATRICK LEAHY OF VERMONT, 2004

The tone of these paintings has a lot to do with the devolution of contemporary language, its corruption in public and political discourse in ways that even George Orwell could not have imagined. There is an implicit critique in tracking this downward spiral from the polite and respectful to the nasty and insulting. Each painting begins with fairly formal words and degenerates into words and phrases that refer to the body and its functions, from the prim and proper to the crude and vulgar.

These paintings also raise the perplexing question of who is speaking. Does a painting speak in the same voice when it is hanging in my studio, as opposed to in a gallery, museum, or private home? Is it my voice? The reader's voice? Is there perhaps an objectified voice, a voice without intonation, or even a voice without a speaker? Can the emotionalism of the words—strident or passive, serious or silly—be neutralized by the way the words pile up, one after another after another? One thing is certain: I will never hear the voice inside your head reading my painting. Which brings us back to the problem of other minds.

*If you laugh, it's funny.*
CHARLIE CHAPLIN

*If it isn't funny, it isn't true.*
BERTOLD BRECHT

There is an enormous literature on the subject of humor that only demonstrates the futility of trying to explain a joke. For me humor is, first of all, a skeptical way of looking at the world. For the skeptic everything is perpetually in doubt. Every answer merely leads to another question. From this point of view the goal of humor is the subversion of certainty. In order to critique unquestioned beliefs and assumptions, jokes use misdirection, surprising shifts in perspective, and the upending of expectations. The various forms that comedy takes—irony, sarcasm, satire, parody, ridicule, pun, double entendre—are all strategies to undermine the domination of reason and logic. There is, however, a dark side to humor. It often leads to the realization that everything may only add up to nothing. But the fact that humor exists, and that nothing is immune to it, makes that realization (slightly) less unbearable.

I'm often asked if my paintings are meant to be funny. Am I *trying* to be funny? That question always reminds me of the exchange in Martin Scorsese's film *GoodFellas* between Henry, played by Ray Liotta, and Tommy, played by Joe Pesci:

HENRY: You're really funny.

TOMMY: What do you mean funny? You mean funny "ha ha"? You mean funny the way I talk? What?

HENRY: It's just . . . you know. You're just funny.

TOMMY: Funny how? What's funny about it? Tell me how I'm funny. Funny like a clown? I amuse you? I'm here to fucking amuse you? What do you mean, funny? How am I funny?

HENRY: You know, how you tell a story.

TOMMY: No, I don't know. You said it. You said I'm funny. How am I funny? What the fuck is so funny about me? Tell me what's funny.

HENRY: Get the fuck out of here, Tommy.

TOMMY: Motherfucker! I almost had you there.

*The Joys of Yiddish* was designed for the Spertus Institute for Jewish Learning and Leadership in Chicago, to be installed on the traffic barrier during the construction of their new building. Yiddish is the original ghetto language, developed by perpetual outsiders to cope with a foreign and often hostile reality. Capable of expressing the deepest of sentiments, it is also a language of intense self-criticism and moral invective. Reflecting an ironic, unrefined, and frequently scatological view of human nature, it is completely indifferent to polite taste. The Spertus was initially afraid that highlighting such "inappropriate" language on a fifty-foot signboard at a prestigious address in the heart of downtown Chicago was a more transgressive public statement than they wanted to make, but eventually they came around. Personally, having grown up with parents and grandparents who spoke Yiddish, I find the words quite funny.

KIBBITZER Wise guy

KVETCHER Chronic complainer

K'NOCKER Braggart

KUNI LEMMEL Simpleton

NUDNICK Nag

NEBBISH Sad sack

NUDZH Pesterer

GONIF Shady character

DREYKOP Someone who gives you a headache

CHAZZER Greedy person

CHAIM YANKEL Nobody

ALTER KOCKER Cranky old man

MOISHE PUPIK Contrarian

MESHUGENER Crazy person

TUMLER Prankster

TSITSER Useless bystander

SHMOOZER Gossip

SCHMO Fall guy

SHLEMIEL Social misfit

SHLIMAZEL Born loser

SHVITZER Show-off

PISHER Someone who still pees in his pants

PLOSHER Blowhard

PLATKE-MACHER Troublemaker

That many of these words have been anglicized and have entered common usage says a lot about the assimilation of Jews into American society. There is, however, a subtext to this piece. Yellow and black were the colors of the armbands that the Nazis forced Jews to wear. Most contemporary viewers, especially in the United States, do not catch that association—at least, not right away. However, the director of the Jewish Museum in Vienna told me that the work would be impossible to show in Austria because the symbolism of the colors would be understood immediately, antagonizing both the right and the left. I do see this as a political work, but I don't want to put it in quotation marks as "political art." It's best when the politics slip into the cultural stream unannounced, greatly increasing the possibility that the work may alter the status quo by reframing the terms of the discourse. In March 2013, for my exhibition at the Haus der Kunst in Munich, notorious as Hitler's museum of German art, another version of *The Joys of Yiddish* was wrapped in a band across the entire 350-foot cornice of the building's facade, giving a whole new spin to the concept of site specificity.

*Must we* say *what we mean?*
STANLEY CAVELL

Another question I'm often asked is, "What do the *Blah, Blah, Blah* paintings mean?" But the real question is: Must everything mean something?

    We live in a world oversaturated with empty language—small talk, tweets, texts, leet speak, chitchat, pop-up ads, telephone-answering messages ("your call is important to us . . ."), warnings on medicine bottles ("if you have an erection lasting more than four hours . . ."). While there's no escaping this linguistic tsunami, the *Blah, Blah, Blah* paintings subvert it from below. By the incessant repetition of that one innocuous syllable, they seek to escape the gravitational pull of bullshit. They *say* nothing but they can *mean* anything, everything, something, or nothing. Operating at a sublinguistic level, they are simultaneously sublime and ridiculous, aggravating and hilarious. Just one more confirmation that *Language Is Not Transparent.*

# Selected Bibliography

## SOLO EXHIBITION CATALOGUES

Arditi, Fiamma. *Mel Bochner: Opera Recenti.* Rome: Galleria d'Arte il Gabbiano, 2003.

Borchardt-Hume, Achim, et al. *Mel Bochner: If the Colour Changes.* London: Whitechapel Gallery and Ridinghouse, 2012; Ram, 2013.

Burton, Johanna, et al. *Mel Bochner: Language, 1966–2006.* Chicago: Art Institute of Chicago, 2007.

Cherix, Christophe, Laurent Jenny, and James Meyer. *Mel Bochner: Working Drawings and Other Visible Things on Paper Not Necessarily Meant to Be Viewed as Art.* Geneva: Musée d'Art et d'Histoire, Cabinet des Estampes, 1997.

Field, Richard S., ed. *Mel Bochner: Thought Made Visible, 1966–1973.* New Haven: Yale University Art Gallery and Yale University Press, 1995.

Fine, Ruth. *Mel Bochner: Drawings from Four Decades.* New York: Fifth Floor Foundation, 2006.

King, Elaine. *Mel Bochner, 1973–1985.* Pittsburgh: Carnegie Mellon University Press, 1985.

*Mel Bochner.* Rio de Janeiro: Centro de Arte Hélio Oiticica, 1999.

Meyer, James. *Mel Bochner: Colorful Language.* Washington, DC: National Gallery of Art, 2011.

Paul, Frédéric, and Mel Bochner. *Mel Bochner.* Trans. Simon Pleasance. Bignan, France: Centre d'Art Contemporain—Centre Culturel de Rencontre, Domaine de Kerguéhennec, 2009.

Richardson, Brenda. *Mel Bochner: Number and Shape.* Baltimore: Baltimore Museum of Art, 1976.

Rothkopf, Scott. *Mel Bochner Photographs, 1966–1969.* New Haven: Yale University Press, 2002.

Weiss, Jeffrey. "Ad Infinitum." In *Mel Bochner Photographs and Not Photographs.* San Francisco: Fraenkel Gallery, 2010.

——. *Event Horizon: Mel Bochner.* New York: Peter Freeman, Inc., and Paris: Galerie Nelson-Freeman, 2007.

## GROUP EXHIBITION CATALOGUES

*Documenta 5.* Kassel, Germany: Documenta GmbH, 1972.

Gintz, Claude, Juliette Laffon, and Angeline Scherf, eds. *L'Art Conceptuel: Une Perspective.* Paris: Musée d'Art Moderne de la Ville de Paris, 1989.

Halbreich, Kathy. *Mel Bochner/Richard Serra.* Cambridge, MA: Hayden Gallery and MIT Press, 1980.

Iles, Chrissie, et al. *2004 Whitney Biennial.* New York: Whitney Museum of American Art, 2004.

Krauss, Rosalind E. *Line as Language: Six Artists Draw.* Princeton, NJ: Princeton University Art Museum, 1974.

McShine, Kynaston, ed. *Information.* New York: Museum of Modern Art, 1970.

Pascale, Mark. *Drawings from the Collection of Irving Stenn, Jr.* Chicago: Art Institute of Chicago, 2011.

Rales, Emily Wei, and Jeffrey Weiss. *If We Could Imagine.* Potomac: Glenstone Foundation, 2009.

Szeemann, Harald. *When Attitudes Become Form.* Bern: Kunsthalle Bern, 1969.

## ANTHOLOGIES

Battcock, Gregory, ed. *Minimal Art: A Critical Anthology.* New York: Dutton, 1968.

Godfrey, Mark. *Abstraction and the Holocaust.* New Haven: Yale University Press, 2007.

Goldstein, Ann. *A Minimal Future? Art As Object, 1958–1968.* Los Angeles: Los Angeles County Museum of Art, and Cambridge, MA: MIT Press, 2004.

Goldstein, Ann, and Anne Rorimer, eds. *Reconsidering the Object of Art: 1965–1975.* Cambridge, MA: MIT Press, 1995.

Lippard, Lucy. *Six Years: The Dematerialization of the Art Object from 1966 to 1972.* New York: Praeger, 1973.

Meyer, James. *Minimalism: Art and Polemics in the Sixties.* New Haven: Yale University Press, 2001.


**ARTICLES AND REVIEWS**

Artner, Alan G. "Mel Bochner Has a Way with Words." *Chicago Tribune,* October 12, 2006, sec. 5, 3.

Ashton, Dore. "New York Commentary." *Studio International* 179 (March 1970): 118–19.

Boice, Bruce. "The Axiom of Indifference." *Arts Magazine* 47, no. 6 (April 1973): 66–68.

——. "Mel Bochner at Hartford Art School." *Artforum* 11 (December 1972): 86–87.

Buchloh, Benjamin H. D. "Conceptual Art, 1962–1969: From the Aesthetic of Administration to the Critique of Institution." *October* 55 (Winter 1990): 105–43.

Chandler, John. "The Last Word in Graphic Art." *Art International* 12 (November 1968): 25–28.

Cullinan, Nicholas. "Critics' Picks: Mel Bochner." *Artforum* (February 2013).

Danto, Arthur C. "Introduction." In Ludwig Wittgenstein, *On Certainty/Über Gewissheit.* San Francisco: Arion, 1991.

de Bruyn, Eric. "Alfaville, or the Utopics of Mel Bochner." *Grey Room* 10 (Winter 2003): 76–111.

Edit, Deak. "Mel Bochner at Sonnabend." *Art in America* 62 (January–February 1974): 100–102.

Flanders, Judith. "Joyous, Pointless Information," *TLS* (November 9, 2012).

Grabner, Michelle. "Mel Bochner: The Art Institute of Chicago." *Frieze* 105 (March 2007): 191.

Graham, Dan. "Models and Monuments: The Plague of Architecture." *Arts Magazine* 41, no. 5 (March 1967): 62–63.

Heartney, Eleanor. "Mel Bochner at Sonnabend." *Art in America* 89 (June 2001): 126.

Kalina, Richard. "Measure for Measure." *Art in America* 84 (September 1996): 88–93.

Kennicott, Philip. "Critics Review: National Gallery's 'In the Tower: Mel Bochner.'" *Washington Post*, November 4, 2011.

Krauss, Rosalind E. "Sense and Sensibility: Reflection on Post '60s Sculpture." *Artforum* 12 (November 1973): 43–52.

LeWitt, Sol. "Paragraphs on Conceptual Art." *Artforum* 5 (Summer 1967): 79–83.

Markus, David. "Mel Bochner." *Brooklyn Rail* (June 7, 2008).

McKinnon, John. "Critics' Picks: Chicago, Mel Bochner Spertus Museum." *Artforum* (November 2006).

"Mel Bochner and Ludwig Wittgenstein." *Print Collector's Newsletter* 22 (July–August 1991): 98.

Meyer, James. "Best of 2000: 13 Top Tens. Mel Bochner, 'If the Color Changes.'" *Artforum* 39, no. 4 (December 2000): 114.

Ollman, Leah. "Art Review: Mel Bochner at Marc Selwyn Fine Art." *Los Angeles Times,* March 5, 2010.

Pincus-Witten, Robert. "Mel Bochner: The Constant as Variable." *Artforum* 11 (December 1972): 28–34.

Post, Ari. "'Amazing!' Mel Bochner in the Tower." *Georgetowner,* November 30, 2011.

Rotman, Brian. "Mel Bochner: Visible Thinking." *Trans* 1–2, 3–4 (1997): 167–69.

Schwabsky, Barry. "Mel Bochner, Gravats: Représentation des Premières Oeuvres." *Exposé* (Paris) 2 (1995): 134–43.

Smith, Roberta. "Art in Review: Mel Bochner." *New York Times,* June 16, 2006, 33.

——. "A Calculus with Chalk, Stones, and Walnuts." *New York Times,* May 24, 2013, 28.

——. "Mel Bochner." *New York Times,* May 2, 2008, sec. E30.

——. "Mel Bochner at Sonnabend." *Artforum* 12 (December 1973): 82.

Thompson, Anne. "Critics' Picks: Mel Bochner." *Artforum* (June 2010).

Vogel, Carol. "Inside Art." *New York Times,* June 29, 2012, 24.

Weiss, Jeffrey. "Language in the Vicinity of Art: Artists' Writings, 1960–1975." *Artforum* 42 (Summer 2004): 212–17.

Westfall, Stephen. "Bochner Unbound." *Art in America* 73 (July 1985): 108–13.


**WRITINGS BY THE ARTIST**

"Alfaville, Godard's Apocalypse." *Arts Magazine* 42 (May 1968): 14–17.

"Anyone Can Learn to Draw." Press release for "Drawings," Galerie Heiner Friedrich, Munich, 1969.

"Art in Process-Structures." *Arts Magazine* 40, no. 9 (September–October 1966): 38–39.

"Bullshit (Response to Tim Ulrich)." *Artforum* 9 (October 1970).

"Conditions." *Bulletin 27.* Amsterdam: *Art & Project,* September 15, 1970.

"10 Hypothèses de Travail." *VH–101* (Autumn 1970): 46–47.

"The Domain of the Great Bear." With Robert Smithson. *Art Voices* 5 (Autumn 1966): 44–51.

*11 Excerpts (1967–1970)*. Paris: Édition Sonnabend, 1971.

"Excerpts from Speculation." *Artforum* 8 (May 1970): 70–73.

*Mel Bochner*. Milan: Toselli, 1971.

*Mel Bochner/Notes on Theory*. Kingston: University of Rhode Island, 1970.

*Mel Bochner: (toward) Axiom of Indifference, 1972–1973*. New York: Sonnabend Gallery, 1974.

"Mel Bochner: Venticinque Anni, Scritti e Interviste, 1966–1990." Trans. Cecilia Casorati, Stefano Chiodi, and Giovanni Iovane. *Carte d'Arte: Internazionale Rivista d'Arte Contemporanea* 3 (September 1993).

*Misunderstandings (A Theory of Photography)*. In *Artists and Photographs*. New York: Multiples Gallery, 1970.

"Parenthetical Reflections on Five Earlier Statements." *Arts Magazine* 46, no. 8 (Summer 1972): 38.

"Photography Before the Age of Mechanical Reproduction." Press release, Two Palms, New York, 2011.

"Primary Structures: A Declaration of a New Attitude as Revealed by an Important Current Exhibition." *Arts Magazine* 40, no. 8 (June 1966): 32–35.

*Primer: The Complete Catalog of Twenty-One Demonstrations from "A Theory of Sculpture: Counting."* Milan: Flash Art, 1973.

"Review: Eccentric Abstraction." *Arts Magazine* 41, no. 1 (November 1966): 57–58.

"Review: Sol LeWitt." *Arts Magazine* 40, no. 9 (September–October 1966): 61.

"Secrets of the Domes: Mel Bochner on 'The Domain of the Great Bear.'" With an introduction by Tim Griffin. *Artforum* 45 (September 2006): 340–45.

"Serial Art Systems: Solipsism." *Arts Magazine* 41, no. 8 (Summer 1967): 39–43.

"The Serial Attitude." *Artforum* 6 (December 1967): 28–33.

"Six Years: The Dematerialization of the Art Object." *Artforum* 11 (June 1973): 74–75.

*Solar System & Rest Rooms: Writings and Interviews, 1965–2007*. Cambridge, MA: MIT Press, 2008.

*Spéculations: Écrits, 1965–1973*. Ed. Christophe Cherix and Valérie Mavridorakis, trans. Thierry Dubois. Geneva: Musée d'Art Moderne et Contemporain, 2003.

"Systemic Painting." *Arts Magazine* 41, no. 1 (November 1966): 57–58.

"Ten to 10." *Some Recent American Art*. New York: International Council of the Museum of Modern Art, 1973, p. 21.

"Theory of Boundaries." *Arts Magazine* 44, no. 6 (April 1970): 44.

"Three Statements for Data Magazine." *Data Magazine* 2 (February 1972): 62–67.

## INTERVIEWS WITH THE ARTIST

"The Archeology of Doubt: Mel Bochner in Conversation with Jacopo Benci." *891 International Artists Magazine* 3 (June 1986): 8–13.

"Art in Conversation: Mel Bochner with Phong Bui." *Brooklyn Rail* (May 2006): 16–17.

Coplans, John. "Mel Bochner on Malevich: An Interview." *Artforum* 12 (June 1974): 59–63.

"From Idea to Experience: Interview with Fréderic Valabrèque." *Artefactum* (June–August 1988): 14–17, 58, 62–63.

"How Can You Defend Making Paintings Now? A Conversation Between Mel Bochner and James Meyer." In Philip Armstrong et al., *As Painting: Division and Displacement*. Columbus: Wexner Center for the Arts, Ohio State University, and MIT Press, 2001, 74–79, 199–204.

"Language Factory: Mel Bochner Talks to Mark Godfrey About Words, Portraits, Roget's Thesaurus, Color, Jorge Luis Borges, Humour, Nostalgia and Political Engagement." *Frieze* 87 (November–December 2004): 102–5.

Marano, Lizbeth. "Mel Bochner Interview." Archives of American Art, May 1994.

Varian, Elayne. "Interview" (1969). In Mel Bochner, *Solar System & Rest Rooms: Writings and Interviews, 1965–2007*. Cambridge, MA: MIT Press, 2008, 56–60.

# Selected Exhibition History

## SOLO EXHIBITIONS

**2012–13**
Whitechapel Gallery, London; Haus der Kunst, Munich; and Museu de Arte Contemporânea de Serralves, Porto, Portugal
Egeran Gallery, Istanbul

**2011**
National Gallery of Art, Washington, DC
Peter Freeman, Inc., New York

**2010**
Galerie Nelson Freeman, Paris
Marc Selwyn Fine Art, Los Angeles
Fraenkel Gallery, San Francisco

**2009**
Rhona Hoffman, Chicago
Lawrence Markey, San Antonio

**2008**
Peter Freeman, Inc., New York

**2007**
Domaine de Kerguéhennec, Bignan, France

**2006**
Spertus Museum (now Spertus Institute for Jewish Learning and Leadership), Chicago
Peter Freeman, Inc., New York
Art Institute of Chicago

**2003**
Galleria d'Arte il Gabbiano, Rome
Sonnabend Gallery, New York

**2001**
Bound & Unbound, New York

**2000**
Sonnabend Gallery, New York

**1997**
Cabinet des Estampes du Musée d'Art et d'Histoire, Geneva
Musée d'Art Moderne et Contemporain, Geneva

**1996**
Société des Expositions du Palais des Beaux-Arts, Brussels
Städtische Galerie im Lenbachhaus, Munich

**1995**
Yale University Art Gallery, New Haven

**1976**
Baltimore Museum of Art

**1972**
Sonnabend Gallery, New York and Paris

**1971**
112 Greene Street, New York
Museum of Modern Art, New York

**1970**
Sperone Gallery, Turin
Toselli Gallery, Milan
Art and Project Gallery, Amsterdam

**1969**
Heiner Friedrich Gallery, Munich
Konrad Fischer Gallery, Düsseldorf

**1966**
School of Visual Arts Gallery, New York

## GROUP EXHIBITIONS

**2013**
"When Attitudes Become Form: Bern 1969/Venice 2013," Fondazione Prada, Venice
"Merci/Mercy," Restoin Roitfeld Gallery, New York

**2012**
"Second Nature: Abstract Photography Then and Now," deCordova Sculpture Park and Museum, Lincoln, Massachusetts

**2011**
"Art = Text = Art," University of Richmond Museum, Richmond, Virginia
"Light Years: Conceptual Art and the Photograph, 1964–1977," Art Institute of Chicago
"Drawings from the Collection of Irving Stenn, Jr.," Art Institute of Chicago

**2010**
"Third Thoughts," CCA Andtrax, Majorca
"Sammlung Herman und Nicole Daled, 1966–1978," Haus der Kunst, Munich
"Double Bind/Stop Trying To Understand Me," Villa Arson, Nice

**2009**
"If We Could Imagine," Glenstone Foundation, Potomac, Maryland

2008
"Mel Bochner, Alighiero Boetti, Hanne Darboven," Collège Jacques Cartier, Chauny, France

2007
"If Everybody Had an Ocean: Brian Wilson, an Art Exhibition," Tate St Ives, UK
"Magritte and Contemporary Art: The Treachery of Images," Los Angeles County Museum of Art

2005
"Open Systems: Rethinking Art c. 1970," Tate Modern, London
"Rub Out the Word," Dumbo Arts Center, Brooklyn, New York
"Looking At Words," Andrea Rosen Gallery, New York

2004
"Whitney Biennial," Whitney Museum of American Art, New York

2001
"Art Express: Art Minimal et Conceptual Américain," Cabinet des Estampes du Musée d'Art et d'Histoire, Geneva
"Saying Seeing," Leo Castelli Gallery, New York
"As Painting, Division and Displacement," Wexner Center for the Arts, Columbus, Ohio

2000
"Contemporary Drawings from the Sarah-Ann and Werner Kramarsky Collection," Southern Methodist University, Dallas

1999
"Circa 1968," Museu de Arte Contemporânea de Serralves, Porto, Portugal
"After Image: Drawing Through Process," Museum of Contemporary Art, Los Angeles
"Drawings from the 1960s," Curt Marcus Gallery, New York

1998
"The Serial Attitude," Addison Gallery of American Art, Andover, Massachusetts; Wexner Center for the Arts, Columbus, Ohio

1997
"Drawing Is Another Kind of Language," Fogg Art Museum, Harvard University, Cambridge, Massachusetts
"Magie der Zahl," Staatsgalerie Stuttgart

1996
"L'Informe: Mode d'Emploi," Centre Georges Pompidou, Paris

1995
"1965–1995: Reconsidering the Object of Art," Museum of Contemporary Art, Los Angeles

1994
"A Century of Artists' Books," Museum of Modern Art, New York

1991
"Motion and Document/Sequence and Time: Eadweard Muybridge and Contemporary American Photography," Addison Gallery of American Art, Andover, Massachusetts (traveling)

1990
"Amerikanische Zeichnungen in den Achtziger Jahren," Graphische Sammlung Albertina, Vienna, and Museum Morsbroich, Leverkusen, Germany

1989
"L'Art Conceptuel: Une Perspective," Musée d'Art Moderne de la Ville de Paris and Fundación Caja de Pensiones, Madrid

1988
"Collection Sonnabend," Museo Nacional Centro de Arte Reina Sofía, Madrid

1984
"Vanishing Points," Moderna Museet, Stockholm

1980
"Mel Bochner/Richard Serra," Massachusetts Institute of Technology, Cambridge

1979
"Pittura Ambiente," Palazzo Reale, Milan

1976
"Drawing Now," Museum of Modern Art, New York

1974
"Line as Language," Princeton Art Museum, Princeton, New Jersey
"Some Recent American Art," Museum of Modern Art, New York; National Gallery of Victoria, Melbourne; West Australian Art Gallery, Perth; Art Gallery of New South Wales, Sydney; Art Gallery of South Australia, Adelaide; and City of Auckland Art Gallery, New Zealand

1973
"Contemporanea," Parcheggio di Villa Borghese, Rome

1972
"Documenta 5," Kassel, Germany
"Konzept-Kunst," Kunstmuseum Basel

1970
"Information," Museum of Modern Art, New York
"Conceptual Art/Arte Povera/Land Art," Museo Civico d'Arte Moderna, Turin
"Using Floors, Walls, and Ceilings," Jewish Museum, New York
"Language IV," Dwan Gallery, New York
"Artists and Photographs," Multiples Gallery, New York

1969
"Art in Progress IV," Finch College Museum of Art, New York
"When Attitudes Become Form," Kunsthalle Bern
"Konzeption/Conception," Museum Leverkusen, Leverkusen, Germany

1968
"Language II," Dwan Gallery, New York

1967
"Art in Series," Finch College Museum of Art, New York
"Scale Models and Drawings," Dwan Gallery, New York

The photographers and the sources of visual material other than the owners indicated in the captions are as follows. Every effort has been made to supply complete and correct credits; if there are errors or omissions, please contact Yale University Press so that corrections can be made in any subsequent edition.

Photographers of Mel Bochner's work: Lawrence Beck, Mel Bochner, James Dee, Richard Goodbody, Inc., Nicholas Knight, Lizbeth Marano, Laumont Photo Labs, James Powers, Douglas Volle, Joy Whalen.

Other credits and copyrights:
Page 11: Eva Hesse, *Untitled:* artwork © Estate of Eva Hesse, courtesy of Hauser & Wirth, Zurich and New York; photograph by Light Blue Studio, Inc., provided courtesy of Craig F. Starr Gallery, New York. Page 12: Dan Flavin, *Monument for V. Tatlin:* artwork © 2013 Stephen Flavin / Artists Rights Society (ARS), New York. Page 14: Guillaume Apollinaire, *The Mandolin, Carnation, and Bamboo:* photograph © CNAC/MNAM/Dist. RMN–Grand Palais / Art Resource, NY. Sonia Terk-Delaunay, prospectus for *The Prose of the Tran-Siberian and of Little Joan of France:* artwork © Pracusa 2013035; photograph © 2013 Museum Associates/LACMA. Page 15: Robert Smithson, *A Heap of Language:* artwork © Estate of Robert Smithson/licensed by VAGA, New York, NY, photograph provided courtesy of James Cohan Gallery, New York and Shanghai. Carl Andre, *words men word court proofs years hair men cell:* artwork © Carl Andre/licensed by VAGA, New York, NY, digital image © 2006 The Museum of Modern Art, New York. Richard Serra, *Verb List:* artwork © 2013 Richard Serra / Artists Rights Society (ARS), New York. Page 84: *The Joys of Yiddish,* 2012: The Jewish Museum, New York, Purchase: The Muriel and William Rand Collection Gift, by exchange, and Hyman and Joan C. Sall Gift, 2012-22a-b. Page 91: originally published in *Art in America,* December 2012. Courtesy of BMP Media Holdings, LLC.